Revitalizing American Cities

THE CITY IN THE TWENTY-FIRST CENTURY

Eugenie L. Birch and Susan M. Wachter, *Series Editors*

A complete list of books in the series
is available from the publisher.

REVITALIZING AMERICAN CITIES

Edited by

Susan M. Wachter

and

Kimberly A. Zeuli

PENN

UNIVERSITY OF PENNSYLVANIA PRESS

PHILADELPHIA

Published by
University of Pennsylvania Press
Philadelphia, Pennsylvania 19104-4112
www.upenn.edu/pennpress

Printed in the United States of America
on acid-free paper
10 9 8 7 6 5 4 3 2 1

Library of Congress Cataloging-in-Publication Data
Revitalizing American cities / edited by Susan M. Wachter and Kimberly
A. Zeuli. — 1st ed.
    p.   cm. — (The city in the twenty-first century)
    Includes bibliographical references and index.
    ISBN 978-0-8122-4555-4 (hardcover : alk. paper)
    1. Urban renewal—United States—History—21st century. 2. City
planning—United States—History—21st century. 3. Urbanization—
United States—History—21st century. 4. Urban renewal—United
States. 5. City planning—United States. 6. Urbanization—United States.
I. Wachter, Susan M. II. Zeuli, Kimberly. III. Series.
HT175.R475   2014
307.3'4160905—dc23   2013024695

CONTENTS

Introduction

Small and mid-sized cities played a key role in the Industrial Revolution in the United States. Well-positioned cities like Allentown and Bethlehem in Pennsylvania, with easy access to coal from the north and railroad connections to the east, became ground zero for manufacturing the steel that built the nation. New England towns, like Beverly and Southbridge in Massachusetts, imported British technology and produced cheap fabrics for the textile industry. Newly built canals in the 1820s turned Dayton, Ohio, and Erie, Pennsylvania, into hubs for shipping, warehousing, and distributing manufactured products.

The rise and fall of the steel industry in particular reflect not only manufacturing trends in the United States but also the fate of older industrial cities. During the second half of the nineteenth century and the first half of the twentieth, Pittsburgh-based Carnegie Steel Company, Bethlehem Steel, and its neighbors the Allentown Iron Company and the Allentown Rolling Mills in Allentown all thrived, supplying the steel used in building skyscrapers and in the growing manufacturing sector. Bethlehem Steel's warships were a critical contribution to World War I and II victories. As late as 1964, Bethlehem Steel was building its largest plant to date. Clearly, the steel companies and their communities expected manufacturing to retain its vibrant and predominant position in a growing economy and in the cities that produced the product. While manufacturing was dominant, northeastern and midwestern cities, by processing raw materials and manufacturing products, prospered and grew.

And then it changed. Transportation became cheaper, communication became easier, foreign companies became more competitive, and the U.S. manufacturing industry seemed to be down for the count. In 2001, Bethlehem Steel filed for bankruptcy. By 2003, it no longer existed. Other factories closed. Imported foreign steel hit cities like Allentown and Bethlehem particularly hard. Manufacturing profits tumbled and the cities that relied on these industries declined. In response to these broad economic changes, since the 1970s, local governments have developed policy interventions to bring growth (both economic and demographic) back to cities.

There was and is, of course, an important regional component to the growth and decline of cities, with population declining in older industrial cities in the Northeast and Midwest and growing in cities across the South and West. From 1980 to 1990, in the Northeast and Midwest, thirty-one cities lost population, and twenty-eight cities gained population. The older industrial cities such as Allentown and Bethlehem experienced dramatic losses in population. The following decade saw a similar pattern. But in the most recent decade, 2000 to 2010, these patterns began to turn around. The most recent census data, showing growth between 2010 and 2011, confirm a pattern of renewed strength in cities: for the nation as a whole, core areas grew at .08 percent, while outlying areas grew at .06 percent.

American cities have "a history of being remarkably resilient," says Charles Plosser, president of the Federal Reserve Bank of Philadelphia. Even in a period of slow national growth, in the aftermath of the Great Recession, cities are being reinvented, particularly the older industrial cities in the Midwest and Northeast. Today, Allentown and Bethlehem are experiencing strong population growth for the first time in decades—and they are not alone. Many small and mid-sized cities are reinventing their present and future and reversing their trajectory of decline.

For some cities, this rebirth is taking hold in a reinvented manufacturing sector. In 2010 and 2011, manufacturing employment increased for the first time since the late 1990s, providing some evidence that manufacturing is coming back. But other cities are seeking new growth in a re-envisioned economy centered on arts, downtown renaissance, and knowledge-based jobs. Among today's educated young adults, "Rust Belt chic"—which refers to the gritty, underdog allure of struggling manufacturing cities—has become an attractive antidote for some to overly neat, expensive, and boutique-filled cities. Old industrial hubs across the nation—from Springfield to Wichita, from Providence to Columbus—have started to experience a shift in their fortunes. While this demonstrates that turnarounds can happen, whether they happen or not depends on a city's underlying conditions, as well as its policy choices.

Deindustrialization wrought broad changes to the fabric of America's older industrial cities and had far-reaching consequences for those who lived in these cities. Declining cities have concentrated poverty and decreased opportunities for the urban poor. This issue, and the policy responses engendered, is the object of much research and debate, particularly on the role of the federal government. Following World War II to the 1960s, the federal government was at the center of urban renewal efforts but later modified and limited its financial support for urban revitalization initiatives (Fainstein and Fainstein 1986; Mollenkopf 1978).

One reason for this shift is a greater understanding of concentrated urban poverty and of governments' historic responses, which have fallen short and, in some cases, reinforced this concentration. Research and experience show that policy interventions need to be put into place both at and beyond the local level and that, when a city itself is in decline, providing the services that matter for quality of life is challenging. This book focuses on successful strategies, examining how they have been put into place and how they can be replicated and scaled up to revitalize urban economies and provide increased economic opportunities for people who live in cities.

The chapters in this volume investigate the decline and growth of older cities, with the aim of providing insights into new drivers and forces of change and into the barriers that stand in the way. The authors analyze the severity of urban decline and the drivers of urban growth and offer tangible steps to inform the reinvention of declining cities. Today, many cities (and the federal government) face fiscal constraints that are due in part to slow or no growth; while we do not address these constraints specifically, strategies for stabilizing decline and for fostering growth are the central focus of this volume.

The volume is separated into four sections. The first section (City Decline and Revival) explores what we know from the research literature about city decline and revitalization in America, discussing national patterns of growth and decline as well as factors that may influence the trajectories of regions and of particular cities. The second section (Discovering Resilience) presents case studies and comparative analyses demonstrating the repercussions of different approaches to decline, again with a focus on the small, industrial cities that represent many of the country's declining cities. Because many of the nation's struggling cities were once industrial and manufacturing centers, the third section (Land and Neighborhood Policy) addresses a challenge common to such urban areas: vacant land and the struggling neighborhoods burdened with blight. The fourth section (The New Economy and Cities) identifies citywide strategies for reinvention in the new economy.

The chapters include strategies that have proven effective in successful urban reconfigurations as well as characteristics of flawed approaches. For example, while it is clear that infrastructure spending on roads is important for metropolitan employment and population growth, suburban growth may be promoted at the expense of city growth. However, the enduring role of clusters in center cities as job generators for both cities and their surrounding suburbs is demonstrated. In particular, the importance of a dense central business district to economic productivity, through the exchange and diffusion of ideas as well as through the consumption activity arising from the "bright lights" of a vibrant center, are clear. Insights are also drawn from local government responses to manufacturing dependency and transitions to alternative sources of growth. As noted, the need to respond to legacy issues such as vacant and blighted land in declining former manufacturing cities brings its own challenges. How to deal with the vacant land and industrial brownfields remains a question. Does land banking help stabilize declining neighborhoods and cities? Is transformation to skilled manufacturing, new service industries, and the arts possible for renewed urban growth? What is the role of anchor institutions in helping to bring this about? How can critical educational and workforce training gaps be addressed as jobs are reinvented in our cities? Is there a role for the green economy in local employment? The themes that run throughout the book point to the importance of human capital and public and private entrepreneurship.

Our nation's cities continue to evolve. Change is inevitable and therefore reinvention is necessary. When Alexis de Tocqueville toured America in the early nineteenth century, he was struck by this uniquely American quality. "The greatness of America lies not in being more enlightened than any other nation," he wrote, "but rather in her ability to repair her flaws" (de Tocqueville 1835). This is true for America's cities as well.

PART I

City Decline and Revival

CHAPTER 1

The Historical Vitality of Cities

Edward Glaeser

At the start of the nineteenth century, Americans left dense enclaves on the eastern seaboard to populate the empty spaces in the hinterland; at the start of the twenty-first century, Americans are moving back to cities. After a period of net losses in the second half of the twentieth century, many older cities are again experiencing population growth. But not every urban area is thriving, and many of our urban areas are a shadow of their former selves— why have some cities been able to adapt and thrive as conditions have changed, while others have not? This chapter will discuss the historic factors that allowed certain cities to thrive, factors key to growth in cities today, and contemporary approaches to foster revitalization. I will argue that—while it is easy to be distracted by infrastructure—cities are, fundamentally, the people within them. It is people who envision and implement change. Thus, the route to urban vitality lies in adopting policies that help people to thrive and to innovate; in other words, the route to revitalization lies in promoting human capital. While the federal government has a role to play in this, local governments play the biggest role in bringing people together in cities.

History of the Growth of America's Communities

At the beginning of the American experience, transportation drove the development of cities. Some cities fostered adaptability and innovation, while others struggled to survive as conditions changed. This section will outline two stages of city development—first around infrastructure (as hubs of transportation), later around human capital (as hubs of innovation)—and the repercussions of technological changes for those cities that did not make a transition from infrastructure-focused development to human capital-focused development.

Cities as Hubs of Transport

In 1816, it cost as much to ship goods thirty miles over land as it did to ship them across the entire Atlantic Ocean, which is the reason our major cities clung to the eastern seaboard. But over the course of the nineteenth century, we built an amazing transportation network of canals (like the Erie and the Illinois and the Michigan) and of railroads (like the Pennsylvania Main Line) that supplemented the canals. Cities grew up as part of this network. In 1900, the twenty largest American cities were all on major waterways. From the oldest (such as New York and Boston), typically where the river met the sea, to the newest (such as Minneapolis at the northernmost navigable point on the Mississippi), our cities existed because of access to transportation. Industry grew up around those transportation networks (Glaeser and Kohlhase 2004).

The three largest industries in New York City in the 1900s, for example, were printing and publishing, the garment trade, and sugar refining. Because New York City was a great center for trade with the Caribbean, sugar came in through New York's port, and it made sense to reap economies of scale by refining that sugar in a central location. An enormous amount of textiles flowed through the port, so the garment trade grew as well. Even the printing and publishing trade grew out of New York's port. At that time, we did not recognize European copyright: successful publishers relied on being the first to print a pirated copy of a new book. Because Harper and Lee and other New York City-based publishers had access to new books coming in to the port before their rivals in Philadelphia, for example, they had the great advantage of timely publication that enabled their firms to prosper (Glaeser 2011).

Cities as Hubs of Innovation

Cities that formed as a result of the port then, once formed, often fostered amazing leaps of innovation. The story of Henry Ford in Detroit exemplifies this. In the nineteenth century, Detroit Dry Dock—a cutting edge industrial plant at the time—provided education for young people like the young Henry Ford. He learned how engines worked from working at Detroit Dry Dock and working for Thomas Alva Edison—and then Ford embarked on a quest to produce the mass-produced automobile. While, in the 1890s, New York was the largest center of auto production, Detroit was abuzz with automotive entrepreneurs (Henry Ford, the Dodge brothers, the Fisher Brothers, David Dunbar Buick, Ransom Olds, and Billy Durant in nearby Flint), so it was Detroit that ultimately built the first mass-produced car (Glaeser 2011).

According to legend, Ford followed the car of Charles Kirby—the first person to build a car in Detroit—in a bicycle to figure out how it worked. While the story may be apocryphal, the essential characteristic of cities that it illuminates is true. This characteristic was captured eloquently 120 years ago by English economist Alfred Marshall (1890: iv.x,3): in dense clusters, "the mysteries of the trade become no mysteries but are, as it were, in the air." Today we see this in the fact that patents are more likely to cite other patents that are physically close to them; in other words, people developing patents are more likely to learn from nearby inventors (Jaffe, Trajtenberg, and Henderson 1993; Glaeser, Kerr, and Ponzetto 2010).

Detroit in the nineteenth century brought together people who learned from one another in their efforts to mass produce cars. Their success resulted in the creation of the River Rouge plant, which produced massive numbers of Model Ts. On one level, this was a tremendous triumph, both for those Americans who wanted inexpensive cars and for those workers who worked for five dollars a day in those plants. By the 1950s, Detroit was one of the world's most productive places.

While the static efficiency of the River Rouge plant in the 1950s was remarkable, it was a terrible model for long-term city success. River Rouge was a vast, vertically integrated plant employing overwhelmingly less-educated Americans who were walled off from the outside world; this model did not and does not lead to urban sustainability because it does not need the city: it does not give to the city, it does not take from the city, and it is an empire unto itself. When conditions change—and they always do—it can simply be moved somewhere else, leaving the city behind. For cities that developed as hubs of transportation, changes in transportation costs over the twentieth century were the hurdle to which some cities would adapt and others would not. Whether the city's human capital was walled off or integrated across firms and industries would matter in this adaptation (Glaeser 2011).

Implications of Changes in Transportation Costs over the Twentieth Century

Over the twentieth century, transportation costs dropped (Glaeser and Kohlhase 2004). The costs of moving a ton by rail declined by 90 percent, so while proximity to inputs like the wood of Michigan or the coal mines of Pittsburgh was valuable in 1910, it was less important in 1970. Detroit's waterways and rails had, in 1910, given it a comparative advantage in producing cars, but, as transportation became cheaper, this advantage lost value (Glaeser and Kohlhase 2004; Glaeser and Ponzetto 2010). Plants could be moved where wages and other costs were cheaper. Thomas Holmes compares counties on opposite sides of the right-to-work line—pro-union policies on one side, pro-business policies on the other—and finds a large increase in industrial growth after 1947 on the pro-business side of the line. Plants moved to the pro-business side of the border, as costs were lower (Holmes 1998).

As a consequence of declining transportation costs, Americans became free to move to places that brought them higher levels of amenities. Data show that one of the strongest predictors for where people choose to move is January temperature: no variable better predicts metropolitan area growth during the twentieth century. Figure 1.1 shows population growth and the January temperature of the major city in the metropolitan area from 1910 to 2010; Figure 1.2 ranks counties by temperature over the last ten years. Other factors were at work—including relatively pro-business policies south of the Mason-Dixon Line (Holmes 1998), relatively lax policies toward constructing new homes (Glaeser, Gyourko, and Saks 2006)—but the temperature itself is a significant variable in predicting migration patterns (Glaeser and Tobio 2008).

Concomitant with the move to sun came a move to a landscape built around the car. On the one hand, this is predictable: we have always built our living spaces around the dominant form of transportation. Our oldest spaces are walking cities, with narrow streets, short blocks, and often curving roadways (for example, Beacon Hill in Boston, New York City around Wall Street, or the oldest European cities). As transportation progressed, we built cities around grids to accommodate wheeled transport and streetcar

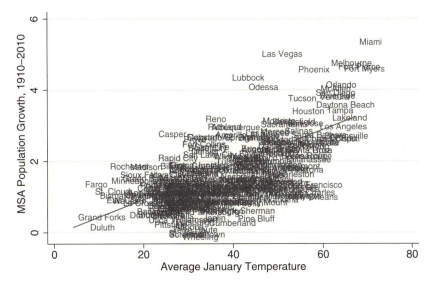

Figure 1.1. MSA population growth, 1910–2010, versus average January temperature. U.S. Census Bureau.

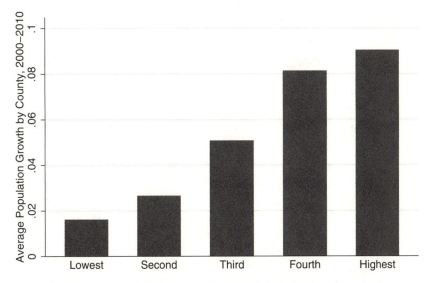

Figure 1.2. Average population growth, 2000–2010, by quintiles of average January temperature. U.S. Census Bureau.

suburbs along mainlines. The car became another transportation technology around which America rebuilt its space. With access to cars, Americans moved toward driving: as of 2009, the average commute by car was 24 minutes, while the average commute by public transit was 48 minutes (U.S. Census Bureau 2009).

The move to cars and away from cities was and is subsidized by government. Nathaniel Baum-Snow (2007) finds that each highway that cut into the center of a metropolitan area after World War II reduced the central city's population by about 18 percent relative to the metropolitan area as a whole. With the move to sun and sprawl, all our older, colder cities went into decline. Thus, the oversized federal role in highway funds, and the role of the federal government in transportation spending generally, contributed to the migration away from cities to newly developed suburbs.

Components of Vitality

Some communities have proved themselves remarkably adaptable, while others have endured decades of pain. What makes some cities able to rebuild while others struggle? I argue that it is the strength of a city's human capital—its education and level of entrepreneurship—coupled with the fundamentals of city government that foretells urban success. First, however, I will present an overview of what we know of how declining cities differ from thriving cities.

Differences Between Declining and Thriving Cities

Density and income levels are strongly related, as illustrated in Figure 1.3, which ranks the 3000-odd counties in the United States by density (people per square mile), with each dot representing a tenth of the counties. The bottom line shows that the densest tenth of American counties have incomes that are on average 50 percent higher than the least dense half of America's counties. The three densest metropolitan areas in this country produce 18 percent of America's GDP while including only 13 percent of America's population. The top line illustrates America's recent move back to cities. It represents population change between 2000 and 2010, again related to density as of the year 2000.

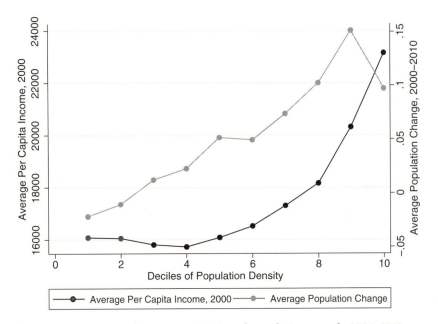

Figure 1.3. Average median income, 2000, and population growth, 2000–2010, by deciles of MSA population density, 2000. U.S. Census Bureau.

Table 1.1 shows the ten largest cities in the United States as of 1950. Today, eight of those ten have lost 23 percent or more of their population. The three most extreme declines—Cleveland, St. Louis, Detroit—have lost 56 percent or more of their population. Detroit lost another 25 percent of its population over the last decade alone. So, while we can take note of the triumph of the city in some general sense, many cities continue to face enormous challenges. Of the 235-odd cities in the country with more than 100,000 people in 2000, 38 have lost more than 1 percent of their population in the last ten years. On average, those cities are substantially poorer than the national norm: their income levels and income growth, between 2000 and 2008, are about 20 percent below the national average.

Figure 1.4 shows population growth between 2000 and 2010 and housing values (reported by the census) in 2000. The chart illustrates the one way in which all declining cities differ from growing cities: housing prices. Declining cities are all relatively inexpensive to live in; that is one of the reasons people stay. Even after a city declines, the homes endure. Cities built during a previous era stick around in part because they have an enduring

Table 1.1. Ten Largest Cities in the United States as of 1950

City	1950 population	2000 population	Change (%)
New York	7,891,957	8,175,133	4
Chicago	3,620,962	2,695,598	−26
Philadelphia	2,071,605	1,526,006	−26
Los Angeles	1,970,358	3,782,621	92
Detroit	1,849,568	713,777	−61
Baltimore	949,708	620,961	−35
Cleveland	914,808	396,815	−57
St. Louis	856,796	319,294	−63
Washington	802,178	601,723	−25
Boston	801,444	617,594	−23

U.S. Census Bureau.

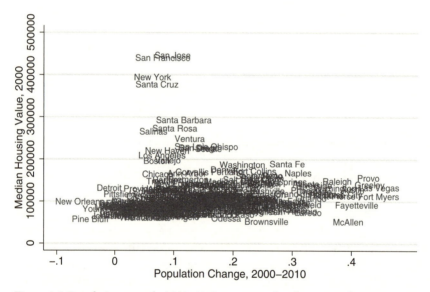

Figure 1.4. Population growth, 2000–2010, versus median housing value, 2000. U.S. Census Bureau.

housing infrastructure. Year by year, decade by decade, housing lapses into obsolescence, but it remains cheap housing, which remains one of the chief attractions of these cities (Glaeser and Gyourko 2005). While these factors define declining versus thriving cities, the question is what factors determine growth or decline.

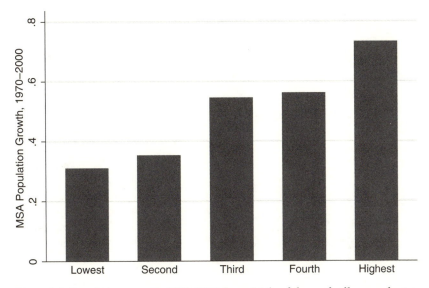

Figure 1.5. Population growth, 1970–2000, by quintile of share of college graduates in 1970. U.S. Census Bureau.

Education

Human capital is the bedrock on which urban growth rests (Rauch 1993; Simon and Nardinelli 2002; Glaeser and Saiz 2004). Education has been a critical component to city success across the country. Figure 1.5 shows the positive, robust relationship across metropolitan areas between the share of the population with a college degree in 1970 and subsequent population growth. In the Northeast and Midwest, the areas hit with cataclysmic changes, this relationship is even stronger, as shown in Figure 1.6. In the top quintile, growth exceeds 50 percent, while, in the bottom quintile, growth is below 10 percent. Figure 1.7 ranks the population growth of all the counties in the United States by share of the population with a college degree. Education is close to being destiny. Human capital is central.

Enrico Moretti (2004) finds that having a land grant college in a metropolitan area prior to 1940 has a powerful effect on recent income levels, income growth, and population growth. Education is, in part, central to population growth because it is central to economic well-being. Figure 1.8 illustrates the relationship between per capita GDP and education across metropolitan areas. As the share of population in a metropolitan area with a

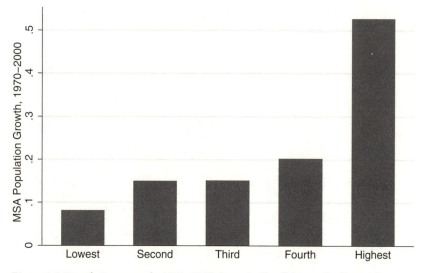

Figure 1.6. Population growth, 1970–2000, by quintile of share of college graduates, 1970, for Northeastern and Midwestern MSAs. U.S. Census Bureau.

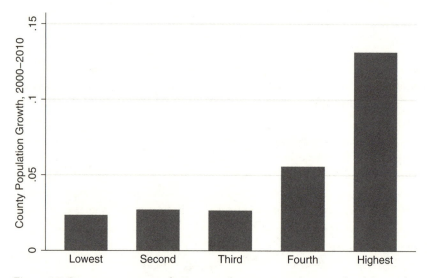

Figure 1.7. County average population growth, 2000–2010, by quintile of share of college graduates in 2000. U.S. Census Bureau.

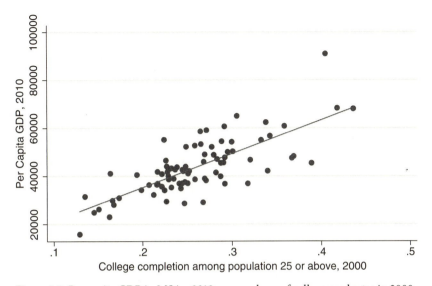

Figure 1.8. Per capita GDP in MSAs, 2010, versus share of college graduates in 2000. U.S. Census Bureau and BEA.

college degree goes up by 10 percent, wages go up by 8 percent (holding years of schooling constant). The value of being in a skilled metropolitan area is enormous. In his chapter in this volume, Gilles Duranton reports on some of the studies that establish a causal effect between concentration of skills in a metropolitan area and higher wages.

Inequalities in skills have been growing over time. Figure 1.9 shows the strong, positive relationship between the share of the population with a college degree in 1940 and the growth in the share of the population with a college degree between 1940 and 2000. The graph shows that those places that started more skilled have become more skilled. This divergence of skill levels across space is part of the challenge our most disadvantaged communities face. This issue is addressed by Laura Perna in her chapter in this volume.

Entrepreneurship

While education levels serve as a marker for the education, idea, and intellectual intensity of a place, the important skills learned in cities may not be those learned in school. The most important skills are those most often

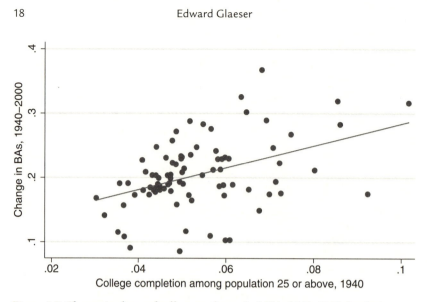

Figure 1.9. Change in share of college graduates in MSA, 1940–2000, by share of college graduates in 1940. U.S. Census Bureau.

learned after the workplace: the skills and inclination to be an entrepreneur, to find new opportunities, and to find new business models. Fifty years ago, economist Benjamin Chinitz (1961) compared New York City and Pittsburgh and saw that New York appeared to be more diversified and therefore more successful than Pittsburgh. He argued that New York's success reflected a culture of entrepreneurship embedded in the city's industrial history. The garment trade allowed anyone with a good idea and a couple of sewing machines an opportunity to start a business. It was an industry in which it was easy to get started, and those who started there might then move on to something else.

In contrast, what did Pittsburgh have? Pittsburgh had U.S. Steel, and U.S. Steel had company men. Company men are skilled at extracting value from a large organization, but when that model of production disappears they lack the skills to find new opportunities. The company men at U.S. Steel, like the company men at General Motors, were part of the machine. They did not have the skills to adapt to change (Chinitz 1961).

Our measures of entrepreneurship are mediocre, yet they still predict urban success very well (Glaeser, Ponzetto, Tobio 2011). Figure 1.10 shows metropolitan areas ranked by the average size of their firms in 1977. Those metropolitan areas with the smallest firms have had subsequent employ-

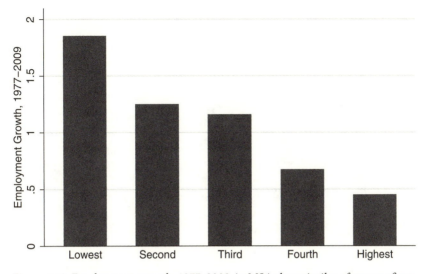

Figure 1.10. Employment growth, 1977–2009, in MSAs by quintiles of average firm size in 1977. County Business Patterns.

ment growth more than three times higher than those areas with the largest firms. The same is true when entrepreneurship is measured by the share of employment in start-ups or in long-time historical variation such as proximity (or not) to a mine. The connection between various measures of entrepreneurship and urban success is very robust (Glaeser et al. 1992; Audretsch 1995; Glaeser, Kerr, Ponzetto 2010).

Some evidence also suggests that an economy concentrated in a few big industries is not as adaptable as one that is more diverse. Figure 1.11 shows the influence of the degree of industrial concentration on employment growth at the county level. Counties that had a higher level of industrial concentration in 1977 experienced lower levels of employment growth between 1977 and 2000 than did counties with a lower level of industrial concentration. New ideas are formed by combining old ideas, so having a bevy of different sources of these old ideas—in other words, a diversity of industries—appears to be conducive toward urban success. Small, nimble firms coming from many different industries seem to be critical for successful urban development (Glaeser et al. 1992). Globalization and new technologies have not spelled the death of cities for a very simple reason: they have increased the complexity of the world; therefore they have increased the returns to being smart.

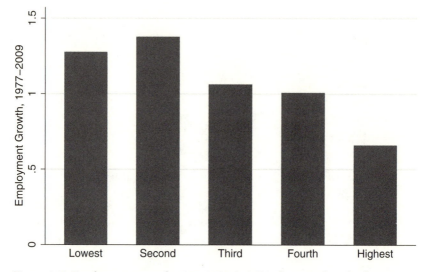

Figure 1.11. Employment growth, 1977–2009, in MSAs by quintiles of industry concentration in 1977. County Business Patterns.

Cities enable us to learn from each other, to pick up unplanned pieces of information that are learned by being around people, watching their failures and their successes. The more complicated the world is, the easier it is for information to be lost in translation. We have evolved over millions of years to have queues for communicating comprehension or confusion that are lost when we are not in the same room. This is part of what makes face-to-face contact so important; it is part of the reason Google built the Googleplex. Cities that want to succeed need to build on this. But building on this means first having the human capital to implement and capitalize on knowledge innovation through the communication that cities naturally enable (Berry and Glaeser 2005).

What Should We Do About Decline?

What should cities do to attract human capital? To retain and attract jobs and residents, in short, to make cities livable, there is no substitute for providing the basics of city government. Since the dawn of history, cities have been dealing with the demons that come with density. If two people are close enough to give each other an idea face to face, they are also close enough to give each other a contagious disease, and, if two people are close enough to buy and sell a newspaper, they are close enough to rob each other (Glaeser and Sacerdote 1999). The research demonstrates the importance of government provision of public safety as a basic urban good in order to retain and attract new residents (Gould Ellen and O'Reagan 2009).

Public safety, in the broadest sense, including public health, is historically a key factor in urban growth. Historically, the most important job of city government has been to provide clean water. Remarkably, cities that were once dreadful have become quite pleasurable, something that happened only through massive investments by local government to provide fundamental urban services such as water and sanitation. In 1900, the life expectancy for a boy born in New York City was seven years less than the national average; today, life expectancies in New York are more than two years above the national average (Glaeser 2011).

The relative safety of cities did not happen easily. Cities and towns were spending as much on clean water at the start of the twentieth century as the federal government was spending on everything except the post office and the army. Cities and towns historically played an essential role in creating safe cities, and local government continues to be the place to be for those who care about improving the lives of ordinary people.

Beyond the provision of basics including public safety, what should be done about decline? I will discuss four different approaches: the physical capital approach, the tax incentive approach, the shrinking to greatness approach, and the human capital approach.

Physical Capital Investments

Do infrastructure investments make a difference—can we change the tides of history with major infrastructure investments? Do they meaningfully help local residents? Do they meet cost-benefit analysis? I believe the federal government is playing too great a role in financing local infrastructure and is, essentially, pretending that cities are structures rather than people. This has proven to be a curse for our urban areas. However, the federal government does have an infrastructure role to play toward cities, in helping cities care for people with fewer resources.

Urban poverty is rarely a sign that cities are making mistakes. Rather, cities attract poor people with a promise of economic opportunity, a more humane social safety net, and the ability to get around without a car. If you build a new subway line, you find that poverty rates go up around subway stops (Glaeser, Kahn, and Rappaport 2008). Is the subway line impoverishing its neighbors? No, the subway is doing exactly what it should: providing a means of getting around for those Americans who cannot afford a car for every adult.

But caring for the less advantaged is a role for the federal government—not for localities. When a local welfare state is created, the rich move out, leaving pockets of poverty. In the 1960s, city after city faced social distress; often, they tried to handle the distress locally, but the firms and the wealthy left, leaving behind an urban crisis.

After the Federal Aid Highway Act of 1973, the federal government funded transportation infrastructure. But Detroit, like other struggling cities, did not need transportation infrastructure; it needed investment in children, safety, and schools. Table 1.2 shows that the transportation infrastructure investments had relatively little impact on urban growth in the following decades (Gottlieb and Glaeser 2008).

Tax Incentives

Tax incentives do seem to make a difference. Busso and Kline (2008) find 2 to 4 percent increases in employment rates in empowerment zones, while Greenstone and Moretti (2004) find significant impact in luring million-dollar plants.

The work suggests that keeping tax rates as low as possible is appropriate. But are these results applicable to cities? Greenstone and Morreti's results (2004) focus mostly on gains in America's rural areas, as these areas are actually winning battles for million-dollar industrial plants. Rural areas may indeed have a comparative advantage in old-style industry or manufacturing; these activities left our cities decades ago. It is very hard to imagine that cities have a comparative advantage in this arena relative to an arts scene, to an ideas economy, to creativity, to the things that actually take advantage of the proximity of people that enables the spread of ideas. Nonetheless, tax policy in general does matter, as do federal policies that support

Table 1.2. Historical Regressions of Population and Income Growth on Metropolitan-Area Transportation Measures and Controls*

	Dependent variable					
Independent variable	Population growth, 1850–60	Population growth, 1850–1900	Population growth, 1960–90	Income per capita growth, 1960–90	Population growth, 1990–2000	Income per capita growth, 1990–2000
Log of initial population	−0.335	−0.629	−0.101	−0.038	−0.007	−0.02
	(0.011)	(0.017)	(0.023)	(0.010)	(0.007)	(0.004)
Distance in miles to ocean or Gulf of Mexico	0.04	0.037	−0.021	−0.013		
	(0.003)	(0.005)	(0.004)	(0.002)		
Dummy for county accessible by rail in 1850	0.144	0.203				
	(0.023)	(0.036)				
Congregationalists per capita in 1850	0.925	0.96				
	(0.181)	(0.286)				
Log of new miles of highway, 1960–90			0.111	0.039		
			(0.026)	(0.009)		
Dummy for top-50 airport					0.046	0.027
					(0.021)	(0.011)
Percent of population with college degree in 1990					0.337	0.093
					(0.088)	(0.047)
Constant	3.154	6.431	1.309	2.412	0.136	0.65
	(0.100)	(0.158)	(0.245)	(0.109)	(0.086)	(0.045)
Unit of observation	Counties	Counties	MSAs	MSAs	MSAs	MSAs
No. of observations	1,517	1,517	205	205	318	317
Adjusted R^2	0.53	0.57	0.15	0.22	0.07	0.1

Gottlieb and Glaeser 2008.

*Metropolitan statistical areas (MSAs) are under the 1999 definitions, using primary rather than consolidated MSAs where applicable and New England county metropolitan areas where applicable. Population, income, and Congregationalists data are from the U.S. Census Bureau. Data on proximity to rail transportation are from Craig, Palmquist, and Weiss (1998). Distance to ocean or Gulf is from Rappaport and Sachs (2003) and is the distance from the closest county in the MSA. Highway data are from Baum-Snow (2007). Airport data are from Bureau of Transportation Statistics (1996). Standard errors are in parentheses.

the poor and vulnerable, who are concentrated in cities, and that counteract the associated heavy fiscal burden on cities.

Shrinking to Greatness

For some cities, the best course may not be returning to a former state by growing back their population to 1950s levels. Instead, cities like Cleveland, Detroit, Saint Louis, or Youngstown have started to embrace the vision of "shrinking to greatness." The governments and populations of these localities recognize that their housing stock and their public infrastructures cannot be sustained with their current population and economic activity and that they are not going to get back the population level that requires such infrastructures. The concept of shrinking to greatness is to shrink the physical footprint of the area to reduce the costs of city services and potentially produce more usable land. Recognizing that people will not come back to repopulate once-dense neighborhoods, cities that adopt this approach develop plans to destroy empty and often unsound homes and replace them with parks, open space that is less costly to maintain and does not pose hazards. While this approach does not immediately bring back economic activity and people, it can make these cities more attractive and less costly to maintain. This approach is difficult, and significant opposition exists to any plans that displace residents. Nonetheless, some city leaders, including mayors David Bing in Detroit and Dayne Walling in Flint, have made a commitment to do some targeted demolition and have allocated funds and made use of eminent domain to do so.

Accepting that sustainability entails downsizing their physical footprints, sharing or consolidating urban services between adjacent communities, and concentrating redevelopment efforts on the remaining core of density and activity will not bring cities back to their former states but will make them more efficient in delivering services and better able to provide a good quality environment for their residents (Glaeser 2011).

Human Capital

The most difficult and promising approach is to focus directly on human capital: on attracting, retaining, and empowering skilled people. This is not just about appealing to twenty-seven-year-old poets and artists; it is also about appealing to thirty-eight-year-old moms who work in research labs and care about the safety, education, and commutes of their children. We cannot ignore the basics of city government and get sidetracked by the idea of glitzing our way to successful redevelopment. Fundamentally, attracting and retaining smart people means providing basic city government services well.

That, of course, also requires innovation directly in education. The challenge of providing better schooling, for example, requires innovative models and the development of a better understanding of how to deliver education in an urban environment that counteracts the differential that exists today in educational outcomes in cities versus suburbs (Jacob and Ludwig 2011). The success of older cities in reinventing themselves lies in their capacity to develop their human capital through education and prepare a skilled workforce that will be able to demonstrate the creativity required by the knowledge economy.

*   *   *

America's cities continue to face challenges. But the ability of our nation and our species to endure and innovate because we are connected by our cities, because we are more than the sum of our parts, because we learn from the people around us, because we innovate in the urban milieu—that track record is remarkable and it will continue.

CHAPTER 2

The Growth of Metropolitan Areas in the United States

Gilles Duranton

Between 2000 and 2010, the population of metropolitan areas grew on average by 10.8 percent in the United States. This average masks considerable heterogeneity. Of 366 metropolitan areas, 42 lost population while 65 grew by 20 percent or more during this decade.

City decline leads to calls for a policy response. In the United States and other developed countries, a wide variety of revitalization policies have been proposed, from the construction of major infrastructure to high-tech clusters to various types of urban beautification policies to attempts to attract "talent."

In the absence of a good understanding of what drives city growth, many of these initiatives are likely to prove futile. This chapter provides a brief summary of what is known regarding the drivers of the growth and decline of cities. Given its breadth, this chapter will focus mostly on U.S. cities.[1] The exposition attempts to remain accessible to the nontechnical reader; a more technical exposition of the issues surrounding the growth of cities can be found in Duranton and Puga (2013).

The chapter explores six mains "engines" of metropolitan growth uncovered in the literature: roads, amenities, human capital, entrepreneurship, industry clusters, and land regulations. Given space constraints, the exposition can focus on only a few key papers for each engine of growth. Other potential engines of city growth—such as non-road transportation infrastructure like airports or the quality of local governments—may also matter, but the extant literature does not provide significant empirical support for these alternative drivers of city growth. This does not imply that the six engines of city growth explored here are exclusive: We simply know extremely little outside these six engines of city growth.

Roads and Land Use

To understand why we expect roads—and particularly roads within cities— to matter, returning to the core model of cities as developed by Alonso (1964), Mills (1967), and Muth (1969) is useful (for a historical perspective on transportation as a driver of city growth, see Edward Glaeser's chapter in this volume). This model represents cities as a central business district surrounded by residential areas. Potential residents, before moving to a city, consider the wage the city offers and the cost to live there. This cost of living is determined by the cost of housing and of commuting to the central business district where jobs are located. While arguably primitive in its representation of the geography of cities, this model highlights the importance of "accessibility" and the endogenous determination of housing costs. More specifically, higher housing costs close to the center offset shorter commutes, while higher commuting costs offset cheaper housing on the outskirts of a city. Keeping population constant, a transportation improvement should, thus, lead to both lower commuting costs (a direct effect) and lower housing costs (an indirect effect, given that accessibility is now less binding). Both effects serve to make the city more attractive to potential residents since it now offers higher wages net of urban costs.

This simple argument predicts that transportation improvements within cities should cause city population and city employment to grow.[2] However, we expect city population and employment to increase only gradually after an increase in roadways since new construction and other adjustments to housing stock do not happen overnight. Together, this suggests looking at city population (or employment) growth over time as a function of initial roads and population.

Roads, and more specifically the development of the U.S. interstate system, are arguably the quintessential transportation improvement of the second part of the twentieth century. Duranton and Turner (2012) gather data about the mileage of interstate highways in U.S. metropolitan areas in 1983 (the earliest available year of data) and employment in these metropolitan areas in 1983 and 2003. They first perform a simple regression using employment growth between 1983 and 2003 as a dependent variable and miles of interstate highways in 1983 and employment at the same date as explanatory variables. They measure an (apparent) elasticity of population with respect to interstate highways of about 7 percent. That is, doubling the roadway in a city is associated with an increase in employment of about 7 percent over the subsequent twenty years.

Regressing employment growth in cities on a measure of urban roads raises a fundamental inference problem: that doubling the roadway is associated with a 7 percent growth in employment over the subsequent twenty years is only a statistical association. We cannot make any causal statement here, unless we are confident that roads are allocated to cities in a way unrelated to their subsequent growth. This is doubtful. One hopes that roads are given to cities to accommodate their expected growth. One also fears that roads may be allocated to struggling cities to help them. Alternatively, roads may be associated with another, missing variable that explains city growth. In any of these scenarios, roads and city growth are jointly determined, and one cannot interpret the coefficient on roads in the regression as causal.

To determine the causal effect of roads on city growth, we need to use a "surrogate" variable that explains the presence of interstate highways in 1983 but is otherwise uncorrelated with the growth of cities between 1983 and 2003.[3] Economists refer to such a variable as an instrumental variable. We can use variations in this instrumental variable to assess the causal effect of roads on city growth. The procedure is as follows. First, we can measure the effect of this instrumental variable on 1983 interstate highways. Second, we can assess the effect of this instrumental variable on employment growth between 1983 and 2003. We can then find the effect of 1983 interstate highways on 1983–2003 employment growth by "dividing" the latter effect by the former. For instance, if a 10 percent higher value of the instrument predicts 20 percent more miles of actual 1983 highways and if this same 10 percent higher value is associated with 3 percent more growth between 1983 and 2003, we can deduce that 10 percent more miles of 1983 interstate highways cause 1.5 percent more employment growth between 1983 and 2003.

Again, this calculation is only valid if the instrument affects employment growth only through highways.[4] This is really the fundamental condition on which this type of approach relies. It is called an exclusion restriction. It is easy to understand that if the instrument affects another engine of growth, the above calculation of the effect of road on growth is invalid. For instance, if the instrument affects roads and education and both roads and education affect urban growth, it becomes impossible to isolate the effect of roads on urban growth.

To construct an instrumental variable that explains roads in 1983 but is not otherwise correlated with city growth over 1983–2003, Duranton and Turner (2012) propose using the 1947 map of planned interstate highways from which they compute planned miles of interstate highways for each metropolitan area in 1947. This variable predicts interstate highway miles in 1983 well. Proving this formally is easy, but showing that this variable is associated with employment growth between 1983 and 2003 *only* through 1983 interstate highways, and thus satisfying the exclusion restriction, is much more difficult. To resolve this, Duranton and Turner first examine the mandate given to the committee that drew this plan and the conditions surrounding the committee's work. The mandate that underlies the 1947 highway plan is straightforward: to link major U.S. cities for defense and trade purposes. Importantly, planned 1947 highways were not supposed to address commuting, and those developing this plan were not instructed to be forward looking. This latter point can be easily verified: miles of planned interstate highways do not correlate with city growth at the time.

This said, larger cities clearly received more planned interstate highways in 1947 than did smaller cities, and, since city population in 1947 may be related to employment growth between 1983 and 2003, the instrumental variable may be associated with employment growth over this period through this alternative channel. To rule out this possibility, one needs to condition out population in 1947 from the regression, for instance, by using population of U.S. metropolitan areas in 1940 and 1950 as control variables. We must address other objections to the validity of the use of planned 1947 highways as an instrumental variable, such as the idea that these planned highways may have depended on the geography of cities or their location. For instance, coastal cities (or warmer cities) may have received more (or fewer) miles of planned interstate highways in 1947. At the same time, being on a coast (or being warm) may cause city growth. As with population, we need to preclude these possible linkages by controlling directly for these alternative channels through which the instrument might affect urban growth.

Despite these efforts, this attempt to estimate the effects of interstate highways on city growth using an old map of the interstate highway system may create uneasiness. One can never make absolutely sure that an instrument affects an outcome only through the explanatory variable of interest. Planned 1947 highways affect 1983 highways and, in turn, 1983 to 2003 population growth. Unfortunately, 1947 highways may affect contemporaneous population growth through another variable we have not thought about.

Finding other instrumental variables and checking those results against the results when using the planned 1947 highways as an instrumental variable is a way to reduce such worries. So, in addition to using planned interstate highways, Duranton and Turner (2012) propose using kilometers of railroad tracks in U.S. metropolitan areas around 1900. Old railroad tracks predict 1983 interstates well because many of these tracks were eventually converted into highways or had highways built alongside them. The chosen date (circa 1900) corresponds to the peak of railroad expansion in the United States. The robber barons that built the U.S. railroad system were more interested in making a quick profit by moving people across the continent and shipping coal, grain, and cattle than in promoting employment growth a century later: That is, miles of railroad tracks circa 1900 make a plausible instrument for miles of interstate highways in 1983. Finally, Duranton and Turner (2012) also propose using old exploration routes dating back to 1528. A road that was good for horses and carriages centuries ago is likely to be good for the automobile today. The fact that several instruments of a different origin all yield the same result is reassuring since, for this to occur, they can be all valid or they need to be invalid in exactly the same way (an unlikely possibility).

Using the three instruments just described, Duranton and Turner (2012) estimate the elasticity of city employment over twenty years with respect to miles of interstate highways to be about 15 percent. Put differently, one standard deviation in interstate highways in 1983 explains nearly two-thirds of a standard deviation in employment growth over the subsequent twenty years. This elasticity of 15 percent—estimated with instrumental variables—is about twice as high as the elasticity estimated directly from the data. This suggests that interstate highways allocated exogenously have a much higher effect on employment growth than do interstate highways allocated by the current political process. Put differently, the simple association between urban roads and the growth of cities in the data reflects both the causal effect of roads on growth and the fact that roads tend to be built when growth is low. Duranton and Turner (2012) provide independent evidence about this last point by showing that, indeed, more roads are built in cities when they are doing poorly.

Amenities

The second major engine of population growth for U.S. cities is amenities. As argued by Glaeser, Kolko, and Saiz (2001) and in Glaeser's chapter in this volume, weather—as measured by January and July temperatures—is one of the most reliable predictors of city growth in recent U.S. history. Warmer temperatures in January and cooler temperatures in July are both associated with city growth.

Before dwelling deeper on this, one may wonder why amenities should affect city growth. Following Roback (1982), economists define urban amenities as local characteristics that affect the well-being of residents but are not paid for directly. Instead, residents pay for amenities indirectly through higher housing costs and, perhaps, even more indirectly through lower wages. Put differently, more desirable cities are in greater demand, which translates into higher land prices, which affects housing costs. Higher land prices also affect the costs of production for firms that are thus more constrained in their abilities to pay high wages (at least when they compete on a national market). Amenities are, thus, expected to capitalize into property prices and wages. This reasoning tells us that amenities should affect city population size—but it is not clear why they should affect city population growth. For amenities in general and good weather in particular to account for city growth, at least one of the following three explanations must be brought to bear.

First, amenities are normal goods, and, as such, households are willing to pay more for them as they get richer. In this context, migration to high-amenity cities reflects economic growth. Second, past constraints on the urban landscape have been relaxed by technological change. For instance, cities that once benefited from proximity to coal no longer profit from this setting, since the cost of shipping coal and the coal's economic importance have both fallen dramatically. As a result, households have moved out of coal cities (with their poor climates) to cities with better weather. Third, amenities may be correlated with something that is both missing from the regression and is correlated with the population growth of cities. For instance,

Sunbelt cities offer mild winters (a positive amenity). But these cities also have less stringent land use regulations that allow for cheaper housing and more construction (Glaeser and Tobio 2008). Lax land use regulations could be the true engine of the growth of Sunbelt cities. This third possibility brings up an important problem and raises some doubts about how much of the association between amenities and city growth is causal.

When trying to understand the effect of amenities on city growth, defining "amenities" is problematic. It is unclear what "amenities" really are. We could write down a long list of what urban amenities might be—from the availability of good restaurants to nice architecture to low crime, and so forth—but most of these amenities are likely to be endogenous to city growth. Whether good restaurants cause city growth or result from it is unclear. We suspect the latter, but finding a good instrument for each possible amenity is a hopeless task.

To solve these problems of causality and define what amenities are, recent research has taken two different directions. The first focuses on the weather. Although it may be correlated with a variable missing from the analysis, most manifestations of the weather are not a consequence of city growth. In addition, pleasant weather is highly valued by households when they choose where to live. Albouy (2008) provides an estimate of the total value of amenities for each U.S. city using a Roback (1982) approach, as described above. When he performs a regression of aggregate amenity values on a vast number of amenity variables, he finds that weather variables explain a large fraction of aggregate amenity values in U.S. cities.

Rappaport (2007) focuses on the relationship between city growth and nice weather (in the form of mild winters and summers that are not too hot) and finds that nice weather is a major engine of population growth for U.S. counties between 1970 and 2000. More specifically, he shows that a standard deviation in January temperature is associated with a 0.6 standard deviation in population growth. For July temperature, one standard deviation is associated with a 0.2 standard deviation in population growth. Overall, the effect of weather on city growth is large, even larger than that of roads.

The second direction taken by recent research is to look instead for a "summary variable" that would proxy for the entire bundle of amenities in a city. Carlino and Saiz (2008) propose using the number of leisure visits as collected by a consultancy in the tourism industry. They first show that leisure visits correlate well with alternative measures of amenities and quality of life, including Albouy's (2008). Second, they regress population growth between 1990 and 2000 for U.S. metropolitan areas on leisure visits and find that the elasticity of population with respect to leisure visits is about 2 percent over this ten-year period. This coefficient is robust to the inclusion of many other control variables. This said, we can again imagine a number of ways leisure visits might be correlated with city growth without having a causal effect on the latter. Tourism is itself a strong growth industry. However, the correlations are robust to the exclusion of the likes of Las Vegas and Orlando. In addition, fast-growing cities receive a greater inflow of newcomers who, in turn, may receive more visits from family and friends. We can again use an instrumental variable approach to circumvent this simultaneity problem. Carlino and Saiz (2008) use two exogenous determinants of leisure visits: the number of historic places and the coastal share within a ten-kilometer radius of the central city. This instrumental variable approach leads to an even higher elasticity of city population with respect to amenities of 4 percent.

Taken together, these findings strongly indicate the positive effect of amenities, and particularly of nice weather, on city growth.

Human Capital

The third key engine of the population growth of cities is human capital. The strong association between human capital as measured by the education of the workforce and city growth has been noted for a long time; Glaeser, Scheinkman, and Shleifer (1995) and Simon and Nardinelli (2002) present early formal evidence. (Glaeser, in his chapter in this volume, argues for the centrality of human capital to city vitality.)

Before proceeding, understanding how human capital may affect city growth is important. First, human capital may affect productivity through human capital externalities: The notion that smart people benefit from being surrounded by other smart people has received support in the literature (for one example, see Moretti 2004). If those benefits take place over time through learning spillovers, we expect more educated cities to enjoy faster productivity growth, which, in turn, translates into faster wage and population growth. Second, entrepreneurs may be overrepresented among more educated workers. If this is the case, a more educated city is also a more entrepreneurial city, where firms grow faster. Stronger population growth then naturally follows. Finally, more educated cities may develop better amenities. These are attractive to workers from other cities, particularly educated workers. Note that these last two channels of transmission for the effect of education overlap with the engine of city growth that we just discussed (amenities) and with the one that we discuss next (entrepreneurship).

In a thorough investigation of the relationship between human capital and city growth across U.S. metropolitan areas, Glaeser and Saiz (2004) conclude that one standard deviation in the share of university graduates in the city workforce at the beginning of a decade is associated with a quarter of a standard deviation of population growth during this decade. Put differently, for an average city, a 1 percentage point higher share of university graduates is associated with around 0.5 percent population growth over the subsequent decade. They also show that most effects of human capital percolate through a productivity channel, either learning and human capital externalities or entrepreneurship and firm growth. The amenity channel seems much less important.

The strong association between human capital and city growth might be spurious for many reasons. For instance, more educated workers may be more mobile (or equivalently have stronger incentives to move) and as a result be overrepresented in fast-growing cities. Glaeser and Saiz (2004) perform a number of robustness checks to show that this is not the case and that the effect of human capital on city growth is most likely causal. First, they show that education levels affect city growth even after controlling for a wide array of city characteristics. Second, they show that the relationship between education and city growth holds when looking only at variations in growth and human capital within cities over time. That is, a given city tends to grow faster when its population is more educated. This indicates that the relationship between human capital and city growth is not driven by unobserved permanent characteristics that make cities grow faster and attract more educated workers. Finally, to account for the possibility of a common determinant of both city growth and human capital, they use instrumental variables. To obtain an exogenous determinant of human capital in cities, they follow Moretti (2004) in using the existence of land grant colleges as an instrumental variable. Starting in 1862, land grant colleges were created in each state to foster agricultural and engineering education. They were usually placed in cities that were conveniently located (typically, a central location in a state). Shapiro (2006) shows that these cities were not more educated before 1900 but gradually became more so as the grant colleges developed, often turning into major universities. Glaeser and Saiz (2004), like Shapiro (2006), find that instrumenting city human capital by the presence of land grant colleges strongly suggests that the effect of education on city growth is causal and, if anything, leads to higher coefficients than indicated by the simple association in the data.

Entrepreneurship

The fourth key engine of the population growth of cities is "collective entrepreneurship." This expression attempts to capture the notion that, while entrepreneurship alone affects city growth, collectively, entrepreneurs represent more than the sum of their parts because of agglomeration effects. (For further discussion of the role of entrepreneurship in urban growth, see Edward Glaeser's chapter; for discussion of how density may affect knowledge exchange see Kyle Fee and Daniel Hartley's chapter.) The recognition of the importance of entrepreneurs to understand urban evolution goes back to Chinitz (1961) and was later forcefully highlighted by Glaeser, Kallal, Scheinkman, and Shleifer (1992). In their celebrated paper, Glaeser and colleagues find that a standard deviation of their measure of entrepreneurship and urban diversity for a given city and industry is associated with up to one-fifth of a standard deviation of employment growth for this city and industry over 1956–87.

Understanding how entrepreneurship might affect city growth is important. First, entrepreneurs may generate dynamic externalities. Entrepreneurial skills may be a specific form of human capital. As with the previous engine of city growth, one can then conjecture that the clustering of entrepreneurs may lead to faster learning that is self-reinforcing. This is not far from the mechanism suggested by Alfred Marshall long ago:

> The mysteries of trade become no mysteries; but they are as it were in the air, children learn many of them unconsciously. Good work is rightly appreciated, inventions and improvements in machinery, in process and the general organization of the business have their merits promptly discussed: if one man starts a new idea, it is taken up by others and combined with suggestions of their own; and thus becomes the source of further new ideas. (Marshall 1890: iv.x,3)[5]

An alternative explanation for the effect of entrepreneurs on city growth assumes static externalities. In a city with many entrepreneurs, producers have easy access to many small firms in a diversity of industries, which makes it easier for them to hire specialized workers or find specialized inputs (as modeled by Duranton and Puga 2001). Firms operating in such environments enjoy higher productivity. More productive firms may invest more and, in turn, grow more over time, which fosters city growth. While these explanations differ, they lead to the same conclusion: A cluster of entrepreneurs may act as a powerful engine for city growth.

Although the notion that clusters of entrepreneurs foster city growth is appealing, proving this fact is extremely difficult. First, entrepreneurship is a disputed concept that is not easily captured in the data. In their initial investigation, Glaeser, Kallal, Scheinkman, and Shleifer (1992) used a measure of average employment per manufacturing establishment to proxy for entrepreneurship (since more entrepreneurs should lead to smaller establishments). Their results were confirmed by Glaeser and Kerr (2011) who use, instead, employment in new start-ups to measure entrepreneurship.

Beyond this measurement problem, establishing the direction of causality between entrepreneurship and city growth is a major challenge. Indeed, the strong association between local entrepreneurship and city growth could alternatively be explained by greater entrepreneurial entry in the presence of growth opportunities in a city. After all, this is what we expect entrepreneurs to do. To establish that causality runs from entrepreneurs to growth, Glaeser and Kerr (2009) first confirm that much of local entrepreneurship can be explained by the presence of many small suppliers in line with Chinitz's (1961) initial suggestion.[6] Second, Glaeser, Kerr, and Ponzetto (2010) look at whether the presence of many small firms in a city and sector is driven by the demand for entrepreneurship or by its supply. To the extent that the demand for entrepreneurship can be captured by higher sales per worker, it does not appear to matter. Their findings point instead to the importance of the supply of entrepreneurship.

Finally, Glaeser, Kerr, and Kerr (2012) tackle this causality issue head on, again using instrumental variables. Returning to Chinitz's (1961) initial comparison of Pittsburgh and New York, they use the idea that cities closer to mines have developed or have been influenced by large mining firms. In turn, large firms are expected to reduce entrepreneurship by providing attractive employment opportunities for highly skilled workers. Large firms may also breed a local culture of "company men," which also reduces entrepreneurship. Indeed, proximity to historical mines is associated with larger establishments today even in completely unrelated sectors. Using this instrument, they estimate an even larger effect of entrepreneurship on city growth than the one measured directly from the data. Because a mining past can be associated with a general decline in manufacturing, Glaeser, Kerr, and Kerr (2012) replicate their main findings for cities outside the Rust Belt. These findings also hold when, instead of focusing on overall employment, they look only at service sectors remotely tied to mining. Overall, these results are supportive of the notion that entrepreneurship is an important engine of city growth.

Industry Clusters and Shocks

"Historical accidents" and "shocks" of various sorts, especially industry shocks (positive or negative), seem to play an important role in explaining the evolution of cities. That is, an industry location that may have begun as the result of an historical accident may result in a cluster of firms that gives rise to growth overtime (in her chapter, Kimberly Zeuli describes how two cities responded differently to similar shocks, with different results).

Unfortunately, shocks are hard to measure, making it difficult to demonstrate their role in the evolution of cities. One imperfect way to measure them is to think of shocks and luck as residual explanations for city growth after conditioning out everything else. The fact that regressions that attempt to explain city growth over a ten- or twenty-year period often struggle to explain more than a third or half of the variation in growth despite controlling for a wide variety of engines of city growth suggests, indeed, that shocks may be important. Of course, one must remain cautious when interpreting a low R^2 in a regression since it can always be due to noisy measures of the dependent variable and missing explanatory variables.

Jacobs (1969) provides further evidence for the importance of shocks with an interesting collection of anecdotes. She reports that, in the late nineteenth century, New York City was the capital of the photographic industry, whereas Rochester, New York, led the production of precision instruments. George Eastman, while working at improving optical instruments in Rochester, invented an emulsion-coating machine that enabled him to mass produce photographic dry plates. His company soon took over the market for photographic films, and, as a consequence, Rochester replaced New York as the main center of the photographic industry. Fifty years later, Rochester retained that distinction, while New York was the center of the duplication

industry. Then, the Haloid Company—a firm specializing in the manufacturing of photographic papers and operating in the shadow of Eastman
Kodak—came up with a new process for making copies without the need for
developing. The process, called xerography, made Rochester the new capital
of the duplication industry, displacing New York with its leadership in the
previously dominant technology, the Varityper. These two industries came
to represent an important part of Rochester's employment. Their subsequent
loss is arguably an important cause of Rochester's recent decline. More generally, two important positive shocks can account for much of Rochester's
earlier growth, and two large negative shocks go a long way to explain its
recent decline. Again, caution is needed. Multiple anecdotes are not data.

A third way to make the case for the importance of shocks in a city's
growth or decline is to develop a model in which cities experience industry
shocks leading to the capture or loss of an industry (as with Kodak and
Haloid in Rochester). Duranton (2007) proposes such a model of city growth
where cities are hit by innovation shocks. This model makes a number of
predictions. First, innovation shocks within and across industries should
lead to the fast churning of industries across cities. There is considerable
evidence of such churning in the United States. Second, according to the
model, cities will both gain and lose industries so that they will slowly move
up or down the urban hierarchy. Duranton (2007) provides evidence of this
for twentieth-century American cities. He also provides evidence for more
detailed patterns predicted by the model including the stronger variance in
growth rates for small cities for which industry shocks will have a larger effect. To return to our earlier example, the loss of the photographic industry
was a catastrophe for a small city such as Rochester, whereas the loss of a
similar industry like computing in the New York metropolitan area following the reorganization of IBM around the same time was far less important.
Finally, the model predicts a steady-state distribution of city sizes that is not
far from Zipf's law. Zipf's law is synonymous with a Pareto distribution with
unit shape parameter. In practice, this implies that the population of the second largest city is expected to be half the population of the largest, the third
largest is expected to be a third of the size of the largest, and so forth. This
benchmark is relevant for the distribution of the population size of metropolitan areas in the United States. There is strong evidence that the distribution of city sizes in the United States is fairly still and that Zipf's law is a
good first-order approximation for the size distribution of cities. The caveat
with this modeling approach is that the evidence is only indirect. If the size

distribution of cities is unchanging, cities move slowly up and down the urban hierarchy following net gains or losses of industries. These movements are based on the evolution of the composition of the cluster of industries located in cities caused by innovation-driven shocks that can lead to fast location changes of industries across cities (Duranton 2007).

Finally, we can also use the fact that the sectoral and occupational composition of economic activity of a city strongly conditions its subsequent growth or decline. More precisely, one can construct a strong predictor of the growth of a city over a period of time by interacting its composition of economic activity at the beginning of the period with the national growth of the sectors of activity over the period (excluding, possibly, the city being examined). For instance, the expected employment growth rate of a city specializing in steel production in 1980 is lower than that of a city initially specializing in computing or tourism. Bartik (1991) initially proposed this predictor of city growth. It performs very well and has been widely used since it was originally proposed. More research is, nonetheless, needed here because there are minor unresolved identification issues. For instance, the strong presence of high-growth sectors in growing cities could be caused to some extent by the arrival of new residents.

To conclude, the various pieces of evidence discussed here and casual observation strongly suggest that shocks, and especially industry shocks, are a strong determinant of urban evolution.

Land Use Regulations and Geography

This discussion of city growth has so far ignored housing supply. All these factors can either lead to growth or increased house prices depending on the stringency of supply, though, perhaps with a lag, we may expect the supply of housing in cities to follow the demand of households, in which case the role of housing supply in city growth would be minimal. This explanation, however, neglects an important element: housing supply does not always respond to demand. Stringent land use regulations can make the supply of housing extremely inelastic. We note that cities could use land use regulation to increase the supply through densification schemes, for instance. However, in practice, land use regulations in the United States are, in most cases, geared toward restricting housing supply through, among others, minimum lot size regulations, maximum building height, green belts, and lengthy and cumbersome approval processes. The literature discussed below attempts to measure all these aspects within one aggregate index such as the the Wharton Residential Land Use Regulatory Index (Gyourko, Saiz, and Summers 2008).

Properly speaking, land use regulations are not an engine of population growth in cities. Rather, they are a necessary condition for city population growth, and they determine whether an increase in the demand for labor in a city will lead to higher wages or to more population. In the short run (where we take city population to be fixed), an increase in the demand for labor leads to higher wages. In turn, higher wages attract to the city new workers who need to live somewhere. With lax land use regulations, new construction will occur, and wage increases will remain in check while population expands. With stringent regulations, new workers must outbid current residents since the stock of housing is fixed. In this case, a higher demand for labor leads to higher wages, higher housing prices, and little or no population growth.

This argument demonstrates that measures of the stringency and restrictiveness of land use regulations cannot be used directly as explanatory variables in a city growth regression. Instead, the stringency of land use regulations should be interacted with predictors of city growth. In cities that are predicted to grow, we expect strong population growth when land use regulations are lax and strong wage and housing price growth when they are stringent. In their analysis of U.S. metropolitan areas between 1980 and 2000, Glaeser, Gyourko, and Saks (2006) use two robust predictors of city growth to demonstrate this process. They selected the first predictor—the share of the population with a bachelor's degree—because human capital is a strong engine of city growth. The second predictor is an index that exploits the idea proposed above, that cities differ in the sectorial composition of their employment and sectors do not grow nationwide at the same rate over time. For a given predicted employment growth, Glaeser, Gyourko, and Saks (2006) show that highly regulated cities experienced lower population growth, higher income growth, and higher growth in housing prices.

This type of analysis raises again an inference problem. We expect land use regulations to be more stringent in fast-growing cities. In addition, current land owners may lobby hard for stricter regulations when they expect housing prices to appreciate, whereas employers may lobby for laxer regulations when they expect their activities to expand. Increases in income per capita in cities may also be a consequence of housing price appreciation since only richer households may be able to afford more expensive houses. All this casts doubts on the direction of causality in the findings reported above.

While a complete disentangling of the stringency of land use regulations and population growth in cities has escaped the literature so far, Saiz (2010) offers interesting findings about the exogeneity of land use regulations. Most important, land use regulations are more stringent in cities where there is less "usable" land. Usable land is defined as all land minus bodies of water and land with a steep slope. By that measure, cities like San Francisco and Miami have very little usable land, whereas cities like Atlanta and Columbus are largely unconstrained in their development. Saiz (2010) shows a strong link between these natural constraints and stringent land use regulations. Ultimately, the limits on city growth imposed by land use regulations are geographical limits.

The Asymmetry of City Growth and Decline

As just shown, land use regulations affect housing construction, which may constrain the population growth of cities. However, once a house is built, it is built for a long time. The durability of housing also has important implications for city growth. People can move out of a city. Houses cannot.

When a negative labor demand shock hits a city, one expects workers to leave that city for cities where labor demand is expanding. However, as workers leave a city, house prices fall, and, when there are more houses than households, house prices can fall very low, sometimes well below construction costs; this extremely cheap housing slows the outflow of workers. Even when a city offers poor job prospects, workers may find the very low cost of living attractive. This suggests an interesting asymmetry between city growth and city decline. Growing cities may grow very fast. For example, Las Vegas, Nevada, and Raleigh, North Carolina, both enjoyed more than 40 percent growth between 2000 and 2010—and these are only two examples among seventeen metropolitan areas that grew by more than 20 percentage points above the mean of 10.8 percent that decade. On the other hand, New Orleans saw its population decline by more than 10 percent between 2000 and 2010, and this is the only city that is more than 20 percentage points below the mean. Being 20 percentage points below the mean is thus much rarer than being 20 percentage points above it. New Orleans, having suffered the sudden and massive destruction of its housing stock by a natural event, is the rare exception that confirms the rule. Even Youngstown, Ohio, and Johnstown, Pennsylvania—which come just before New Orleans at the bottom of the growth ranking for 2000–2010—did not decline by more than 6 percent over a decade. Glaeser and Gyourko (2005) confirm this fact more systematically for 321 U.S. cities for each decade between 1970 and 2000.

Glaeser and Gyourko (2005) also argue that those who stay in declining cities because of low housing prices are likely to be those with the lowest labor market prospects if they were to move to other cities. Hence, cities that decline in population are also expected to decline in human capital. Glaeser and Gyourko provide evidence of this phenomenon for their sample of U.S. cities. Given the evidence discussed above, a decline in human capital does not help the growth prospects of declining cities. Aside from this decline in human capital, there is an even more fundamental reason urban decline is highly persistent: housing is durable but not permanent. It depreciates slowly over time. Hence, after a negative shock in labor demand in a city, some households will leave, and housing prices will collapse—but many other households will stay because of the availability of inexpensive housing. Then, over time, the housing stock depreciates, and housing supply declines. Since housing prices, that is, the market values of properties, may be well below their construction costs, houses that depreciate are not likely to be refurbished. Households will, thus, slowly leave the city as the housing stock slowly depreciates. Put differently, housing decline is expected to be very persistent. Indeed, urban decline one decade is a strong predictor of urban decline for the following decade whereas city growth one decade is not such a strong predictor of city growth for the following decade (Glaeser and Gyourko 2005). Finally, we note that urban decline leaves cities with large stocks of derelict housing and developed but unoccupied land. The management of such underutilized land is an important policy challenge for these cities, a topic taken up by the authors of the chapters in this book's next section.

Conclusion: Which Role for Policies?

The evidence about the drivers of city growth is still incomplete and tentative but strongly points toward roads, amenities, human capital and entrepreneurship, shocks, and land use regulations. This limited knowledge may be viewed as a sad state of affairs in absolute terms, but, relative to how little we know about the much bigger but related question of the determinants of economic growth across countries, it is not so bad. It is also comforting to note that much of what we know today was learned after 2000 as a result of trying to establish causality.

Where does all this leave us in terms of implications for urban policy? The first message should be one of caution. The state of our knowledge does not really allow us to defend any policy to reverse urban decline as a "no-brainer." Second, the diversity of engines of urban growth suggests that there is no such thing as a "magic bullet." As already mentioned, Las Vegas and Raleigh were among the fastest-growing cities in the United States between 2000 and 2010. Las Vegas combines lots of roads, very mild winters, a specialization in a strongly expanding sector, and lax land use regulations. Raleigh also combines a variety of engines of city growth, albeit in a different way with a greater importance of human capital and entrepreneurship. Third, trying to reverse urban decline is an uphill battle. As argued above, negative shocks to cities translate into slow, persistent decline. Attempting to reverse urban decline thus means attempting to reverse the effects of large negative shocks to a city that will likely persist for decades.

Considering specific policy areas does not make the case for strongly activist policies more encouraging. Quite the opposite. For instance, Duranton and Turner (2012) argue that greater road provision would be an extremely expensive way to achieve urban growth. Others propose amenities; but, unfortunately, nice weather seems to be key and local policies cannot change the weather. Other amenities or quasi-amenities—such as better delivery of local public services—are certainly worth pursuing. But all cities, not only cities interested in reversing their decline, should be doing this. As for major beautification projects—such as establishing a world class museum or a large-scale rejuvenation of a brownfield area—the jury is still out. For one successful museum in Bilbao, Spain, how many white elephants have we seen? Human capital is also worth pursuing, but this should be true, again, for all cities. Better local education at all levels is certainly fundamental, but this is unlikely any time soon to bridge the skill gap that many declining cities face. Attracting skilled workers from elsewhere sends us back to the difficulty of providing amenities, something especially challenging for poor, unskilled cities with cold winters. The many attempts to establish new high-tech clusters have an appalling success record (Duranton, Martin, Mayer, and Mayneris 2010). Only the not-so-glamorous bidding for big assembly plants appears to bring significant employment and productivity benefits (Greenstone, Hornbeck, and Moretti 2010). Even there, whether this passes any cost-benefit analysis is unclear.

Finally, lax land use regulations are only a necessary condition and cannot achieve anything on their own.

This is not to say that nothing can be done. Often, the problem of urban decline is ill posed. Urban decline has important negative consequences for the less-skilled residents of declining cities (as Laura Perna points out in her chapter in this volume). Maybe these less-skilled residents should be the prime target of policies, not the cities in which they live. If their skills can be upgraded, then where they decide to take their skills may be their decision.

CHAPTER 3

The Relationship Between City Center Density and Urban Growth or Decline

Kyle Fee and Daniel Hartley

One striking characteristic of shrinking metropolitan statistical areas such as Detroit and Cleveland is the amount of vacant land and number of abandoned buildings in close proximity to the central business districts (CBDs) of their central cities. This lies in stark contrast to growing MSAs such as New York, Chicago, San Francisco, or Boston. Yet, in many shrinking MSAs, such as Detroit and Cleveland, one can find suburbs that do not show the same signs of decline as can be seen within the city limits of the central city. The spatial patterns of population decline observed in Detroit and Cleveland are typical of MSAs that experience net population loss: of the 345 MSAs we studied, the 36 that experienced population loss from 1980 to 2010 showed, on average, the steepest drop in population density in areas close to the CBD.

Almost all the MSAs that have lost population since 1980 were more heavily concentrated in manufacturing than the average MSA (as discussed in the chapter by Cochrane et al. in this volume). On average, 30 percent of employment in these declining MSAs was in the manufacturing sector in 1980, while this average was about 20 percent across all other MSAs in the same year. With only a few exceptions, these MSAs are located in the region of the United States sometime referred to as the Rust Belt, stretching from upstate New York through Pennsylvania, Ohio, Michigan, Indiana, and Illinois to the eastern edge of Iowa. Employment and population decline in these places is connected with shifts in manufacturing activity to the South and overseas.

The population decline associated with the loss in manufacturing jobs was concentrated in the areas close to the CBD of these regions. Thus, we ask in this chapter whether the drop in population density that we observe in shrinking cities reinforced the negative manufacturing employment shock, becoming an additional factor in the decline of these cities. We also ask what other demographic changes accompanied drops in population density near the CBD and whether these drops are particularly detrimental to the MSA in terms of productivity or merely symptoms of a changing industrial landscape.

The chapter compares demographic changes within growing cities to those within declining cities and explores the relationship between these cities and their suburbs, particularly focusing on population density near the CBD and MSA-level income growth. We assemble a constant MSA boundary and constant census tract boundary data set for the years 1980, 1990, 2000, and 2010 and perform the first part of our analysis, documenting how population density and other demographic variables evolved as a function of distance to the CBD in growing versus shrinking MSAs. In the second part of our analysis, we construct MSA-level variables by summing and taking weighted means of the tract-level data to aggregate the variables of interest to MSA-level variables. We find that, from 1980 to 2010, changes in population density near the CBD are positively associated with MSA-level income growth, while controlling for changes in population density for the MSA as a whole and initial characteristics of the MSA. This result points to a connection between MSA-level productivity growth and changes in population density near the CBD.

The first part of our analysis, which looks at within-MSA changes in population density and demographics in shrinking and growing cities, relates to a large body of literature on urban growth and suburbanization. Several examples include Rappaport (2003); Glaeser and Kahn (2001b); Boustan and Shertzer (2010); and Baum-Snow (2007). Our work also relates to a set of recent papers that examine spatial patterns within cities such as Guerrieri, Hartley, and Hurst (2013, 2012) and Glaeser, Gottlieb, and Tobio (2012).

The second part of our analysis concerns the question of whether the drop in population density that we observe in shrinking cities might act to reinforce the negative shock that is the root cause of the MSA's decline. This question is related to a large body of literature on economies of agglomeration.[1] As Elvery and Sveikauskas (2010) point out, much of the recent empirical evidence on agglomeration points toward agglomeration effects that are present at short distances.[2] These short distance effects point in the direction of the importance of the exchange and diffusion of ideas as opposed to benefits purely driven by forces that are likely to operate at greater distances, such as labor market pooling and supply linkages. (See Glaeser's chapter for a discussion of the importance of proximity in fostering entrepreneurship and Duranton's chapter for clustering and agglomeration economies.) A dense CBD may serve as a coordination mechanism by guiding people and firms to a place where these exchanges are most likely to happen. While polycentric MSAs may provide this as well, it seems plausible that having many diffuse areas of economic activity would make it harder for these informational spillovers to occur.

Given the importance of short-distance agglomeration effects, we run ordinary least squares (OLS) regressions of growth in MSA-level income on changes in population density near the CBD and changes in population density for the entire CBD and a host of initial-year MSA-level controls. We find that increases in population density near the CBD are associated with higher MSA-level income growth, while increases in population density for the entire MSA are associated with lower income growth. This evidence points to a connection between density near the CBD and agglomerative benefits.

Methodology

In order to take a detailed look at within-MSA changes in population density and other demographics, we use the Neighborhood Change Database (NCDB) in conjunction with the Longitudinal Tract Database (LTDB) to construct measures of population and demographic variables for the years 1980, 1990, 2000, and 2010 that conform to 2010 census tract boundaries and 2008 MSA boundaries. The use of constant geographical boundaries is especially important when considering growing MSAs, which may appear to lose population density as less populated counties farther from the CBD are developed and become part of the MSA.

For each MSA or metropolitan division (in cases when an MSA is broken into metropolitan divisions, we use the metropolitan divisions rather than the entire MSA), we identify the latitude and longitude of the CBD by taking the collection of census tracts listed in the 1982 Census of Retail Trade[3] for the central city of the MSA (the city in the MSA with the largest population) and finding the centroid of that cluster of census tracts. We

identify the CBD latitude and longitude for 268 MSAs in this manner. For
the remaining 117 MSAs, whose central city was not listed in the 1982 Census of Retail Trade, we use the latitude and longitude found by geocoding the
MSA's central city found using the ArcGIS 10.0 North American Geocoding
Service. ArcGIS returns points that are, on average, very close to the CBDs
from the Census of Retail Trade; for the 268 cities for which we have both,
the mean distance between the two is 0.39 miles. One of the MSAs with the
largest distances between the two is New York City, for which the Census of
Retail Trade CBD corresponds to midtown, while ArcGIS returns a point in
Lower Manhattan (on Chambers, halfway between Broadway and Church).
When calculating distance to CBD, we calculate the distance from the centroid of each 2010 census tract in the MSA to our central city CBD point.

Our sample consists of all census tracts in the continental United States
that were part of an MSA in 2008 and that were fully covered by census
tracts in 1980. To construct our sample, we start with the NCDB produced
by Geolytics. The NCDB provides census tract level summary variables
similar to those that can be found in U.S. census tract level summary files
for 1980, 1990, and 2000. The benefit of the NCDB is that the data from years
prior to 2000 (1970, 1980, and 1990) have been normalized to the year 2000
tract boundaries. Dropping observations associated with MSAs that were not
completely covered by census tracts in 1980 eliminates 1,776 tracts (about 3.4
percent of the total); we begin with 1980 rather than 1970 because, if we began in 1970 and dropped observations associated with MSAs that were not
covered by census tracts in 1970, we would have had to drop about 15 percent
of the sample.

Next, we convert the 1980, 1990, and 2000 tract level tabulation variables
to census 2010 tract boundaries using the 2000 to 2010 tract conversion tool
discussed in Logan, Xu, and Stults (2012).[4] The conversion tool uses population and land area weighting to reweight count or mean variables to adjust
for census tracts that have changed from 2000 to 2010. After converting
the NCDB data to 2010 tract boundaries, we merge it with census tract
population, race, and age tabulations from the 2010 census and education,
income, and poverty rate census tract estimates from the 2006–2010 American Community Surveys (ACS). We limit our sample to 345 MSAs in the
continental United States for which we have at least ten census tracts. Our
final sample contains a set of consistently defined variables for 1980, 1990,
2000, and 2010 for 57,403 consistently defined census tracts in 345 MSAs. It

is important to note that our MSAs are defined using the 2008 MSA definitions and the boundaries we use do not change over time.

The Relationship Between Growth and City Center
Density and Other Demographics

We break our sample of 345 MSAs into three groups. The first group consists of the 36 MSAs that lost population between 1980 and 2010 (see Table
3.1 for a list of these); the second group consists of the 272 MSAs with population growth between 0 and 100 percent from 1980 to 2010; the third consists of the 37 MSAs whose populations grew in excess of 100 percent over
the same period (see Table 3.2 for these). We refer to these groups as shrinking, moderate growth, and fast growth MSAs throughout the chapter.

We find that shrinking MSAs display markedly different patterns in
population density and demographic changes near their CBDs compared to
the moderate and fast growth MSAs. In particular, from 1980 to 2010,
shrinking MSAs lost about a third of their population density near the CBD,
on average. In contrast, moderate growth and fast growth MSAs had slight
gains in population density near the CBD. In conjunction with the loss of
population density, compared to growing MSAs, tracts near the CBD in
shrinking cities also experienced smaller gains in educational attainment,
less growth in average household income, greater increases in poverty rates,
and an increase in the fraction of the population who are African American.

Figure 3.1 presents plots of locally weighted mean population densities
(census tract population per square mile) in 1980 and 2010. In each plot (and
all subsequent figures), the line with short dashes indicates the mean for the
group of shrinking MSAs, the solid line indicates the mean for the group of
moderate growth MSAs, and the line with long dashes and dots indicates
the mean for the group of fast growth MSAs. Figure 3.2 shows mean changes
in population density for each of the three groups. The figure displays plots
of population changes for 1980–1990, 1990–2000, 2000–2010, and the entire
period 1980–2010.

A number of features of these plots are worth noting. First, in each decade, and as a result for the period as a whole, population density in the
group of shrinking MSAs fell the most near the CBD and fell very little or
not at all thirty miles from the CBD. In contrast, population density in

Table 3.1. MSAs That Shrank (in Population) 1980–2010

Anderson, IN Metropolitan Statistical Area
Battle Creek, MI Metropolitan Statistical Area
Bay City, MI Metropolitan Statistical Area
Binghamton, NY Metropolitan Statistical Area
Buffalo-Niagara Falls, NY Metropolitan Statistical Area
Cleveland-Elyria-Mentor, OH Metropolitan Statistical Area
Danville, IL Metropolitan Statistical Area
Danville, VA Metropolitan Statistical Area
Davenport-Moline-Rock Island, IA-IL Metropolitan Statistical Area
Decatur, IL Metropolitan Statistical Area
Detroit-Livonia-Dearborn, MI Metropolitan Division
Dubuque, IA Metropolitan Statistical Area
Duluth, MN-WI Metropolitan Statistical Area
Elmira, NY Metropolitan Statistical Area
Flint, MI Metropolitan Statistical Area
Huntington-Ashland, WV-KY-OH Metropolitan Statistical Area
Johnstown, PA Metropolitan Statistical Area
Kokomo, IN Metropolitan Statistical Area
Lima, OH Metropolitan Statistical Area
Mansfield, OH Metropolitan Statistical Area
Muncie, IN Metropolitan Statistical Area
New Orleans-Metairie-Kenner, LA Metropolitan Statistical Area
Niles-Benton Harbor, MI Metropolitan Statistical Area
Parkersburg-Marietta-Vienna, WV-OH Metropolitan Statistical Area
Peoria, IL Metropolitan Statistical Area
Pine Bluff, AR Metropolitan Statistical Area
Pittsburgh, PA Metropolitan Statistical Area
Pittsfield, MA Metropolitan Statistical Area
Saginaw-Saginaw Township North, MI Metropolitan Statistical Area
Springfield, OH Metropolitan Statistical Area
Toledo, OH Metropolitan Statistical Area
Utica-Rome, NY Metropolitan Statistical Area
Waterloo-Cedar Falls, IA Metropolitan Statistical Area
Weirton-Steubenville, WV-OH Metropolitan Statistical Area
Wheeling, WV-OH Metropolitan Statistical Area
Youngstown-Warren-Boardman, OH-PA Metropolitan Statistical Area

moderate growth cities grew slightly at all distances from the CBD, and population density of fast growth MSAs grew the most ten to fifteen miles from the CBD. Second, while the shrinking MSAs were higher density than the growing MSAs in 1980, by 2010 growing and shrinking MSAs have very similar density versus distance to CBD profiles. Third, while the 1980s and

Table 3.2. MSAs That Grew by More Than 100% (in Population), 1980–2010

Athens-Clarke County, GA Metropolitan Statistical Area
Atlanta-Sandy Springs-Marietta, GA Metropolitan Statistical Area
Austin-Round Rock-San Marcos, TX Metropolitan Statistical Area
Bakersfield-Delano, CA Metropolitan Statistical Area
Blacksburg-Christiansburg-Radford, VA Metropolitan Statistical Area
Boise City-Nampa, ID Metropolitan Statistical Area
Bradenton-Sarasota-Venice, FL Metropolitan Statistical Area
Cape Coral-Fort Myers, FL Metropolitan Statistical Area
Charlotte-Gastonia-Rock Hill, NC-SC Metropolitan Statistical Area
Charlottesville, VA Metropolitan Statistical Area
College Station-Bryan, TX Metropolitan Statistical Area
Colorado Springs, CO Metropolitan Statistical Area
Dallas-Plano-Irving, TX Metropolitan Division
Fayetteville-Springdale-Rogers, AR-MO Metropolitan Statistical Area
Fort Collins-Loveland, CO Metropolitan Statistical Area
Fort Worth-Arlington, TX Metropolitan Division
Greeley, CO Metropolitan Statistical Area
Hanford-Corcoran, CA Metropolitan Statistical Area
Laredo, TX Metropolitan Statistical Area
Las Cruces, NM Metropolitan Statistical Area
Las Vegas-Paradise, NV Metropolitan Statistical Area
Madera-Chowchilla, CA Metropolitan Statistical Area
McAllen-Edinburg-Mission, TX Metropolitan Statistical Area
Naples-Marco Island, FL Metropolitan Statistical Area
Ocala, FL Metropolitan Statistical Area
Olympia, WA Metropolitan Statistical Area
Orlando-Kissimmee-Sanford, FL Metropolitan Statistical Area
Phoenix-Mesa-Glendale, AZ Metropolitan Statistical Area
Port St. Lucie, FL Metropolitan Statistical Area
Provo-Orem, UT Metropolitan Statistical Area
Raleigh-Cary, NC Metropolitan Statistical Area
Reno-Sparks, NV Metropolitan Statistical Area
Riverside-San Bernardino-Ontario, CA Metropolitan Statistical Area
Sebastian-Vero Beach, FL Metropolitan Statistical Area
West Palm Beach-Boca Raton-Boynton Beach, FL Metropolitan Division
Wilmington, NC Metropolitan Statistical Area
Yuma, AZ Metropolitan Statistical Area

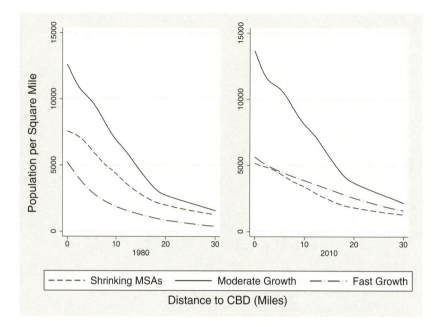

Figure 3.1. Locally weighted mean population densities in 1980 and 2010.
U.S. Census Bureau.

2000s saw big drops in center city density for shrinking cities, the 1990s also
saw a drop in density near the CBD for shrinking MSAs in the 1990s, but it
was smaller. Economists have found that denser places are more productive
than more diffuse places.[5] Thus, a decline in population density near the
CBD of a city could potentially exacerbate productivity declines that are being caused by external factors.

Given the marked differences in density changes, we next investigate
how the spatial patterns have changed for a series of variables related to urban growth literature. Figure 3.3 contains a different variable in each column.
The left column shows the fraction of the population with a bachelor's or
higher degree in 1980 and 2010 and the change in that fraction from 1980 to
2010. The right column shows the fraction of the population aged twenty-
five to thirty-four for the same time period.

Several interesting features stand out in the education plots. First, in
1980, the group of MSAs that subsequently shrink already have much lower
levels of educational attainment at all distances than the MSAs that subsequently grow. This is particularly true at distances within five miles of the

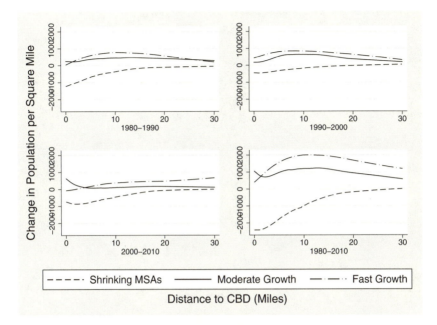

Figure 3.2. Mean changes in population density for 1980–1990, 1990–2000, 2000–2010, and 1980–2010. U.S. Census Bureau.

CBD. By 2010, educational attainment in the moderate growth cities was the highest of the three groups at most distances. It is also interesting that between five and fifteen miles from the CBD, educational attainment in the shrinking cities caught up with that of the fast-growing cities by 2010. However, at distances farther than fifteen miles from the CBD and also between zero and five miles of the CBD, the growing MSAs had higher educational attainment in 2010 than the shrinking MSAs. In fact, near the CBD, the gap in educational attainment between the shrinking and growing MSAs widened from about 10 percentage points in 1980 to about 15 percentage points in 2010, as shrinking MSAs saw increases of only 10 percentage points near the CBD compared to roughly 17 percentage points for both types of growing MSAs. Economists have found that more highly educated cities tend to be more likely to recover from negative shocks.[6] It may be that low educational attainment of the population near the CBD hindered the adoption of new industries as manufacturing declined in the set of cities that shrank.

The right column of Figure 3.3 shows how the fraction of the population aged twenty-five to thirty-four varies with distance to the CBD in 1980 and

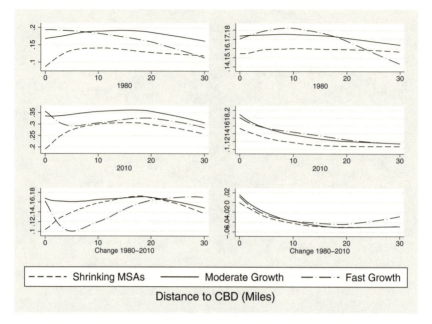

Figure 3.3. Changes in fraction of the population with a bachelor's degree or higher (left) and age twenty-five to thirty-four (right) in relation to distance from the CBD in 1980, 2010, and 1980–2010. U.S. Census Bureau.

2010 and how that has changed from 1980 to 2010. The plots for 1980 and 2010 reveal a gap near the CBD between the growing and shrinking MSAs in the fraction of people ages twenty-five to thirty-four. This gap stayed fairly constant between 1980 and 2010. The striking feature of the plots is that, in all three groups of MSAs, the fraction of the population aged twenty-five to thirty-four has fallen more in tracts that are farther from the CBD. The fact that the fraction of the population in this age range is shrinking in most places is likely to be a result of the aging of the "baby-boom" generation. At the same time, the pattern also shows that, in all, young people have become more likely to locate near the CBD in shrinking cities as well as in growing cities.

Figure 3.4 shows the log of mean household income (real, in terms of 2010 dollars) in the left column and the poverty rate in the right column. Average household income and poverty rates were similar in the three groups of MSAs in 1980. For all three groups of MSAs, income rose with distance to the CBD, and poverty rates fell with distance to CBD. The same patterns held

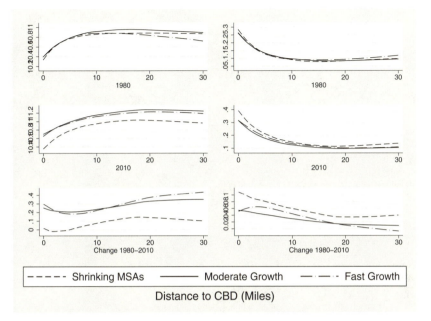

Figure 3.4. Changes in log of average household income (left) and poverty rate (right) in relation to distance from the CBD in 1980, 2010, and 1980–2010. U.S. Census Bureau.

in 2010, except that, while average household income rose by about 0.3 log points in the growing MSAs, the growth was much lower in shrinking MSAs. In fact, close to the CBD, shrinking cities experienced roughly zero growth in average household income from 1980 to 2010. While poverty rates in all three groups of cities rose from 1980 to 2010, the largest increase was among the shrinking MSAs. This pattern of lower income and higher poverty levels could potentially be a problem for shrinking MSAs as tax bases decline and the need for services increases as poverty levels increase.

Figure 3.5 shows how the fraction of African American (left column) and Hispanic (right column) residents vary with distance to the CBD in 1980 and 2010 and how that has changed over the period. In 1980, the fraction of residents who were African American was around 30 percent near the CBD for the shrinking MSAs. In contrast, African Americans made up closer to 20 percent or less of the population near the CBD in the moderate and fast growth MSAs. This is likely a legacy of the African American migration into northern factory towns and the subsequent decline of

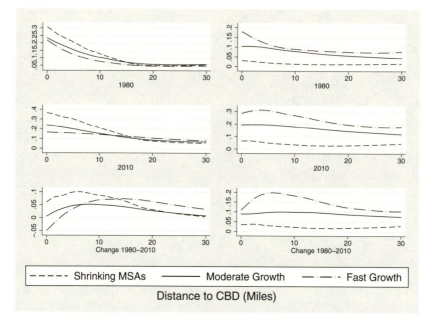

Figure 3.5. Changes in fraction of the population that is African American (left) and Hispanic (right) in relation to distance from the CBD in 1980, 2010, and 1980–2010. U.S. Census Bureau.

the manufacturing industry over the past thirty years, as our shrinking MSAs list has a large share of Rust Belt cities. From 1980 to 2010, the fraction of residents who are African American rose most within ten miles of the CBD for shrinking MSAs, 5 to 10 percentage points. For the fast growth MSAs this fraction fell within two miles of the CBD but rose farther from the CBD.

The Hispanic share of the population was greatest in the fast-growth MSAs in 1980 and increased the most in the fast growth MSAs from 1980 to 2010, expanding by at least 10 percentage points at all distances from the CBD. The moderate growth MSAs also saw substantial increases in the Hispanic population over this period. The shrinking MSAs had least growth in the fraction of the population who are Hispanic, increasing by fewer than 5 percentage points at all distances from the CBD. It is also interesting to note that, in 1980, shrinking MSAs possessed a lower fraction of Hispanics at all distances from the CBD compared to the growing cities. Lack of existing social networks and lack of economic opportunity may both play a role in explaining the slower growth of Hispanic population in shrinking compared to growing MSAs.

Changes in City-Center Density and MSA Income Growth

The first part of our analysis focused on differences in population density and demographic changes as a function of distance to the CBD between shrinking, moderate growth, and fast growth MSAs from 1980 to 2010. A natural question that arises from this analysis is whether changes in population density and other demographics near the CBD are associated with broader MSA-wide changes in productivity. In this section, we examine the relationship between the growth of average MSA household income and changes in population density near the CBD. The question we would like to answer is whether increases in near-CBD population density are related to MSA income growth above and beyond the relationship of MSA income growth to MSA population (or population density) growth. The answer to this question has implications for cities and regions. If density near the CBD is important for MSA productivity, then it may be in the interest of other jurisdictions in the MSA to implement policies that help strengthen the CBD of the central city. To address this question, we analyze an MSA-level dataset created from the constant geography tract-level data described above. Specifically, we run OLS regressions of MSA income growth on changes in population density near the CBD and for the MSA as a whole while controlling for the initial demographic and occupational characteristics of the MSA.

Table 3.3 presents summary statistics for the variables of interest: MSA income growth and changes in population density as well as the initial year demographic controls. The first row reveals that the mean growth rate of real per capita income from 1980 to 2010 for our sample of 345 MSAs was 2.78, meaning that per capita income almost tripled over the period. The standard deviation was 0.66. The next three rows show the mean population density within 2.5, 5, and 7.5 miles of the CBD respectively. These measures are constructed by dividing the total population (measured in thousands of people) living in census tracts with centroids within the boundary by the total land area (measured in square miles) within those census tracts. Rows 2 through 4 show that the mean population density for our sample of MSAs fell with distance from the CBD, although the standard deviations indicate a large amount of variation, each standard deviation larger than its respective

Table 3.3. Descriptive Statistics

	Mean	Std Dev.
Growth of average per capita income 1980–2010	2.78	0.66
Population density w/in 2.5 miles of CBD 1980	4.22	4.31
Population density w/in 5 miles of CBD 1980	2.57	3.11
Population density w/in 7.5 miles of CBD 1980	1.77	2.58
MSA population density 1980	2.58	2.65
Change in population density w/in 2.5 miles of CBD 1980–2010	0.02	1.25
Change in population density w/in 5 miles of CBD 1980–2010	0.19	0.84
Change in population density w/in 7.5 miles of CBD 1980–2010	0.23	0.64
Change in MSA population density 1980–2010	0.35	0.86
Log MSA population 1980	12.47	1.03
Log MSA per capita income 1980	8.78	0.18
Fraction of population with bachelor or higher degree 1980	0.16	0.06

Population density measured in 1000/sq. mi.

mean. The average MSA population density was 2.58 thousand people per square mile (fifth row).

The next four rows of Table 3.3 show the mean changes in the same four population density measures from 1980 to 2010. On average, the increase in population density within 2.5 miles of the CBD was only about twenty people per square mile. However, the mean masks a large amount of variation revealed by the standard deviation. The mean changes in population density increase as the area considered increases from within 2.5 miles of the CBD up to the whole MSA. The last four rows of Table 3.3 show the means and standard deviations of the initial year (1980) MSA demographic characteristics used as controls: log population, per capita income, fraction of population with a bachelor's or higher degree. In addition to these controls, our preferred specification also includes MSA occupational shares. These shares are defined as the fraction of employed people sixteen years and older who work in the following occupations: 1. Professional and technical occupations; 2. Sales workers; 3. Administrative support and clerical workers; 4. Precision production, craft, and repair workers; 5. Operators, assemblers, transportation, and material moving workers; 6. Service workers; 7. Nonfarm laborers. (Farm, forestry, and fishing workers are the omitted share.)

Overall, the summary statistics reveal that MSAs were on average denser closer to their CBD in 1980, but that density increased from the CBD from 1980 to 2010; however, there was much variation in both initial density and the changes in density.

Table 3.4 presents the results of OLS regressions of MSA income growth on changes in population density near the CBD and changes in population density for the MSA as a whole. Column 1 presents the simplest specification: a regression of MSA per capita income growth on the change in population density within 5 miles of the CBD and the change in population density in the MSA as whole. All three variables are defined over the period from 1980 to 2010. The coefficient on change in population density within 5 miles of the CBD is positive and statistically significantly different from zero. The value of 0.171 implies that a one standard deviation increase in population density within 5 miles of the CBD (0.84 thousand more people per square mile) is, on average, associated with 14 percentage points more in income growth over the thirty-year period, which translates to about 5 percent higher income growth compared to the mean of 278 percentage points. In contrast, the coefficient on the change in population density for the MSA as a whole is negative and statistically different from zero. The value of −0.116 implies that a one standard deviation increase in population density at the MSA level (0.86 thousand people per square mile) is associated with a 10 percentage point decrease in per capita income growth, or a 3.6 percent reduction in the growth rate of income per capita.

Column 2 of Table 3.4 presents the results of a similar specification, except that controls for initial year (1980) population density (within 5 miles of the CBD and MSA-level) and log population have been added. The coefficients on the change in population density near the CBD and the change in population density for the MSA as a whole increase slightly in magnitude and remain statistically different from zero. The coefficients on the initial population controls are not statistically different from zero. Column 3 adds additional initial year demographic controls: log 1980 per capita income and the fraction of the population with a bachelor's or higher degree, both defined for the entire MSA. The addition of these controls reduces the magnitude of change in population density near the CBD, though it remains statistically different from zero. With these controls, initial log population is now positively associated with per capita income growth. The new controls, log initial income and the fraction of the population with a bachelor's or higher degree, are significantly negatively and positively associated with per capita

Table 3.4. Dependent Variable: Growth of Per Capita Income 1980–2010

	(1)	(2)	(3)	(4)	(5)	(6)
Definition of near CBD (radius)	5 Miles	5 Miles	5 Miles	5 Miles	2.5 Miles	7.5 Miles
Change in population density near CBD 1980–2010 (population density measured in 1000s of people per sq. mi.)	0.171 (0.060)	0.203 (0.087)	0.144 (0.071)	0.143 (0.065)	0.102 (0.041)	0.135 (0.085)
Change in MSA population density 1980–2010 (population density measured in 1000s of people per sq. mi.)	−0.116 (0.049)	−0.147 (0.066)	−0.142 (0.062)	−0.195 (0.061)	−0.182 (0.059)	−0.168 (0.063)
Population density near CBD 1980		0.029 (0.041)	−0.010 (0.028)	−0.024 (0.026)	0.032 (0.019)	−0.011 (0.032)
Population density in MSA 1980		−0.026 (0.047)	0.018 (0.029)	0.035 (0.027)	−0.038 (0.032)	0.026 (0.028)
Log MSA population 1980		−0.006 (0.040)	0.178 (0.077)	0.199 (0.077)	0.158 (0.069)	0.167 (0.077)
Log MSA per capita income 1980			−2.375 (0.800)	−3.041 (0.861)	−3.025 (0.857)	−3.031 (0.880)
Fraction of population with bachelor or higher degree 1980			4.327 (0.762)	4.453 (2.020)	4.174 (1.966)	4.431 (2.006)
Occupational shares 1980	No	No	No	Yes	Yes	Yes
R-squared	0.02	0.02	0.37	0.48	0.48	0.47
Observations	345	345	345	345	345	345

income growth, respectively. The addition of these controls helps explain a lot more of the variation in income growth. The *R*-square increases from 0.02 in columns 1 and 2 to 0.37 in column 3.

Column 4 of Table 3.4 adds the eight occupational share variables mentioned in the discussion of the summary statistics. The addition of these variables does not have much of an impact on the coefficient on population density near the CBD but does increase the magnitude of the coefficient on the change in the population density of the MSA as a whole. This is our preferred specification. The aim is to see how changes in near-CBD population density and overall MSA population density correlate with MSA income growth while controlling for a number of initial year differences in demographics and occupational structures that might be correlated with subsequent income growth. The coefficients imply that after controlling for all of these initial year demographic and occupational factors, a one standard deviation increase in near CBD population density is associated with about a 12 percentage point increase in income per capita, roughly 4 percent of the mean growth in per capita income. The coefficient on MSA-level change in population density implies that a one standard deviation increase is associated with a 17 percentage point decrease in per capita income, roughly 6 percent of mean income growth.

Columns 5 and 6 present estimates of the same specification as column 4, except that, instead within 5 miles, "near" is defined as within 2.5 and 7.5 miles of the CBD in columns 5 and 6 respectively. While the coefficient on the change in population density near the CBD is smaller in magnitude than it is in column 4, it is still significantly different from zero, and a one standard deviation increase in population density near the CBD still implies about the same 12 percentage point increase in income growth as it did in column 4. However, changing the definition of "near" to "within 7.5 miles" (in column 6) results in a coefficient harder to distinguish from zero and implies that a one standard deviation increase in population density near the CBD is associated with less than a 9 percentage point increase in per capita income at the MSA level.

Discussion

We find that growth in population density near the CBD is positively associated with income growth at the MSA level. While this finding appears to be robust to adding a number of initial year demographic controls and to some variation in the definition of proximity to the CBD, it is unclear what mechanisms may underlie this relationship. One explanation is that loss of density near the CBD might adversely affect MSA-level income growth by decreasing short-distance agglomerative benefits, such as the exchange of ideas and information. An alternative explanation is that the causality runs in the opposite direction. It could be the case that rising income, especially at the upper end of the income distribution, results in a segment of the population who value a short commute so much that they trade the space available in the suburbs for the reduced commute of the area near the CBD. If the market responds by adding residential housing units near the CBD, then population density near the CBD could increase.[7] If population density near the CBD plays an important role in MSA-level productivity, then it may be in the interest of municipal jurisdictions throughout the MSA to pursue policies that lead to increased density near the CBD.

A desire to differentiate between these two possible scenarios led us to consider potential instruments that might be correlated with near-CBD population density and that would not be expected to influence MSA-level income growth except by way of their influence on near-CBD population density. One potential instrument is the measure of area (land or water) unavailable for development within fifty kilometers of the CBD as calculated in Saiz (2010). This fraction of the area within fifty kilometers of the CBD that is unavailable for development is associated with increases in population density within 2.5 miles of the CBD. Taking our column 5 specification and altering it so that changes in population density within 2.5 miles of the CBD is instrumented with the fraction undevelopable variable and dropping the initial year population density variables, results in a first stage F statistic of 10.37 and a t statistic on the unavailable variable of 3.22. However, including the initial population density measures using the 5 or 7.5 mile definitions of "near the CBD" result in much lower first-stage F and t statistics, indicating a potential weak instrument problem. The fact the findings are not robust to variation in the definition of "near the CBD" is a reason to be cautious about interpreting the results as an indication that higher population density near the CBD increases MSA-level productivity.

The other issue is whether it is plausible that the fraction of area unavailable for development within fifty kilometers of the CBD could influence MSA-level income growth in some manner other than by way of population density near the CBD. Saiz (2010) discusses why one would expect productivity to be correlated with the fraction of area unavailable for development: with many possible places to develop a city, places where development is more costly must have some natural advantage in productivity or amenity. Higher productivity could result in a correlation between area unavailable for development and income levels. However, it is unclear whether one would expect area unavailable to have an effect on income growth. For these reasons, we do not put much emphasis on the IV results.[8] However, we find the robustness of the association between changes in population density near the CBD and MSA-level income growth interesting. We think that exploring the mechanisms that may link changes in population density near the CBD to MSA-level productivity is an area for future policy-oriented research. If core density is important for productivity, then policymakers across the entire MSA might want to consider measures aimed at keeping the center city densely populated.

Conclusion

Anecdotal evidence from Detroit and Cleveland suggests that shrinking MSAs have lost the most population density near their CBDs. We find that, on average, this is true for the 36 MSAs that have lost population from 1980 to 2010. We find steep drops in population density for shrinking cities close to the CBD, which tail off as distance from the CBD increases. This pattern is not evident in growing MSAs. In conjunction with the drops in population density near the CBDs of shrinking MSAs, we find a smaller increase in educational attainment than in places farther away from the CBD in shrinking MSAs and a smaller increase in educational attainment than in places near the CBD in growing cities. On average, shrinking MSAs also have lower increases in income, higher increases in poverty rates, and higher increases in the African American fraction of the population near the CBD than do growing MSAs. Changes in the Hispanic fraction of the population are larger in growing MSAs than in shrinking MSAs, but these changes do not display much of a relationship with distance to the CBD in either type of MSA. Finally, the fraction of the population between ages twenty-five and thirty-four falls more as distance to the CBD increases. This pattern is very similar in growing and shrinking MSAs. This similarity may reflect an across-the-board increase in the desire of young people to live closer to the center of cities.

In the second part of our analysis, we turn to the question of whether changes in population density near the CBD are related to changes in MSA-level productivity that are reflected in the growth of income per capita in the MSA. Alternatively, it may be that changes in MSA-level productivity lead to increased desire to locate near the center of CBDs. In OLS regressions, we find a positive partial correlation between changes in population density near the CBD and MSA-level income growth from 1980 to 2010 while controlling for changes in overall MSA-level population density over the same period and controlling for a number of initial-year (1980) MSA characteristics. We explore a potential instrument for changes in population density but are not convinced that it is a strong enough instrument. It may be the case that a legacy of specialization in manufacturing has left these cities with old (and possibly abandoned) industrial facilities near the CBD that tend to make people prefer to live farther away from the CBD. We hope that further research uncovers the mechanisms that underlie the positive association between changes in population density near the CBD and MSA-level income growth, allowing leaders to craft informed policies that may help in the revitalization of cities that have experienced steep drops in population close to their cores. And while which explanation predominates (they are not mutually exclusive) matters, we should note here that both support the competitive advantage of central cities that attend to their core.

CHAPTER 4

Central Cities and Metropolitan Areas: Manufacturing and Nonmanufacturing Employment as Drivers of Growth

Steven Cochrane, Sophia Koropeckyj, Aaron Smith, and Sean Ellis

Over the past forty years, metropolitan areas have grown in both population and employment (see Figure 4.1), with suburban growth within metros outpacing that of central cities. This chapter examines trends in employment and population growth in cities and suburbs of the nation's metro areas, in particular focusing on the historical deindustrialization and the loss of manufacturing jobs in cities.[1]

To analyze these population and employment shifts for the four decades since 1970, we use county-level data from the one hundred largest metropolitan areas. In each metro area, we use the central county containing the largest principal city as a proxy for the central city,[2] with the rest of the counties serving as a proxy for the suburbs. With this approach, we are able to compare population growth, manufacturing employment, nonmanufacturing employment, and wages across central cities and suburbs at a national and regional level, dividing the nation into its four census regions.

It is clear that, historically, manufacturing was concentrated in cities and deindustrialization has occurred primarily in the Rust Belt cities of the Northeast and Midwest. In 1970, nearly 63 percent of metro-area manufacturing employment was located in central cities; in 2011, the share was 53 percent. Manufacturing employment fell in central cities by 48 percent between 1970 and 2011; the suburban decline was 23 percent.

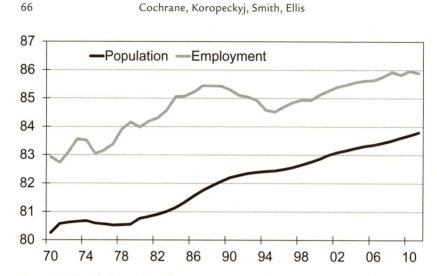

Figure 4.1. Population and employment in metropolitan areas, percent of U.S. total, 1970–2010. Bureau of Labor Statistics, U.S. Census Bureau, Moody's Analytics.

We find that the decline of manufacturing and the exodus from central cities has slowed and, in some cases, reversed with the onset of the Great Recession. We also note a reversal in population and nonmanufacturing employment growth rates in central cities versus suburbs and conclude with these data and their regional components.

3

The Decline of Manufacturing

The industrial structure of the U.S. economy has been undergoing a shift for decades: Manufacturing output and employment in absolute numbers and as a share of total output and employment have been declining since the late 1970s, while service employment has grown steadily. Manufacturing employment is now about 40 percent lower than it was at its peak in 1979, while service employment has nearly doubled. As a result, manufacturing now employs only 9 percent of the workforce, down from 22 percent in 1979, while the service share has grown from 54 to 69 percent (see Figure 4.2).[3] This shift has presented a tremendous challenge to the cities, where manufacturing was historically concentrated.[4]

The timing of the decline has not been steady but rather has accelerated during recessions. In the aftermath of the recession of the early 1980s, man-

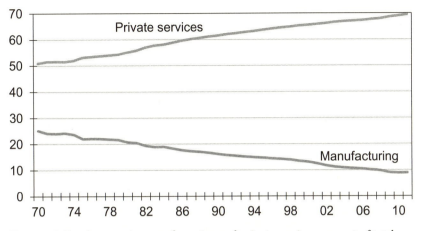

Figure 4.2. Employment in manufacturing and private services, percent of total, 1970–2010. Bureau of Labor Statistics, Moody's Analytics.

ufacturing failed to recover completely for the first time in post-World War II history. Similarly, only partial recovery characterized the rebound from the early 1990s recession. Following the recession of 2001, no rebound occurred. Rather, manufacturers continued to shed jobs throughout the economic expansion that followed. During the 2000s, manufacturing employment declined by one-third—a loss of 5.9 million jobs. This represents nearly three-quarters of the jobs lost since the late 1970s peak. Manufacturing employment bottomed out in early 2010 and has increased by only about half a million jobs since.[5]

One important reason for this significant loss of manufacturing jobs is implementation of labor-saving technologies and equipment (Rowthorn and Ramaswamy 1997: 20–24). Investments and improvements in capital equipment, particularly computer and information technology advancements, as well as more efficient processes, have enabled manufacturers to raise their output and keep pace with increasing demand without a corresponding increase in the number of workers that they employ. Gains in productivity for service industries have been much slower, and the need for workers has not fallen as much.[6] Of course, the role of labor-saving technology in job loss depends on the degree to which capital can substitute for labor and on the availability of a skilled labor force. Germany has been able to maintain manufacturing employment at about 20 percent because it was able to develop a skilled manufacturing labor force.[7]

A second reason for the loss of jobs is the decline of transportation costs and expansion of global trade as the United States outsourced lower value-added, labor-intensive manufacturing production first to lower cost regions in the United States and then to low-wage countries.[8] The huge job losses since the beginning of the last decade coincide with the surge in trade with China, which was able to manufacture goods far more cheaply thanks to its abundant supply of cheap labor. In 1985, the United States imported less than $4 billion worth of products from China. By 2000, the value had surged to more than $100 billion, and, by 2010, it had reached $365 billion (Nichols 2003).

The Shift from Cities to Suburbs

In 1970, central cities employed far more manufacturing workers than did suburban counties (see Figure 4.3). The difference narrowed sharply during the 1980s and 1990s as manufacturers closed down facilities in deindustrializing cities, mostly in the Northeast and Midwest, and relocated to suburbs in the Midwest and to both cities and suburbs in the South and the West as well as to low-wage countries, particularly since 2000.

In the 1970s, central cities, in aggregate, in the South and West enjoyed positive growth in manufacturing employment, strong enough to offset net declines in the Northeast and Midwest, generating a modest but positive growth rate for the sum of central cities (see Figure 4.4). But in the next three decades, cities in aggregate lost manufacturing jobs rapidly.

Central cities in both the Northeast and Midwest hemorrhaged their manufacturing base from the 1980s on. For central cities in the South and the West, this is a much more recent phenomenon; they lost only a small number of manufacturing jobs until the 2000s (see Figure 4.5).

In the South and West, from 1970 to 2000, suburban counties gained jobs (nearly 400,000 manufacturing jobs in the South and 300,000 in the West; see Figure 4.6). Growth of manufacturing in the suburban counties evolved markedly differently in the Midwest than in the South and West. A large increase in suburban growth in the Midwest occurred during the 1990s. Since the Midwest also underwent a substantial contraction of its central county manufacturing base during the 1980s, this suggests that growth in the suburban counties in the decade that followed was related to relocation to and expansion of the suburbs. During the first half of the 1990s,

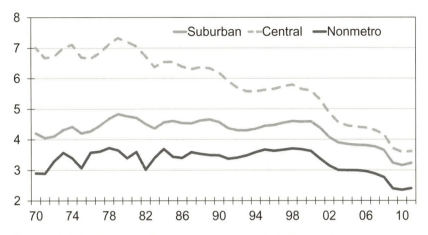

Figure 4.3. Suburban, central, and nonmetro manufacturing employment, in millions, 1970–2010. Bureau of Labor Statistics, Moody's Analytics.

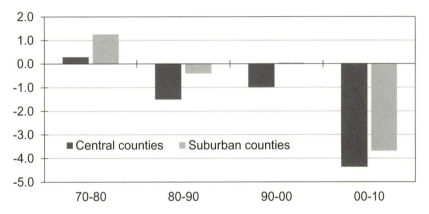

Figure 4.4. Manufacturing employment in central, and suburban counties, ten-year annualized percent change, 1970–2010. U.S. Census Bureau, Moody's Analytics.

the Midwest benefited in particular from expansion in auto parts production in suburban counties (Collins, McDonald, and Mousa 2007: 15–16).

Most (more than 60 percent) of the suburban gains in the South and West occurred during the 1970s. Central cities in the South and West also built up their manufacturing capacity during this period. The growth in the South and West reflected the attractiveness of these regions' costs relative to those in the Midwest and Northeast and declining transportation costs as

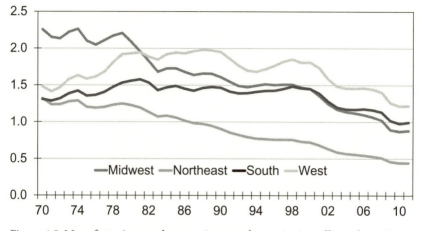

Figure 4.5. Manufacturing employment in central counties in millions, by region, 1970–2010. Bureau of Labor Statistics, Moody's Analytics.

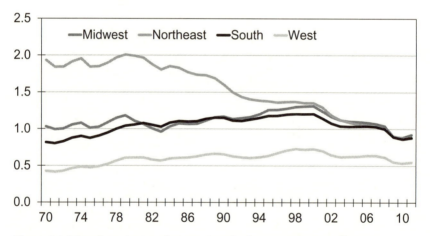

Figure 4.6. Manufacturing employment in suburban counties in millions, by region, 1970–2010. Bureau of Labor Statistics, Moody's Analytics.

well (Glaeser and Tobio 2007: 2). Edward Glaeser also points to the role of costs in regional relocation in his chapter in this volume.

In the decade from 2000 to 2010, manufacturing losses became pervasive. The manufacturing growth that had occurred in the suburbs of the Midwest and the cities and suburbs of the South and the West in the previous decades came to a halt. The losses in the Northeast accelerated during the 2000s, and the gains in the Midwest of the previous decade were wiped out. Indeed, suburban manufacturing employment in the Midwest ended in 2010 below the level of 1970. It was barely above the 1970 level in the suburban areas of the South.

Thus, over the past four decades, manufacturing employment declined in central cities in all four regions of the country, while manufacturing employment expanded in the suburbs of the Midwest, the South, and the West. But, in the 2000s, the combination of the technology bust in the early years of the decade and the deep 2007–2009 recession meant that no region escaped a manufacturing decline even in the suburban counties. The deindustrialization of the suburbs followed upon that of the cities.

While we are focusing on the aggregate manufacturing trends in each region's central cities and suburbs, the reality, of course, is that there is great variation within the regions. In fact, historically, the rate of the decline of central city manufacturing is correlated with each city's concentration of manufacturing; those with the highest concentration generally had larger percentage declines in manufacturing employment. For example, the central cities of Buffalo and Rochester, New York, and Youngstown, Ohio, ranked among the ten most concentrated in manufacturing among the 100 largest metro areas in 1970. Their rate of decline through 2011 was among the top 20.[9]

Trends in Population, Nonmanufacturing Employment, and Wage Income

Central cities' populations on average have grown in the metro areas of each of the four regions of the United States, between 1970 and 2010, although they have done so at much slower rates than those in the suburban counties (see Figure 4.7).

This pattern has held in each of the four broad regions of the country (see Figure 4.8) but with some significant regional differences. The difference in suburban and central city population growth has been less pronounced in the Northeast and West than in the South and Midwest. In all four regions, central cities lost most ground in the 1970s. Thus, population losses, relatively and, in many cases, absolutely, in central cities occurred prior to the decline in manufacturing jobs, although population losses continued as

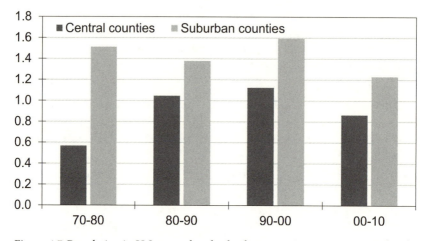

Figure 4.7. Population in U.S. central and suburban counties, ten-year annualized percent change, 1970–2010. U.S. Census Bureau, Moody's Analytics.

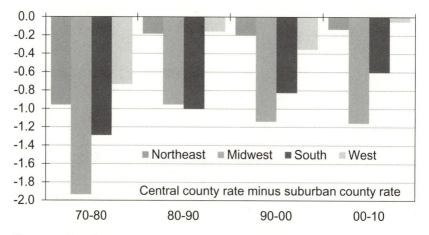

Figure 4.8. Population in metro areas, ten-year annualized percent change, by region, 1970–2010. U.S. Census Bureau, Moody's Analytics.

jobs also declined. As Glaeser and Duranton show in their chapters in this volume, transportation improvements resulted in the growth of suburbs as well, first as bedroom communities, then as job centers.

Nationally, central city and suburban employment trends (measured here as nonmanufacturing employment by place of employment, which today accounts for 91 percent of total payroll employment) over the past forty

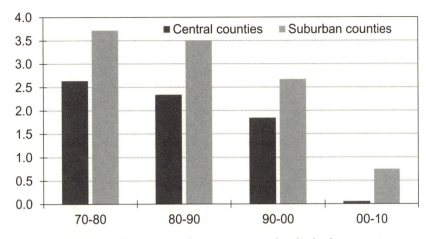

Figure 4.9. Nonmanufacturing employment in central and suburban counties, ten-year annualized percent change, 1970–2010. U.S. Census Bureau, Moody's Analytics.

years are similar to trends in population growth. As with population trends, nonmanufacturing employment grew faster in suburban counties than in central cities in all four decades (see Figure 4.9). The suburban counties gained the most relative to the cities during the 1970s and 1980s; the gap narrowed in the following two decades. From 1980 to 2010, as with population, the suburbs gained the most ground in the South and Midwest (see Figure 4.10).

The comparative performance of central cities within metro areas can also be gauged by wage income. Total resident wage income in central cities was more than double suburban wage income in 1970s. This gap narrowed to 1.5 times the suburban level as wage income in the central cities consistently grew at a slower pace than elsewhere in the metro areas (see Figure 4.11). But the differences between these growth rates have not been nearly as wide as the differences in employment growth rates. This, in part, reflects the highly paid jobs in finance and professional occupations, as well as in some managerial and healthcare occupations, which concentrate in the central cities of metro areas,[10] although note that the wage data we present here are for residents of cities.[11] It is important to note as well that higher aggregate income in the central cities provides no information about income distribution; poverty has been and still is concentrated in central cities, although most recently there has been an increase in poverty rates in suburbs

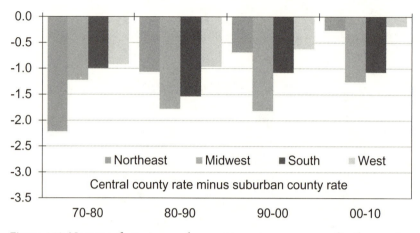

Figure 4.10. Nonmanufacturing employment in metro areas, annualized percent change, by region, 1970–2010. U.S. Census Bureau, Moody's Analytics.

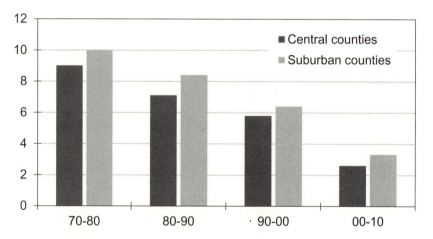

Figure 4.11. Wage income in central versus suburban counties, ten-year annualized percent change, 1970–2010. BEA, Moody's Analytics.

both absolutely and relatively to cities.[12] Moreover, household income is and has been higher in suburbs than in cities (see Table 4.1).

There has been virtually no difference in aggregate wage income growth trends between the central cities and suburban counties in the Northeast region over the past two decades, where some of the highest-paid occupations tend to be clustered (see Figure 4.12).[13] The long-term trends also indi-

Table 4.1. Median Household Income in 2010 Dollars

	Central cities	Suburbs*
1970	42,328	55,280
1980	44,663	59,202
1990	46,992	62,957
2000	48,365	65,638
2010**	44,815	59,878

State of the City Data System: U.S. Census Bureau; Brookings
Institution, State of Metropolitan America: U.S. Census Bureau.
*Suburbs data are defined as the total for the All MSAs/PMSAs less
the sum of data for these cities: All central cities, U.S.
**2010 data are from Brookings State of Metropolitan America.

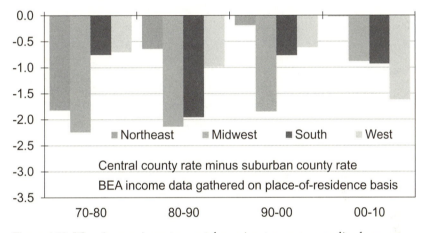

Figure 4.12. Wage income in metro areas by region, ten-year annualized percent
change, 1970–2010. BEA, Moody's Analytics.

cate that the wage income growth rate's discrepancy between urban and
suburban counties in the Midwest has narrowed since the 1980s.[14]

A Brief Interlude: The Great Recession

The Great Recession was felt in both central cities and in suburban metro
area counties. The downturn was the deepest in the Midwest, but no region
escaped the recession's impact, as shown by the data on resident wage

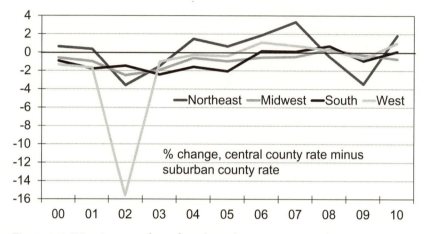

Figure 4.13. Wage income, place of-residence-basis, metro areas, by region, 2000–2010. BEA, Moody's Analytics.

income growth (see Figure 4.13) as well as by household income.[15] By 2009, the central cities and suburbs were hit hard, with central cities faring worse, with income declining 5.2 percent as compared with a 3.8 percent decline in the suburban counties.

The Great Recession was particularly hard on manufacturing industries in both central cities and suburbs (as discussed above). Nationwide manufacturing employment in 2008 fell by 3.2 percent in central cities and by 2.9 percent in suburbs. The worst year was 2009 when manufacturing employment declines accelerated to about 11 percent in both central cities and the suburbs, with the Midwest hit the hardest.[16]

The pattern for nonmanufacturing employment followed a similar time path. Central city employment was virtually flat in 2008 and down by 4.2 percent in 2009, while suburban area employment was down slightly in 2008 and by 3.7 percent in 2009. The Great Recession of 2008–2009 interrupted the longer-term trends of the past several decades, as income and employment across all industries plummeted and the trends spared neither central city nor suburb.

Central City Resurgence?

By 2011 both central cities and suburbs were recovering with growth in both manufacturing and nonmanufacturing employment, with manufacturing taking a stronger role in the suburbs and nonmanufacturing leading in central cities. Interestingly, however, the most recent data show a break in the long-term historical trends of suburban gains outpacing growth in urban areas for much of the country for nonmanufacturing employment and for population. These new findings, described below, show gains for cities relative to suburbs, albeit for a very short period.

The data also indicate that, after decades of steady and steep losses, manufacturing is making a modest comeback in the nation's largest cities. Based on data from the Quarterly Census of Employment and Wages (QCEW), about half of central cities expanded their manufacturing base between the second half of 2009 and the fourth quarter of 2011. More than 60 percent of central cities posted net gains in manufacturing employment during 2011, far exceeding the losses in the other 40 percent. This is a significant change from earlier business cycles in which manufacturing played little or no role in the labor market recovery following recessions. Further, the recent growth of manufacturing was not limited to the auto assembly and parts industries, which received considerable assistance from federal fiscal policy. Export demand and domestic business investment broadened the growth of manufacturing in 2010 and 2011.

Thus, recent data show that the urban cores of many U.S. metro areas are exhibiting signs of revival of manufacturing following the Great Recession. These findings must be considered tentative at this point, given that data remain subject to revision and the period of economic recovery remains limited. However, manufacturing appears to be a factor in recent job growth, particularly in durable goods industries in the Midwest and tech-producing industries in the West. Signs of revival are also present in the Northeast, but to a far lesser degree, and manufacturing plays a much smaller role in the Northeast economy. In the South, manufacturing gains are less often in central urban areas and more frequently in suburban or even nonmetro areas where greenfield locations are available. Once again, the U.S. urban core appears to be a competitive option for technology manufacturing.[17]

Still, as has been the case since the 1970s, manufacturing growth in suburban counties performed better than in central cities in 2010 and 2011 (see Figure 4.14), although a few central cities did outpace suburbs. These show that central cities can be drivers of metro-area manufacturing growth, but the pattern is not widespread.

Most interestingly, central city *non*manufacturing employment, on the other hand, has met or exceeded that of suburban counties in metro areas

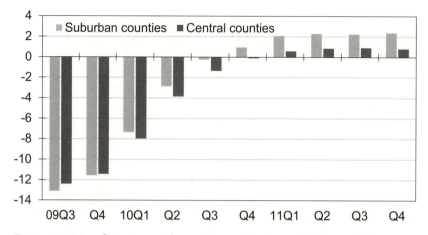

Figure 4.14. Manufacturing employment, annualized quarterly percent change, suburban and central counties, 2009–2011. Bureau of Labor Statistics, Quarterly Census of Employment and Wages, Moody's Analytics.

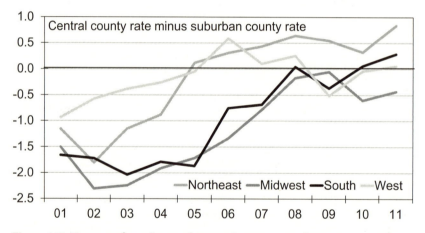

Figure 4.15. Nonmanufacturing employment in metro areas by region, annual percent change, 2001–2011. U.S. Census Bureau, Moody's Analytics.

of the Northeast, South, and West (see Figure 4.15). (Only in the Midwest do the urban counties still lag, although the difference has narrowed since the 2001 recession.) Thus, in the most recent data, urban counties in much of the country have halted what has been a long-term trend of loss of metro nonmanufacturing employment share to the suburbs. The central cities

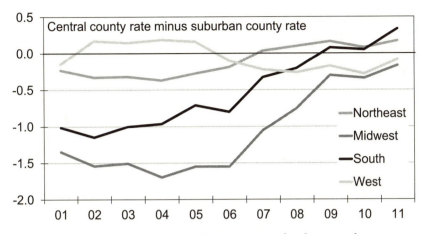

Figure 4.16. Population in metro areas by region, annualized percent change, 2001–2011. U.S. Census Bureau, Moody's Analytics.

have accounted for a steady 59 percent of metro-area nonmanufacturing employment since 2009.[18]

Population growth mirrors this shift. In fact, the recent census found that annual growth in cities surpassed suburbs for the first time in twenty years. From 2010 to 2011, the population increased 1.0 percent in cities, compared to 0.8 percent in suburbs (see Figure 4.16). This trend shift was evident in the Northeast (0.5 percent in central cities; 0.3 percent in suburbs) and in the South (1.6 percent; 1.3 percent). Suburbs still outpaced central cities in 2011 in the Midwest (0.3 percent; 0.5 percent) and in the West (1.1 percent; 1.2 percent).[19]

Conclusion

For all of the twentieth century and into the first decade of the twenty-first, most U.S. economic growth has taken place in metropolitan areas; this has been the case since 1970, as we track here, for both employment and population growth. Within metropolitan areas, from the 1970s to the 1990s, there were stark differences in employment growth rates between the central cities of the country's 100 largest metro areas and their corresponding suburban counties, reflecting a shift in economic activity from central cities to the suburbs. This is also reflected in population growth during the 1970s, when population growth in suburban areas rapidly outpaced that of the central cities. That difference narrowed during the 1980s and thereafter. This pattern is more dramatic in manufacturing employment, where deindustrialization hit cities hard. The aggregate of the central cities has not enjoyed growth in manufacturing employment since the 1970s.

The most recent data, however, show a break in these long-term historical trends, with central city population growth rate 1.0 percent greater than the 0.8 percent growth rate in the suburbs for 2010–2011. Nonmanufacturing employment growth in central cities in the aggregate has also, for the first time in the data, outpaced that of the suburbs in the same time period. Furthermore, more than half of central cities expanded their manufacturing bases between the second half of 2009 through the fourth quarter of 2011. These breaks in the trend are notable for population and nonmanufacturing growth, showing faster gains in cities than in suburbs. This may be an outcome of the recovery from the preceding bubble and bust. While it is too soon to call this a trend, cities throughout the country have recovered from decline and are growing; decline is not inevitable.

This chapter uses a broad approach of studying aggregate trends across the largest metro areas of the country; the next chapters examine specific examples of central city recovery (and decline) in order to understand how urban recovery and growth occurs.

PART II

Discovering Resilience

CHAPTER 5

Lessons from Resurgent Mid-Sized Manufacturing Cities

Yolanda K. Kodrzycki and Ana Patricia Muñoz

Mid-sized manufacturing cities have struggled for decades, suffering the consequences of deindustrialization and suburbanization (Bluestone and Harrison 1982; Glaeser and Kahn 2001a; Krugman 1991). Some cities, however, have been able to reinvent themselves and are recognized as vital communities today. We call these "resurgent cities," and they provide important lessons on the elements necessary to promote and sustain revitalization efforts.

Learning from the path that resurgent cities have followed is of particular importance for cites like Springfield, Massachusetts, New England's fourth-largest city. Known as the "City of Firsts," Springfield was for many years the center of a prosperous 200-mile industrial corridor in the Connecticut River Valley (Forrant 2009). The Springfield Armory manufactured weaponry for the U.S. military from 1794 until its closure in 1968. A number of private metalworking firms made products for both commercial and defense applications. Although some of this activity survives in Springfield, the large American Bosch manufacturing facility closed in 1986, in the process eliminating more than 1,500 jobs. Although a significant number of medical establishments, a Fortune 500 financial services firm, and several higher education institutions remain, Springfield has one of the highest rates of concentrated poverty in the country.[1] Five of the seventeen neighborhoods in the city have poverty rates that exceed 45 percent.[2]

To provide examples of the type of revitalization strategies that can help in Springfield and other struggling older industrial cities across the nation, we studied the economic development of a group of twenty-six mid-sized manufacturing-oriented peer cities over the past fifty years.[3] We selected cities that were similar to each other in 1960 based on three criteria: population ranging from 100,000 to 250,000, share of manufacturing employment of at least 30 percent, and being the city center of their metropolitan areas. Although all of these municipalities have struggled as a result of factors outside their direct control, some have adapted to their economic challenges substantially better than others. Specifically, we identified a subset of ten "resurgent cities" based on broad indicators of the economic and social well-being of their residents: Evansville and Fort Wayne, Indiana; Grand Rapids, Michigan; Greensboro and Winston-Salem, North Carolina; Jersey City, New Jersey; New Haven, Connecticut; Peoria, Illinois; Providence, Rhode Island; and Worcester, Massachusetts. The economic development paths of these cities over the past five decades provide relevant, inspiring insights on development strategies for urban America.

Confirming previous literature, we find that cities with an especially high reliance on manufacturing jobs at the beginning of the period (1960) tend to have lower median family income and higher poverty presently than others in the peer group. However, our research finds virtually no correlation between these cities' current reliance on manufacturing and their current degree of economic prosperity.

Going beyond the factors typically considered in statistical studies, our analysis is based heavily on both historical and more recent narratives. Our study reveals that the resurgent cities offer important lessons concerning the role of civic leadership and collaboration across spheres of influence, as well as the processes for producing economic transformation. These cities formed visions of the future that required them to break with their past identities as makers of items such as refrigerators, furniture, and tobacco products. Quite often, local institutions of higher learning were instrumental players in fostering an economic turnaround—either individually or as members of a larger partnership. The resurgent cities fostered better ties to other geographic areas through improvements in transportation and communication infrastructure. They also took steps to make their downtowns attractive draws for emerging businesses and new residents.

Because the analysis spans five decades, it illustrates that the resurgent cities suffered periodic setbacks. These disruptions continue, most recently in the form of the Great Recession of 2007–2009. These repeated shocks have

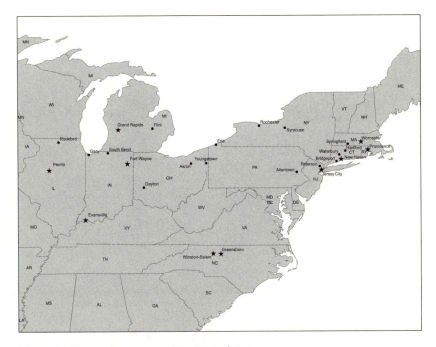

Figure 5.1. Peer and resurgent cities, United States.

served to demonstrate the value of forming durable, wide-ranging, responsive collaborations to support economic development.

The Decline of Mid-Sized Manufacturing Cities

The early 1960s were good times for Springfield, then a municipality with nearly 175,000 residents. Median family income of city residents was slightly higher than the national median, and the city's poverty rate was a little below the U.S. average. About one-third of the city's resident jobholders worked in manufacturing.

Springfield and the twenty-five other peer municipalities selected for our analysis are mapped in Figure 5.1. These cities' populations ranged from about 100,000 to about 250,000 residents from 1960 to 1980. A few—Akron, Dayton, Jersey City, and Rochester—had somewhat larger populations in 1960 but then shrank in size. In 1960, the manufacturing employment

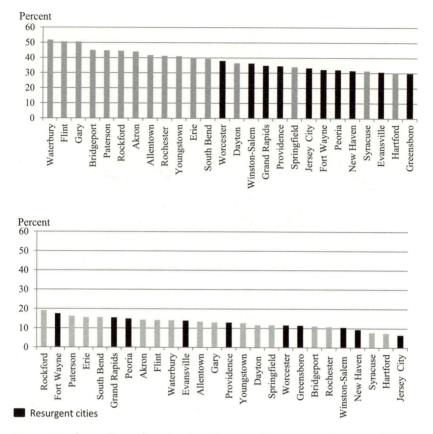

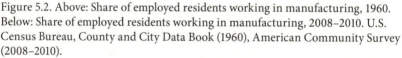

Resurgent cities

Figure 5.2. Above: Share of employed residents working in manufacturing, 1960. Below: Share of employed residents working in manufacturing, 2008–2010. U.S. Census Bureau, County and City Data Book (1960), American Community Survey (2008–2010).

shares among these mid-sized cities ranged from 30 percent to just over 50 percent (Figure 5.2).

Like Springfield, each of the peer cities has remained the primary urban center of its metropolitan area. Thus, in addition to bearing responsibility for the well-being of their own residents, these cities continue to provide job opportunities, medical care, higher education resources, and a range of other services and amenities for the residents of the surrounding region.

Cities were selected on the basis of size and regional role because these characteristics have implications for economic challenges and opportunities. Very large cities often are home to prominent businesses and institutions that have ample financial and civic capacity and that attract or spin off other enterprises. Smaller municipalities located on the fringes of such large cities may find themselves benefitting from these spillovers—or, on the other hand, suffering if the nearby large city falls into economic decline. Although the cities in our mid-sized peer group undoubtedly have been affected by broader regional economic trends, they have had to chart somewhat of an independent course. At the same time, they have not been able to attract the inevitable attention and resources that large cities can command.

Small cities may benefit from having cohesive social networks that facilitate public decision making. By contrast, medium-sized cities often have more diverse populations. Reaching consensus may be difficult when residents have different backgrounds and life experiences. On the other hand, beyond their inherent value, differing perspectives and skills may foster innovation and creativity and may offset the tendency to build a city economy centered on a single dominant industry or institution.

At the beginning of the time period under study, the residents of Springfield and its peer cities enjoyed good access to well-paying jobs. Apart from temporary cyclical downturns, U.S. manufacturing employment grew steadily in the 1950s and 1960s, and an estimated two-thirds of all jobs in the nation's metropolitan areas were located in central cities (Mieszkowski and Mills 1993). Manufacturing employment has fallen over the subsequent decades, and jobs have migrated further from city centers, especially in industries that are relatively land-intensive (Glaeser and Kahn 2001a). By the mid-2000s, only 21 percent of all jobs and only 14 percent of manufacturing jobs in metropolitan areas were located within three miles of a central business district (Kneebone 2009). Central cities continued to attract well-paying jobs in sectors such as professional, medical, educational, and financial services; but these positions tend to have very different educational and skill requirements than do traditional manufacturing jobs.

Distinguishing Features of Resurgent Cities

We undertook a closer examination of the cities in the peer group that were relatively successful in meeting these economic challenges—our ten resurgent cities. Despite differences in time period and methodology, most of the remaining, nonresurgent cities appear on the list of "weak market" cities developed by Furdell and Wolman (2006).[4]

The most important criteria in selecting the resurgent cities were median family income (both the level and the change in the city's rank within the peer group since 1960) and the poverty rate of the population (both the level and the change since 1980, when the U.S. Census Bureau started making such data available for cities). Secondary criteria included the percent change in the city's population since 1960 and the city's reputation among economic development experts. The reputational measures were drawn both from academic studies and from public awards or other forms of recognition. For the most part, we relied on information prior to the Great Recession of 2007–2009, collecting data from the decennial censuses between 1960 and 2000 and the American Community Survey three-year average estimates for the 2000s.

Prior research has found that expert opinions sometimes accord well with standard statistical measures of urban success but, in some cases, are either more favorable or less favorable than the hard data (Wolman, Hill, and Furdell 2000). We found that subjective indicators were helpful in narrowing the list of resurgent cities but that no single type of recognition was definitive. For example, one particularly prestigious indicator is the All-America City Award of the National Civic League. Since 1949, this annual award has recognized places whose residents work together to identify and make unusual progress in tackling community-wide challenges. Five of the resurgent cities—Evansville, Fort Wayne, Grand Rapids, New Haven, and Worcester—have either won or been finalists for the All-America Award since 2000. Three of the remaining peer cities (Akron, South Bend, and Syracuse) have garnered similar recognition from the National Civic League during the same time frame. Ultimately, we had to make judgment calls in drawing a dividing line between resurgent and nonresurgent cities. For further details on the selection criteria and results, see Kodrzycki, Muñoz et al. (2009a).

Today, the residents of the resurgent cities enjoy a substantially higher average standard of living than those living in the other peer cities (Table 5.1). In the period 2008–2010, median family income in the resurgent cities averaged $51,260, 32 percent ($12,520) higher than in the remaining cities in the peer group. On average, 21 percent of the residents in the resurgent cities were living in poverty versus nearly 29 percent in the other cities. Demographic indicators also point to differing outcomes in the resurgent and the other peer cities. Half of the resurgent cities experienced population growth between 1960 and 2008–2010, suggesting that they offer adequate economic

Table 5.1. Key Economic Indicators for Peer-Group Cities, 1960 and 2008–10

	Median family income (% of U.S. median)		Population poverty rate (%)		Population (000)	
	1960	2008–10	1980	2008–10	1960	2008–10
Resurgent cities						
Evansville	93.6	72.9	12.2	20.0	142	118
Fort Wayne	114.7	86.3	11.0	16.2	162	253
Grand Rapids	107.2	72.8	13.5	26.0	177	189
Greensboro	103.3	84.9	12.8	18.5	120	267
Jersey City	105.1	98.7	21.2	17.4	276	245
New Haven	103.6	73.6	23.2	26.7	152	129
Peoria	105.3	99.0	12.3	20.8	103	114
Providence	89.6	66.3	20.4	27.1	207	178
Winston-Salem	93.9	82.9	16.4	20.3	111	228
Worcester	102.5	87.8	14.4	18.1	187	181
Peer city averages						
All cities	106.3	70.1	16.7	25.9	173.7	154.3
Resurgent cities	101.9	82.5	15.7	21.1	163.7	190.3
Other cities	109.1	62.4	17.3	28.9	180.0	131.8
U.S total	100.0	100.0	11.7	14.4	179*	307*

U.S. Bureau of the Census. County and City Data Book (1960), American Community Survey (2008–2010).
*In millions.

opportunities and amenities to retain and attract residents.[5] By contrast, half of the nonresurgent cities lost more than 20 percent of their population over this period. Cities with severe population losses tend to have difficulty raising enough own-source revenues to fund public services (Bradbury, Downs, and Small 1980).

Although the resurgent cities have fared considerably better than their peers over the past five decades, their economic performance has not been as strong as that of the national economy. In 1960, average median family income in the ten resurgent cities was similar to the U.S. figure. In 2008–2010, their average median family income was only 82.5 percent of the U.S. median. Of the resurgent cities, only Jersey City managed to reduce its rate of poverty over the last half-century (from 21.2 percent in 1960 to 17.4 percent in 2008–2010). Moreover, the lowest poverty rate in the resurgent cities now (16.2 percent in Fort Wayne in 2008–2010) is higher than the U.S. average (14.4

percent in the same three-year period). And, as noted, only half of the resurgent cities have managed to stem population losses over the last fifty years.

Moreover, some of the resurgent cities have struggled considerably with the onset of the Great Recession. Providence, in particular, has not escaped the economic malaise affecting the state of Rhode Island and many of its municipalities in the past several years. The unemployment rate in Providence has doubled since the mid-2000s, and, as of the current writing, the city's finances appear to be in precarious shape.[6]

Lessons from Resurgent Cities

While acknowledging that each of the resurgent cities has benefited from having some unique advantages that cannot be replicated in other locations, we studied these cities' histories in an effort to uncover common themes that could be applied to other mid-sized cities. Our methodology represents a hybrid of the approaches used in previous studies.

Starting with Glaeser, Scheinkman, and Shleifer (1995), the econometric literature has emphasized the effects of initial economic and social conditions (such as industry composition or schooling) and of immutable circumstances (such as region of the country or weather) on urban growth in subsequent decades. Other scholars in diverse fields, including economics, regional studies, and sociology, have engaged in detailed case studies, arguing that certain occurrences in one or several cities proved favorable or unfavorable to their economic and social development. For example, Forrant (2009) exemplifies this approach to studying Springfield, Massachusetts. The current study uses mostly quantitative criteria to measure cities' degree of success, while emphasizing how actions on the part of regional and local policymakers and other actors can affect overall outcomes. By studying roughly two dozen cities that started in similar circumstances, we hope to impose greater analytical rigor than is found in case studies.

As much as possible, we used contemporaneous newspaper and magazine articles so as to obtain accounts that were not biased by knowledge of future events. We also read retrospective studies and interviewed local economic development experts. More recently, our impressions have been updated and sharpened as a result of site visits to selected cities.

Each of the ten resurgent cities has its own story. Understanding how these cities have reinvented themselves requires understanding the context in which the transformation of each of the cities happened and how their unique characteristics influenced their fates. Case studies of individual cities can be found in Kodrzycki, Muñoz et al. (2009a). These accounts summarize the economic history of individual cities, highlighting their inherent advantages and disadvantages and describing their challenges and economic development efforts from 1960 to the present.

Despite the differences across the resurgence cities, we uncovered common themes. Our research strongly suggests that successful transformation was only weakly linked to geography. On the one hand, the group of ten resurgent cities includes the two southern peer cities, Greensboro and Winston-Salem, but none of the cities from Ohio, Pennsylvania, or New York. Otherwise, except for tiny Rhode Island, each of the states in the comparison group has at least one resurgent city and at least one nonresurgent city. In northern New Jersey, Jersey City has been able to parlay its location into an advantage, but nearby Paterson has not. In southern New England, New Haven, Providence, and Worcester have developed more successfully than Springfield, Bridgeport, Hartford, or Waterbury. These findings suggest that, although statewide policies—such as North Carolina's progrowth stance or New Jersey's economic development incentives—may have been a factor in easing economic adjustment, cities ultimately play an important role in determining their own fates.

Changing demographies presented greater challenges in some cases than others, and, in general, the resurgent cities saw less dramatic changes in their racial and ethnic composition than the nonresurgent cities. Nonetheless, two of the resurgent cities—Jersey City and New Haven—went from over 85 percent white in 1960 to having nonwhite majorities in 2005–2007. Furthermore, Springfield and Providence underwent very similar demographic shifts, but the latter was more successful in transforming its economy than the former.[7]

Finally, economic resurgence was virtually uncorrelated with city population size. Gary and Grand Rapids had almost identical populations in 1960, yet their economic performance over the next five decades differed considerably. The same applies to Hartford and Fort Wayne or to Erie and Evansville.

Industry Modernization

Econometric studies have documented that metropolitan areas with a heavy dependence on manufacturing in the past have, on average, experienced lower economic growth in recent decades than those that started with less of their employment in manufacturing (Glaeser, Scheinkman, and Shleifer 1995; Glaeser and Saiz 2004). Steven Cochrane et al (this volume) presents findings on the connection between the share of manufacturing and economic growth). These results are borne out in our sample of municipalities.

By 1960, each of the resurgent cities had a sizeable nonmanufacturing job base. At the higher end, about 70 percent of the employed residents of Evansville and Greensboro worked outside manufacturing in 1960. By contrast, none of the cities where over 40 percent of employed residents had manufacturing jobs in 1960 have yet managed to achieve resurgent status (Figure 5.2, top panel).

Econometric studies have been largely silent on the question of whether retention of manufacturing jobs or aggressive promotion of nonmanufacturing industries has been the more successful strategy for old industrial cities. There is some evidence that the answer may have changed over time. Blumenthal, Wolman, and Hill (2009) found that metropolitan areas with a high location quotient in manufacturing in 1990 tended to have *higher* economic growth in the subsequent decade than other areas, all else being equal. They interpreted their finding as indicative of a turnaround in some segments of manufacturing, following a period in which a high presence of manufacturing was a deterrent to regional growth. Based on a sample of small metropolitan areas during the same decade, Erickcek and McKinney (2006) found that the national performance of a metropolitan area's industries had a major impact on the area's personal income growth. In other words, trying to anticipate which industries are likely to grow—and then working to develop several of those industries—may be the most promising strategy for cities to adopt.

In our sample of mid-sized cities, none relies on manufacturing as much today as it did in 1960 (Figure 5.2, bottom panel). However, resurgent and nonresurgent cities do not differ significantly in manufacturing intensity. In the resurgent cities, 12.4 percent of employed residents worked in manufacturing in 2008–2010, a number very similar to the 13.1 percent average in the nonresurgent cities.

Industry modernization has taken many forms in the resurgent cities. In three of them—Fort Wayne, Evansville, and Grand Rapids—manufacturing continues to employ noticeably more residents than any other single sector. However, the composition of activity within manufacturing has shifted, and these cities have taken additional steps to develop more robust nonmanufacturing sectors.

For example, in 1999, Fort Wayne adopted a long-term economic development strategy that called for a shift toward a diverse range of advanced manufacturing and agroprocessing activities, in addition to building up airport-related services, logistics, and other service industries. In Grand Rapids, once known as the "Furniture Capital of the World," a couple of the leading firms made the decision to shift from manufacturing residential products in favor of commercial furnishings, where they perceived greater competitive opportunities. Another significant early step in turning around the Grand Rapids economy was development of a health research industry. Jay Van Andel, one of the founders of Amway Corporation, created the Van Andel Institute in 1996 to focus on research pertaining to the genetic and molecular origins of cancer and other diseases. Later, additional medical facilities and research institutions joined the Institute and Grand Rapids Medical Education and Research Center to form the "medical mile."

The City of Evansville, the former "Refrigerator Capital of the World," began to diversify its economy earlier than most of its peers. While manufacturing continues to be an important component of Evansville's activities, the city has taken advantage of its strategic location and of improvements in transportation systems. As a result, it has been successful over the years in attracting new manufacturing and nonmanufacturing facilities, boosting tourism, and participating in international markets.

At the other extreme, some resurgent cities—most notably Jersey City and New Haven—now rely proportionately less on manufacturing jobs than does the nation as a whole. Jersey City went from being a heavily industrial city in 1960 to a major financial center in the 2000s. New Haven's largest industries now are educational and health-related services, which together employ about 40 percent of the city's workers.

Leadership and Collaboration

Our examination of the resurgent cities' histories indicates that resurgence involved leadership on the part of key institutions or individuals, along with collaboration among the various constituencies with an interest in economic development. Initial leadership in these cities came from a variety of key institutions and individuals. (See Kimberly Zeuli's chapter comparing two Southern mill towns and Alan Mallach's chapter on resilience in small industrial towns, for further discussion of the importance of leadership.) In some cases, the turnaround started with the efforts of the public sector, while, in other cases, nongovernmental institutions or even private developers were at the forefront. In some instances, the cities appeared to be touching bottom economically and socially, which imbued key constituencies with a sense of urgency. The instigators of city revitalization recognized that it was in their own interest to prevent further deterioration in local conditions, and they took responsibility for bringing about improvement.

Regardless of who initiated the turnaround, economic redevelopment efforts in resurgent cities spanned decades and involved collaborations among numerous organizations and sectors. Collaboration became necessary because economic transformation is complex and because outsiders—such as state and national governments, foundations, and businesses that are potential sources of funding and jobs—often require proof of joint efforts to contribute to a city's development.

In some cities, revitalization stemmed from the mayor's leadership. However, ongoing commitments of business and nonprofit groups provided critical continuity as mayors changed. An interesting illustration is Providence. After World War II, the city fell into a downward spiral, losing population and jobs. In 1974, Vincent Cianci was elected mayor. Although controversial, Cianci brought energy and a strong presence to the city. Working with private partners, he led Providence in carrying out a series of ambitious projects that eventually enabled its successful promotion as the "Renaissance City." After a major personal scandal forced Cianci to leave office, a private-sector coalition—led by the Providence Foundation, the Greater Providence Chamber of Commerce, corporate leaders, and the Rhode Island Foundation—was instrumental in pursuing development initiatives. Collaboration between the public and private sectors was fundamental in completing long-range infrastructure projects that were essential in reconnecting downtown to the rest of the city and in developing the waterfront.

Evansville is another example of a mayor-initiated turnaround. Frank F. McDonald, II, Evansville's mayor from 1959 to 1971, started his period in office by commissioning a study on the city's potential and personally contacting businesses to persuade them to settle in Evansville. During this time, the city benefited from the construction of a civic center, federal buildings, a community center, and the state's first enclosed mall, as well as the beginnings of downtown renewal. Then, in the 1980s, the Metropolitan Evansville Chamber of Commerce launched an aggressive economic development program; more recently, the nonprofit Innovation Pointe and the University of Southern Indiana have cosponsored efforts to develop technology-oriented businesses.

While the revivals of Providence and Evansville can be traced to actions taken in their city halls, in other resurgent cities, businesses, philanthropists, or nonprofit organizations initiated the turnaround, and public officials joined the efforts later. Jersey City's proximity to Manhattan, along with falling land values as a result of the city's industrial decline, kicked off a wave of private sector development starting in the mid-1980s. The private sector could not take on the full burden of the Jersey City turnaround, however. Mayor Bret Schundler, in office from 1992 to 2001, is viewed as making major contributions by reducing corruption and bringing together Jersey City's diverse residents. Moreover, business tax incentives offered by the State of New Jersey and public transportation improvements provided further impetus for firms to locate in the city. As noted already, philanthropists and committed entrepreneurs played a key role in bringing about Grand Rapids's resurgence. More recently, public-private partnerships and donations from the private sector have sparked downtown redevelopment in that city.

In some of the resurgent cities, chambers of commerce and business organizations have been involved in broad aspects of economic development, including education and workforce development programs. A notable example is Winston-Salem, a city that had been synonymous with the tobacco industry for many years but that has diversified its economic base considerably. In 1991, the Winston-Salem Chamber of Commerce developed the Blueprint for Technology, which included initiatives for K-12 public education. The chamber also formed the Winston Works task force that launched a campaign to encourage companies to dedicate at least 1 percent of their discretionary spending to local suppliers.

Although institutional arrangements have varied both across cities and towns and over time, the more successful cities now typically have a private, nonprofit organization heading economic development efforts. Such organizations collaborate closely with local chambers of commerce and other nongovernmental entities, but they have broader mandates including attracting and retaining young professionals, improving the educational system, and working on long-term visioning plans. Economic development organizations have institutionalized relationships with city government, usually in the form of funding and representation on the board of directors.

For example, in Peoria, a group of civic leaders created the Economic Development Council (EDC) for the Peoria Area in 1981. The EDC attracted new companies to the area, helped retain existing companies, and worked to ensure that the entire region was involved in economic development strategies. After going through rough times during the recessions of the early 1980s, community leaders, Peoria's mayor, and the private sector (including Caterpillar, the city's largest employer) joined forces to strengthen the EDC. The following year, Caterpillar and other local businesses and civic leaders formed a membership organization called Peoria Next to promote technology-centered development for the city. Through activities such as networking meetings and business incubation, Peoria Next has built up a "knowledge community network" to foster and sustain an intellectual creative class. One early mark of success, growing out of research at Caterpillar, was the founding of battery developer Firefly Energy Inc., co-winner of the 2007 *Wall Street Journal* Technology Innovation Award.

Foundations and groups of civic leaders have played an active role in revitalizing resurgent cities both indirectly through conversations and collaborations among different stakeholders and directly by developing programs that contribute to transformation of these cities. In Greensboro, local foundations initiated a collaborative process to determine economic development strategies. In 2000, six local foundations financed a study aimed at evaluating Greensboro's economic prospects. As a result of the study, the foundations created the not-for-profit organization Action Greensboro to coordinate the development-related activities of the city's numerous business and civic groups. Action Greensboro became a major player in development, investing in numerous projects—including parks, job recruitment programs, and downtown revitalization—and gauging the progress of the city. In 2008, Greensboro was chosen among *Fortune* magazine's "100 Best Places to Live and Launch."

Our evidence on leadership and collaboration adds insights with respect to the conclusions of Blumenthal, Wolman, and Hill (2009). These authors found that metropolitan areas with older central cities tended to have lower economic growth during the decade of the 1990s than areas with newer central cities, all else being equal. They commented that the age of the central city was indicative not only of "the vintage of infrastructure and optimized mode of transport" but also of "political behaviors and institutional arrangements" (623). The resurgent cities illustrate that modernization of civic infrastructure is a key part of transforming older urban areas.

Long-Term Visioning and Reevaluation

Leadership and collaboration facilitated long-term planning that allowed the resurgent cities to develop more dynamic economies. Their transformation has proved to be a continuing process and has required reevaluating strategies and adapting to ongoing challenges.

Fort Wayne adopted a long-term economic development strategy in 2001 by working with community leaders and professionals in economic development. The Peoria Civic Federation, primarily composed of the leaders of the region's largest employers, sponsored the Greater Peoria Vision 2020, which was released in 2005 after a two-year planning process. Several community councils oversee the implementation of master-plan areas such as quality of life, economic revitalization, youth and education, and leadership. In 2009, the City of Peoria sought community input on an updated comprehensive plan, which develops an overall vision for Peoria's growth and development over the next ten to twenty years.

Grand Rapids has also benefited from working on long-term development plans and from coordination efforts across sectors. In 1992, the city launched Voices & Visions, a planning process that involved a wide range of actors from the Grand Rapids City Commission to the Grand Rapids public schools to the private sector. The city's development plans were praised as rooted in community consensus by the National Civic League in 2003.

Successful collaboration and planning efforts often extend beyond city borders. Winston-Salem and Greensboro have collaborated with each other, and with the city of High Point, to draw businesses and support start-ups in their region. Fort Wayne is part of the Northeast Indiana Vision 2020, a ten-county visioning process in which the private sector has played an essential role. Peoria's visioning process extends over three counties.

The resurgent cities also have illustrated the need to adapt to changing circumstances. In some cases, a given development strategy proved successful in some respects but not in others. For example, working with the Chamber of Commerce and the University of Massachusetts, Worcester established the Massachusetts Biotechnology Institute (MBRI) in the 1980s in order to attract biotech companies. Despite the biotechnology industry boom, the city had to readapt its development approach because biotech companies often employ only small numbers of workers and take a long time to achieve profitability. In 1998, the MBRI changed its name to Massachusetts Biomedical Initiatives as it launched efforts to attract medical devices companies that could become an important source of jobs.

Another striking feature of resurgent cities' stories is the need for continuing innovations in overall development strategy. In the 1980s, Fort Wayne adapted to the shutdown of its largest employer by attracting investments on the part of other large companies. More recently, however, the city's focus has been on becoming a stronger player in high-tech entrepreneurship. Greensboro succeeded in attracting service jobs but, in the 2000s, actively recruited higher-paying employers in aerospace technology as a potential new engine for its economy. Peoria realized in the 1990s that building up its retail and service sectors was insufficient to bring about the desired rate of economic growth. The city turned to new strategies centered on medical research, technology, and entrepreneurship.

Infrastructure and Downtown Revitalization

The stories of the resurgent cities involve fundamental changes in physical infrastructure. (Both Edward Glaeser and Gilles Duranton, in their chapters, discuss the importance of transportation infrastructure to city growth.) Over the last several decades, these cities have focused on modernizing their transportation and communications infrastructures by expanding regional airports, improving roads, and building high-speed broadband networks. Such infrastructure improvements have been important draws for a range of businesses. The resurgent cities have also recognized that downtown renewal is important in creating employment and attracting residents.

Providence offers perhaps the most dramatic example of infrastructure makeovers. The projects undertaken included the relocation of railroad tracks running through the downtown and the removal of the so-called widest bridge in the world that had obscured the two rivers crossing the city. In Greensboro, the opening in 1982 of the Piedmont Triad International Airport terminal just west of the city set off a building boom in the city.

Within two decades, a cluster of semiconductor companies had developed near the airport. In Peoria, the state's overhaul of the city's highway system access and the construction of a new terminal at the Peoria International Airport improved manufacturers' and distributors' access to transportation. Transportation improvements in Worcester, such as the establishment of frequent commuter rail service to Boston and direct access to the Massachusetts Turnpike, encouraged new investments in the city.

Several resurgent cities have come to rely on nonprofit organizations created to develop and implement strategies to revitalize their downtowns. The City of Greensboro looks to the Downtown Greensboro Inc. nonprofit organization to continue development of the urban core. The Downtown Winston-Salem Partnership, a member and advocacy organization, is the lead implementer of the downtown plan developed in 2007. The revitalization plan includes the Restaurant Row Program, introduced by the city with federal and state support to help recruit and finance new eateries. The plan also calls for promoting Winston-Salem as the "City of the Arts" and for attracting businesses in the design industry.

The Role of Higher-Education Institutions

With the continued transition to a knowledge-based economy, development strategies increasingly have emphasized improvements to human capital (see Laura Perna's chapter in this volume for a discussion of strategies for improving education and workforce readiness). A number of econometric studies have documented that cities and metropolitan areas whose populations are highly educated have tended to have higher employment and personal income growth in recent decades (Blumenthal, Wolman, and Hill 2009; Glaeser and Saiz 2004; Glaeser, Scheinkman, and Shleifer 1995; Simon 1998; also see Edward Glaeser's and Gilles Duranton's chapters). Educational attainment has improved considerably in resurgent cities. Recent data indicate that the share of the population twenty-five years and older with a bachelor's degree or more was slightly higher than the national average (Figure 5.3).

Institutions of higher education have participated in reinvigorating the resurgent cities' economies in their roles as major employers and as educators. The examples of Yale University in New Haven, educational institutions in Greensboro, and university partnerships in Worcester stand out.

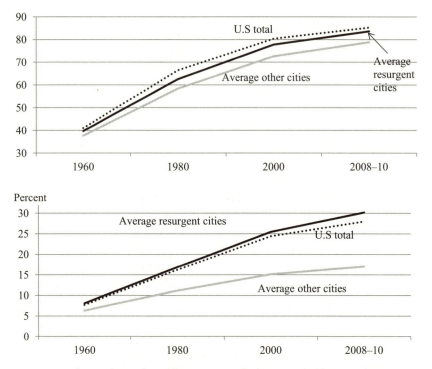

Figure 5.3. Above: Share of population twenty-five years and older completing at least high school. Below: Share of population twenty-five years and older with college degree or higher. U.S. Census Bureau, County and City Data Book (1960), American Community Survey (2008–2010).

Although Yale University was founded in New Haven over three centuries ago, the university's deep involvement in fostering New Haven's overall development is much more recent. Yale partnered with city officials and corporate leaders in the mid-1980s to develop a marketing plan for the City of New Haven that would enhance job opportunities in service sectors. Then, in 1991, Yale reached a formal agreement with the City of New Haven that marked a decisive turning point in the university's participation in civic affairs. The university agreed to make substantial payments to the city in lieu of taxes—amounts equivalent to over 5 percent of the annual municipal budget—and to put its golf course on the property tax rolls. Another major commitment was to fund the Center for the City, an organization aimed at tapping business, government, and other resources to attack the city's social problems. Yale's other initiatives included the redevelopment and/or renovation of downtown properties, subsidies to employees buying a home in the city, and the creation of a venture capital fund to attract biotech companies to the Science Park incubator. The university continues to be active in improving local economic conditions. Along with the city of New Haven and local businesses, Yale contributed to the launching of an Economic Development Corporation in 2008 dedicated to further broadening New Haven's economic base.

Greensboro's various higher education institutions are key players in economic development. Greensboro Community College and Guilford Technical Community College have gained national recognition for job training activities that serve local businesses. The University of North Carolina at Greensboro (UNCG), North Carolina State University, and other schools built the Triad Technology Center to foster cooperation among themselves and with local life sciences firms. In 2007, UNCG and North Carolina AT&T State University announced the creation of a joint research campus and the Joint School of Nanoscience and Nanoengineering.

Worcester is another example of a city with a rich concentration of colleges and universities, although no one institution is dominant. In 2005, Worcester educational institutions formed the UniverCity Partnership to adopt strategies allowing higher education institutions to participate in economic growth by improving local purchasing, employment, real estate development, business incubation, and workforce development. Within the framework of this partnership, institutions have taken on different roles, depending on their individual strengths. Their contributions have included locating new campuses in the downtown area, working on brownfield remediation, and providing support to community organizations. In addition, the Worcester Polytechnic Institute Venture Forum has attracted technology firms to the city.

Does Resurgence Help Low-Income Families and Poor Neighborhoods?

Despite their overall success, the resurgent cities continue to struggle with extending prosperity to a broader share of their populations (Table 5.1). Some of the resurgent cities have implemented distinct efforts to improve opportunities for their poor and minority residents and to narrow the differences between the haves and the have-nots. Although they are separate initiatives, these programs often adopt approaches similar to those used to generate prosperity more generally. Most importantly, they involve collaborations.

The Providence Plan, a not-for profit venture of the city of Providence in Rhode Island, the academic community, and the private sector, focuses on children's well-being, workforce development, and community building. Its successful programs include Ready to Learn Providence, YouthBuild Providence, and the Local Learning Partnership. Moreover, places that exhibit robust collaborations between citywide structures and community-based organizations tend to attract additional capital from national foundations. For example, the New York-headquartered Local Initiatives Support Corporation (LISC) selected Providence as one of six demonstration sites for neighborhood revitalization programs with the participation of local community development corporations, the city, and the community. Similarly, the Annie E. Casey Foundation chose Providence as one of its cities for major investment in the Making Connections initiative, thanks to a strong partnership with the mayor, Rhode Island KIDS COUNT, the Providence Public School District, and other organizations. The goal of this ten-year program is to expand family economic and early grade success strategies.

For many years, the successful redevelopment of Jersey City's waterfront had little in the form of positive spillovers for poor neighborhoods. More recently, neighborhoods have worked with the city in implementing their own economic development projects. Residents of the areas surrounding Martin Luther King Drive, one of Jersey City's poorest neighborhoods, not only participated actively in writing their neighborhood development plan but also controlled its implementation through a neighborhood development corporation. The plan received national and statewide awards and recognition for its innovative use of community outreach and implementation.

Direct involvement of the community in shaping planning efforts has proved to be important in creating comprehensive long-term strategies. In Grand Rapids, the city and the chamber of commerce have partnered with the Neighborhood Business Alliance (NBA) on several occasions to work on economic development strategies. Made up of representatives from all twenty neighborhood associations, NBA meets monthly to coordinate citywide services, share best practices, and advocate on issues affecting neighborhood businesses and districts.

Conclusions and Postscript on Recent Initiatives in Springfield

Fifty years ago, it would have been virtually impossible for the leaders or residents of mid-sized U.S. cities to anticipate the full extent of challenges posed by deindustrialization, suburbanization, and other structural and economic changes. Other than starting from comparatively less dependence on manufacturing jobs, however, the cities that would resurge in later decades did not possess obvious advantages over their peers.

The processes of turning around mid-sized industrial cities have been long and complex. In order to be resurgent, cities needed to modernize their job base, both to develop viable new service sectors and to shift to new types of manufacturing activity. They also needed leaders who worked collaboratively with the various constituents with a stake in economic development. This entailed crafting new and durable partnerships across governments, businesses, and nonprofits. Cities benefited from developing long-range visions for the future but also from having the flexibility to update these plans as conditions warranted. To help attract new businesses and residents, the resurgent cities upgraded their transportation and communications infrastructure, while focusing also on creating a vibrant downtown area. Finally, colleges and universities often played important and varied roles—as employers, educators, redevelopers, and financiers.

Even when these positive conditions were met, the economies of the resurgent cities failed to keep pace with the growth in the U.S. economy from 1960 to 2010. On the whole, incomes in these cities are below the U.S. average, and poverty rates are higher. Periodic nationwide downturns, including the Great Recession of 2007–2009, have repeatedly exposed remaining weaknesses in the resurgent cities' economic structures, making it harder for them to achieve the long-run goals set by their leaders and constituents. Leadership and collaboration continued to play a key role in promoting innovation and growth during these difficult times.

We have mainly focused on the strategies resurgent cities have put in place. Other cities have also been implementing initiatives that promote collaboration and are likely to bear fruit in the long term.

We started this chapter talking about the struggles that the city of Springfield, Massachusetts, has faced over the past five decades. We end by mentioning what has happened in this city in the last couple of years. Springfield has been negatively affected by both the national economic recession and natural disasters, as a tornado and a major snowstorm struck the city in 2011. Nonetheless, the city also has seen the emergence of a number of positive initiatives promoting leadership, collaboration, and community engagement. In 2010, the City-to-City of Greater Springfield program was established to advance collaboration, civic leadership, and peer learning. As part of the program, groups of Springfield leaders have visited four resurgent cities—Winston-Salem, Greensboro, Grand Rapids, and New Haven—learning from local leaders about those cities' strategies to promote economic growth and public-private sector partnerships.

After the 2011 tornado ravaged Springfield neighborhoods, a public-private sector partnership was created to work on a comprehensive multi-year effort to rebuild the damaged areas and help shape the city's vision for the future. Neighborhood and stakeholder meetings were held to integrate the community's input into the master plan. Meanwhile, a number of working groups have been formed to promote collaboration and coordination among higher education institutions, improve workforce development initiatives, and support small business formation and growth. Springfield's increasing collaboration is starting to pay off. In 2012, the city received the All-American City Award from the National Civic League for its efforts to ensure that more children are proficient readers by the end of third grade. Finally, discussions of aid reform that would help cities like Springfield have gained momentum,[8] but, thus far, the state's finances have not recovered enough in the wake of the recession to permit further resources to be channeled to these municipalities without making unpopular sacrifices in other parts of the state budget.

CHAPTER 6

Revitalizing Small Cities: A Comparative Case Study of Two Southern Mill Towns

Kimberly Zeuli

At the start of the twentieth century, the textile industry had started to shift its base from New England to the South; by the 1920s, North Carolina had become the center. At the peak of the industry in the United States, in the late 1940s, 9.3 percent of all textile jobs were located in North Carolina. Many of these jobs were in rural, small towns. Rural manufacturing was at the core of North Carolina's economic development strategy in the twentieth century, and the textile industry has been one of the top two largest employers in rural and small towns since 1940 (Coclanis and Kyriakoudes 2007). By the early 1970s, at the peak in North Carolina, textile jobs accounted for 19.2 percent of the state's employment. The textile industry began a rapid contraction in the United States and North Carolina in 1990. Between 1990 and 2011, the U.S. textile industry lost approximately 1.2 million jobs, 20 percent of them (243,200 jobs) in North Carolina (Bureau of Labor Statistics 2012). By 2011, textile employment in North Carolina had dropped to 1.2 percent of total employment.

Our analysis compares Concord and Eden, two historic mill towns in North Carolina. They had equivalent social and economic positions during the 1970s, at the peak of the textile industry in North Carolina, including a similar level of economic dependence on the textile industry (Table 6.1). Concord and Eden also housed textile mills that eventually became part of the Pillowtex Company. Both communities experienced the loss of their textile base as the industry declined, as well as the closing of local Pillowtex plants in July 2003 when the company went bankrupt. The impact of the

Table 6.1. Concord and Eden in 1970

	Concord	Eden
Total population	18,464	15,871
Land area in square miles	6.9	11.7
Percent persons age 25 or over, 4 years high school or more	35.5	34.1
Percent unemployed	2.6	2.8
Percent below poverty level	16.9	12.3
Real median household income	32,266	41,296
Real per capita income	17,102	15,292

U.S. Census Bureau, Decennial Census Tables (1970).

declining manufacturing industry on national and regional economies has been studied extensively, with special attention given to the Midwest and northeastern parts of the country. The specific case of the textile industry in the South has received far less attention, yet its significance to the region and the distinctive features of a manufacturing industry sited across small towns, versus within a city, afford unique insights into community redevelopment. Few studies have focused on redevelopment and economic revitalization in the context of small cities and towns, which may reveal findings different from those gleaned from analyzing larger manufacturing-dependent cities.

The unique attributes of the textile industry in North Carolina provide us with an opportunity to conduct a comparative study of small city redevelopment. We analyze the redevelopment paths of two similar communities in North Carolina struggling with the same forces of economic transformation—the general contraction of textile manufacturing in the state and the specific closing of local textile plants. Using a mixture of quantitative and qualitative methods, we consider each community's capacity to respond to these events and its economic revitalization to date.

Our qualitative research included interviews and site visits to both communities in early 2012. We interviewed city and county government officials, as well as current and former textile mill employees.

Redevelopment and Revitalization Capacity

The capacity of a community to recover from negative economic events, and perhaps even reinvent itself, may be determined by various social and economic factors. We attempt to identify these variables more precisely by drawing on recent studies of community resiliency, defined as the ability of a community to return to its prior growth path after experiencing an economic "shock." Recent studies on community resiliency identify and test a number of indicators that, in theory, make some communities more likely than others to recover from negative events (Cutter, Burton, and Emrich 2010; Foster 2012; Hill, St. Clair, Wial et al. 2012; Sherrieb, Norris, and Galea 2010). They include a mix of economic and sociodemographic variables. To test Concord and Eden's relative resiliency, we collected a similar set of variables at the community level using publicly available data (Tables 6.2 and 6.3). This allows us to generate a hypothesis about their ability to recover from the textile industry shocks. (For further discussion of shocks, see Duranton's chapter in this volume.)

Concord's History

Concord is located in Cabarrus County just twenty-five miles from downtown Charlotte. Incorporated in 1806, Concord was the home of the textile legend James W. Cannon (1852–1921) (City of Concord n.d.). Cannon started as a cotton buyer for a mercantile company in Concord and built his first textile mill in the town in 1887 (Mock 2013b: 1). In 1906, he began the construction of his "model mill town," Kannapolis, approximately eight miles north of town (North Carolina Research Campus n.d.). Kannapolis developed into the largest unincorporated town in the country, with company houses, schools, churches, etc. (Mock 2013a: 1). In 1928, Cannon Mills was formed from the consolidation of Cannon Manufacturing with several other manufacturing companies and mills (1).

By the early 1980s, the textile industry was already declining, and the mill towns began to change. In 1982, Cannon Mills was sold to a private holding company, and, in 1984, Kannapolis became an incorporated city in North Carolina. In 1986, Cannon Mills was acquired by Fieldcrest (located in Eden), and the new corporation was called Fieldcrest Cannon. As operations were consolidated, there were major layoffs, especially among the executive and administrative ranks, many of whom lived in Concord. In 1997, Pillowtex Corporation in Texas purchased Fieldcrest Cannon.

Table 6.2. Economic Resiliency Variables for Concord and Eden

	1990	2000	2010	1990–2010 average annual % change
Median household income (2010 dollars)				
Concord	42,498	58,369	52,470	1.06
Eden	35,258	35,038	30,600	−0.71
North Carolina	44,457	49,619	45,570	0.12
Per capita income (2010 dollars)				
Concord	22,443	27,254	26,140	1.54
Eden	18,409	19,343	17,407	−0.56
North Carolina	21,497	25,715	24,745	1.42
Poverty rate (all persons)				
Concord	12.1	8.2	11.7	−0.2
Eden	16.2	17.2	24.4	2.1
North Carolina	13.0	12.3	15.5	0.9
Unemployment rate				
Concord	4.1	5.4	9.2	4.1
Eden	4.9	8.3	11.6	4.4
North Carolina	4.8	5.3	8.8	3.0
Manufacturing share of total employment				
Concord	27.2	18.1	10.9	−4.4
Eden	46.3	31.1	23.3	−3.4
North Carolina	26.7	19.7	13.4	−3.4
Textile share of total employment				
Concord	14.6	3.9	—	—
Eden	32.4	17.4	—	—
North Carolina	8.8	3.0	—	—
Services share of total employment (education, health, and social)				
Concord	16.4	18.1	20.7	1.2
Eden	13.9	20.7	22.1	2.4
North Carolina	18.1	19.2	22.6	1.1

U.S. Census Bureau, Decennial Census Tables (1990–2000); American Community Survey (2006–2010, 5 Year Estimates).

Table 6.3. Sociodemographic Resiliency Variables for Concord and Eden

	1990	2000	2010	1990–2010 average annual % change
Population				
Concord	27,347	55,977	79,066	5.5
Eden	15,238	15,908	15,527	0.1
North Carolina	6,628,637	8,049,313	9,535,483	1.8
Population density (persons per square mile)				
Concord	1,254.4	1,085.3	1,311.9	0.2
Eden	1,302.4	1,060.1	1,152.7	−0.6
North Carolina	136.1	165.2	196.1	1.8
High school diploma (%, 25 years and over)				
Concord	27.0	26.6	25.6	−0.3
Eden	28.9	32.1	33.0	0.7
North Carolina	29.0	28.4	28.2	−0.1
Associate degree (%, 25 years and over)				
Concord	7.1	7.3	10.3	1.9
Eden	5.5	5.9	7.4	1.5
North Carolina	6.8	6.8	8.3	1.0
Bachelor degree (%, 25 years and over)				
Concord	10.4	16.9	17.8	2.7
Eden	6.1	7.6	6.9	0.7
North Carolina	12.0	15.3	17.4	1.9
Racial Breakdown, Concord (%)				
Concord				
White	78.6	78.8	70.4	−0.5
Black	20.6	15.1	17.8	−0.7
Other*	0.8	6.1	11.7	14.1
Hispanic	0.5	7.8	12.3	16.8
Racial breakdown, Eden (%)				
Eden				
White	80.8	75.4	71.2	−0.6
Black	18.6	22.2	23.8	1.3
Other*	0.6	2.4	4.9	11.0
Hispanic	0.4	2.3	4.8	12.7

(continued)

Table 6.3. (continued)

	1990	2000	2010	1990–2010 average annual % change
Racial breakdown, North Carolina (%)				
White	75.6	72.1	68.5	−0.5
Black	22.0	21.6	21.5	−0.1
Other*	2.5	6.3	10.0	7.3
Hispanic	1.2	4.7	8.4	10.4
Percent of population of working age (18–64)				
Concord	61.0	62.7	61.0	0.0
Eden	58.7	57.7	59.0	0.0
North Carolina	63.7	63.6	63.1	0.0
Percent of population with disabilities (16–64, with work disability)**				
Concord	9.2	10.7	—	—
Eden	11.8	15.1	—	—
North Carolina	8.7	13.3	—	—
Percent of population born in a different state				
Concord	23.4	34.5	38.3	2.5
Eden	25.1	23.4	22.2	−0.6
North Carolina	27.1	30.8	33.1	1.0
Percent of population foreign born				
Concord	1.2	7.1	10.2	11.3
Eden	0.6	2.1	2.9	8.3
North Carolina	1.7	5.3	7.4	7.6
Percent of population (5 and older) who speak a language other than English at home				
Concord	2.9	9.7	13.0	7.8
Eden	3.3	3.9	4.2	1.3
North Carolina	3.9	8.0	10.4	5.0
Median year housing built				
Concord	1958	1981	1990	—
Eden	1955	1960	1961	—
North Carolina	1971	1978	1984	—
Number of doctors per capita				
Concord	0.010	0.017	0.020	
Eden	0.010	0.009	0.014	
North Carolina	0.012	0.015	0.016	

U.S. Census Bureau, Decennial Census Tables (1990–2000), American Community Survey (2006–2010, 5 Year Estimates)

*Other is calculated as total population minus white and black.

**As percent of civilian noninstitutional population.

Eden's History

Eden is a more isolated community in rural Rockingham County, which borders Virginia in the central part of North Carolina. Eden was incorporated in 1967 by consolidating three mill towns: Leaksville, Spray, and Draper. Each of the three communities has a long history in textiles and other industrial manufacturing. The first documented textile mill in the county was opened in the area in 1764 (City of Eden 2007). The location was favorable because of the significant water resources, a necessity for the operation of textile mills. Both the Dan and Smith rivers flow through Eden. In 1912, Marshall Field from Chicago purchased six large textile mills, renamed the facilities Fieldcrest Mills and established company headquarters in what is now Eden. In the 1920s, Field believed there would be demand for cheaper, mass-produced oriental rugs and built the Karastan mill in Leaksville (a specialized power loom for making the rugs was invented at the mill).

Eden began to experience the effects of the declining textile industry early. In 1971, the town's oldest plant, the Leaksville Woolen Mill, closed (City of Eden 2007: 2). When Fieldcrest purchased Cannon Mills in 1986, it gained 12,900 employees, twelve plants, and fourteen sales offices, becoming the country's fifth largest publicly held textile company (Mock 2013b: 3). According to some of the people interviewed, this move sealed the fate of the company and the community; company headquarters moved to Kannapolis soon after.

Economic Resilience

A review of several variables suggests that Concord had a greater capacity than Eden to respond to the declining textile industry in 1990 (Tables 6.2 and 6.3). Neither town was economically or industrially diverse at that time, but Concord had already diversified away from textile manufacturing and had a stronger economy than Eden. Two industries dominated both towns: manufacturing and services. Concord's labor force employed in manufacturing had dropped to 27.2 percent, compared with Eden's at 46.3 percent. Within that sector, textile manufacturing was still the dominant employer. As a share of total employment, textile employment was at 14.6 percent in Concord, roughly half of Eden's share of 32.4 percent. Unemployment in

Concord was slightly lower than in Eden (4.1 and 4.9 percent respectively), while per capita income and median household income were slightly higher in Concord than in Eden.

Analyzing the towns' socioeconomic variables results in a similar picture. By 1990, both towns were still relatively small, but Concord's population was nearly twice the size of Eden's (27,347 and 15,238 respectively), largely as a result of annexation during the 1980s. A slightly higher percentage of the population in Concord was working age (eighteen to sixty-four). Concord also had a more educated population than Eden. Concord had slightly lower rates of high school graduates than Eden, nearly 27 percent and 29 percent, but a greater share of its population received associate or bachelor degrees. Mill towns are often characterized by a low-skilled labor force. Textile mills did not need a skilled workforce (most positions did not require a high school education); therefore, they did not invest in the education of their workers. As one long-time resident of Eden remarked, "if you could get on at the mill even in the 1980s, you were set for life. You didn't need a high school degree and the job had good benefits. If you lost your job in one textile mill, you could go down the street and get another."

In terms of community cohesion, the relative resiliency of Concord and Eden is mixed. The poverty rate in Concord was lower: 12 percent compared with 16 percent in Eden. However, the communities had similar population densities and racial demographics. Concord was home to a larger share of people born outside the United States, nearly double that of Eden and, accordingly, a larger share of residents who spoke a language other than English at home. Yet, this was a very small percentage of the population in both cases (less than 4 percent). The vast majority of the residents in both Concord and Eden (75 percent) were born in North Carolina.

Textile mills created a paternalistic, but often close-knit, culture in their communities. Generations of families worked at the mills and often lived in company-owned "mill houses." This was true for Concord and the towns that became Eden. By 1990, Concord was primarily home to mill workers in the manager and executive ranks who worked in Kannapolis. They supported a lot of community amenities, including the redevelopment of their historic downtown. Concord joined the North Carolina Main Street revitalization program in 1990 and won the All-America City Award in 2004. In Eden, the textile mill culture created distinct community identity and some long-standing rivalries in the three communities it consolidated. Mill workers of all ranks have always lived in Eden. By all accounts, the executives of

Fieldcrest were also very engaged in the community, providing leadership on many community boards and supporting the development of community amenities. Fieldcrest also fostered the consolidation of Leaksville, Spray, and Draper. Eden has three different historic downtowns and a newer central area where city offices are located. Eden joined the North Carolina Main Street revitalization program in 2003 and won the All-America City Award in 2011.

Leadership, Resource Endowments, and Market Opportunities

Leadership and political institutions are now considered important endogenous factors for economic growth. Stimson, Stough, and Roberts cogently define effective leadership as setting a vision for future development, being proactive in initiating a strategy, and monitoring performance (2006: 325). Such leadership leverages resource endowments for growth, spurs entrepreneurship, and creates a capacity to respond to negative economic events. (For further discussion of the importance of leadership, see chapters by Kodrzycki and Munoz, and Mallach in this volume.)

City leadership in Concord and Eden responded differently to textile industry trends. The government in Concord adopted policies aimed at diversifying the employment base prior to the wholesale loss of textiles as its major employer. Concord's leaders anticipated the decline of the textile industry in the mid-1980s, and the town experienced a significant period of growth during the mid-1980s to 1990s, largely due to annexation. Newly elected council members and new city managers realized that they needed to diversify the local economy. As the mayor of Concord reminisced, "they had the courage to go against conventional wisdom at the time and had the common sense to know that you don't put all of your eggs in one basket."

The annexed areas of Concord increased the town's population and diversified its economic base. By 1990, Concord comprised a large Philip Morris complex and the Charlotte Motor Speedway, with its surrounding motorsports companies. Concord had also supported the development of a private international business park in the mid-1980s and, as noted above, invested in a downtown revitalization campaign. The city also developed the Concord Regional Airport, which opened in 1994. It is still operated by the city and is now the busiest general aviation airport in North Carolina.

The airport is known as the home of the "NASCAR Air Force," referring to the NASCAR teams' use of the airport to travel to races.

As one person we interviewed in Eden stated, "If you had any textile mills in your town, you knew it was only a matter of time. Some businesses will come back, but textiles never will." Yet Eden city leadership did not seem to respond with the same sense of urgency as did leaders in Concord. Some residents we interviewed shared that they felt the city waited too long to react to the declining textile industry; development activities should have started in the early 1990s: "They were waiting for the next white horse, another company or industry to take care of us. They thought that surely someone would come to save us."

Although Concord and Eden share many similar characteristics, their resource endowments and the market opportunities that impact their capacity to recover from negative economic events differ in some important ways. In terms of natural resource endowments, the most significant difference is access to water. As mentioned above, two major rivers flow through Eden. Eden's access to what is essentially an unlimited supply of water makes it an attractive location for industries that rely heavily on water, such as textiles, other types of manufacturing, and brewing. In contrast, Concord does not encompass either a river or lake. In Concord, the limited water access is a constraint, although it also forced the community to diversify to non-water-dependent industries, such as the automotive industry. Both areas also have agricultural industries in their counties, although agriculture is of greater importance to growth and redevelopment in Eden. The county in which Eden is located is one of the top tobacco-producing counties in North Carolina. Income from small tobacco farms has traditionally helped local mill workers diversify their income streams. The city also benefitted from tobacco settlement funds. Although its close proximity to Charlotte has spurred some local food movement development, including a new custom processing plant in the county, Concord's planners did not emphasize agriculture as part of their long-term planning or diversification efforts.

The market opportunities for each town are also clearly a function of their proximity to metropolitan areas and major transportation corridors. Concord's growth reflects in part the growth of Charlotte. Part of the Sunbelt region, Charlotte is one of the fastest-growing metropolitan areas in the country. Some of Concord's residents, especially those who live in some of the newly annexed areas, commute to jobs in Charlotte. Concord is also a member of the Charlotte Regional Partnership, a public-private economic development organization comprised of sixteen counties surrounding Charlotte. Concord's location along Interstate Highway 85, a major transportation route connecting the Northeast to the South, has attracted new businesses and spurred the town's tourist industry.

In contrast, Eden is relatively isolated, with the closest interstate highway at least an hour away. It is adjacent to the Virginia border and is the largest city in the county. It is approximately thirty miles from Greensboro, North Carolina, which is the closest metropolitan area; Charlotte is over one hundred miles away. Its proximity to Virginia allows Eden opportunities to leverage Virginia employment opportunities. It both imports and exports labor from Virginia. In 2001, the city used tobacco settlement funds to support the development of the Berry Hill Regional Mega Park, a partnership between North Carolina and Virginia. Eden provides some water and sewer to the park.

North Carolina is home to numerous community colleges and "four-year" colleges and universities. Concord is within fifty miles of several colleges and universities, including the University of North Carolina at Charlotte. Central Piedmont Community College and Rowan-Cabarrus Community College are both within twenty miles. Eden is also within fifty miles of several colleges and universities, including the University of North Carolina at Greensboro. Rockingham Community College is the closest, located just ten miles from Eden.

Overall, based on the discussion above, in 1990, Concord seems to have had a greater capacity than Eden to respond to the upcoming dual shocks of the sharply declining textile industry and the closure of the Pillowtex plants in 2003. As a result of its proximity to a high-growth urban area and major transportation corridor, Concord had the benefit of more market opportunities than did Eden. It also had strong, visionary leaders who took advantage of these opportunities and began to diversify Concord's local economy before the textile industry's significant decline. As a result, we would expect to see a quicker economic recovery for Concord.

The Shocking Death of an Industry

In the case of the declining textile industry, two types of economic stress, or shocks, present themselves. The multiyear decline of the industry is what Foster (2012) aptly refers to as chronic stress; the significant, unanticipated

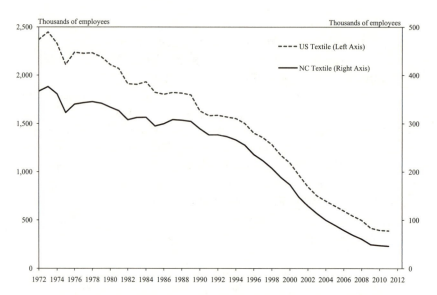

Figure 6.1. Textile manufacturing in North Carolina and the United States, 1972–2011. Note that NAICS replaces SIC beginning 2002. Textile manufacturing prior to 2002 is the sum of textile mill products and apparel and other textiles. After 2002, textile manufacturing is the sum of textile mills, textile product mills, and apparel. Bureau of Labor Statistics/Haver Analytics.

plant closures (single events that happen in a very short time period) are an acute stress. The decline of North Carolina's textile industry started in the early 1970s. The impact was magnified when the steady decline turned into a sharp descent in the 1990s (Figure 6.1).[1] In this chapter, we consider the textile industry decline from 1990 to 2010 as one economic shock to the communities. We also consider the impact of the unexpected textile plant closings in July 2003 stemming from the bankruptcy of Pillowtex Corporation. This was a defining moment in North Carolina; with the loss of 7,650 jobs, it was the largest permanent layoff in the state's history (Minchin 2009; North Carolina Research Campus n.d.: 2). Over 4,300 of the people who worked at Pillowtex lived in Kannapolis and the surrounding communities, including Concord. Pillowtex plants were also shut down in Eden.

In this section, we describe the shocks in greater detail and their impact on each community. A timeline of textile closings and layoffs in Concord and Eden in 1990–2010 illustrates the rapid contraction of the industry during this period both in the United States and North Carolina (Figure 6.2).

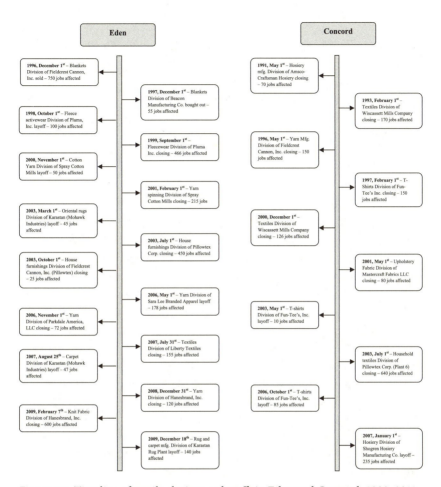

Eden

1996, December 1st – Blankets Division of Fieldcrest Cannon, Inc. sold – 750 jobs affected

1997, December 1st – Blankets Division of Beacon Manufacturing Co. bought out – 55 jobs affected

1998, October 1st – Fleece activewear Division of Pluma, Inc. layoff – 100 jobs affected

1999, September 1st – Fleecewear Division of Pluma Inc. closing – 466 jobs affected

2000, November 1st – Cotton Yarn Division of Spray Cotton Mills layoff – 50 jobs affected

2001, February 1st – Yarn spinning Division of Spray Cotton Mills closing – 215 jobs

2003, March 1st – Oriental rugs Division of Karastan (Mohawk Industries) layoff – 45 jobs affected

2003, July 1st – House furnishings Division of Pillowtex Corp. closing – 450 jobs affected

2003, October 1st – House furnishings Division of Fieldcrest Cannon, Inc. (Pillowtex) closing – 25 jobs affected

2006, May 1st – Yarn Division of Sara Lee Branded Apparel layoff – 178 jobs affected

2006, November 1st – Yarn Division of Parkdale America, LLC closing – 72 jobs affected

2007, July 31st – Textiles Division of Liberty Textiles closing – 155 jobs affected

2007, August 25th – Carpet Division of Karastan (Mohawk Industries) layoff – 47 jobs affected

2008, December 31st – Yarn Division of Hanesbrand, Inc. closing – 120 jobs affected

2009, February 7th – Knit Fabric Division of Hanesbrand, Inc. closing – 600 jobs affected

2009, December 18th – Rug and carpet mfg. Division of Karastan Rug Plant layoff – 140 jobs affected

Concord

1991, May 1st – Hosiery mfg. Division of Amsco-Craftsman Hosiery closing – 70 jobs affected

1993, February 1st – Textiles Division of Wiscassett Mills Company closing – 170 jobs affected

1996, May 1st – Yarn Mfg. Division of Fieldcrest Cannon, Inc. closing – 150 jobs affected

1997, February 1st – T-Shirts Division of Fun-Tee's Inc. closing – 150 jobs affected

2000, December 1st – Textiles Division of Wiscassett Mills Company closing – 126 jobs affected

2001, May 1st – Upholstery Fabric Division of Mastercraft Fabrics LLC closing – 80 jobs affected

2003, May 1st – T-shirts Division of Fun-Tee's, Inc. layoff – 10 jobs affected

2003, July 1st – Household textiles Division of Pillowtex Corp. (Plant 6) closing – 640 jobs affected

2006, October 1st – T-shirts Division of Fun-Tee's, Inc. layoff – 85 jobs affected

2007, January 1st – Hosiery Division of Shogren Hosiery Manufacturing Co. layoff – 235 jobs affected

Figure 6.2. Timeline of textile closings or layoffs in Eden and Concord, 1990–2011. Note that these data are derived from a statewide survey of newspaper accounts of closings and layoffs, and from information supplied to the Employment Security Commission of North Carolina by the employing units experiencing the closings/layoffs. Staff in the Employment Security Commission neither analyze nor evaluate the accuracy of these reports. North Carolina Employment Security Commission, "Announced Business Closings and Permanent Layoffs," http://esesc23.esc.state.nc.us/d4/AnnounceSelection.aspx.

The closing and layoffs started earlier in Concord (in 1991) but ultimately impacted fewer residents than in Eden. Beginning in 1996, Eden experienced almost annual textile plant closings and layoffs through 2009. During our field interviews, we asked the participants to discuss the impact of the declining textile industry and the Pillowtex closures on their communities. We also asked them to identify the most significant textile closing and layoffs impacting their communities since 1990.

Concord

During 1990–2000, the most recently available data, textile employment as a share of total employment in Concord declined dramatically from 14.6 to 4 percent. During the same time period, the manufacturing share of total employment dropped less precipitously, from 27.2 to 18.1 percent. During the years 1990–2010, over 1,700 layoffs in the textile industry were reported in Concord. Ground zero for the Pillowtex bankruptcy was Kannapolis, which borders Concord. In his thorough analysis of the Pillowtex closing, Minchin (2009) discusses how the residents of Kannapolis were left "reeling" after news of the Pillowtex closure, although they were certainly aware that the company was struggling. "This was partly because they could not accept that such a large and long-standing company could ever shut completely. Even when Pillowtex entered bankruptcy, most remained upbeat. . . . Most locals identified strongly with the mill and found it impossible to accept the possibility of closure" (Minchin 2009: 292). Yet, the local residents we interviewed in Concord did not consider it a significant economic shock to Concord. According to those we interviewed, many of the former Pillowtex workers who lived in Concord (generally the managerial and executive ranks) were able to keep their income levels and houses in Concord. Many of the affected local residents were also near retirement. One resident told us, "the town had already moved on, and the new generation was looking for other types of jobs." As textile plants closed in Concord, workers were able to find work in neighboring Kannapolis and Charlotte. By the time Pillowtex closed, textile plants were also a minimum share of tax revenue in Concord.

In Concord, the residents we interviewed cited the closing of the Philip Morris manufacturing facilities in Concord in 2009 as more significant than the Pillowtex closure. The Philip Morris closing was a more significant economic shock because of timing and impact. In 2007, the parent company of Philip Morris, Altria, announced that it would consolidate operations in 2010 but wound up closing the Concord plant a year ahead of schedule. As the mayor noted, the city was surprised because, in 2008, it had provided the company with new incentives to keep the plant open and the city knew that it was one of the company's most modern facilities. Philip Morris was an anchor in the community. Over 1,000 people lost their jobs, although many were eligible for positions in Richmond, Virginia. The City of Concord was hit hard by the tax implications; Philip Morris was the county's largest taxpayer and the city's second-biggest water customer. It also left the city with a very large vacant building on a 2,000-acre site. The residents of Concord also cited the loss of civic leadership and community investment. Philip Morris had donated more than $16 million to local civic and non-profit organizations since 2000.

Eden

Between 1990 and 2000, the most recently available data, textile employment as a share of total employment in Eden also declined dramatically, from 32.4 percent to 17.4 percent. In comparison, during the same time period, the manufacturing share of total employment dropped from 46.3 percent to 31.1 percent. Between 1990 and 2010, nearly 3,500 layoffs in the textile industry were reported in Eden.

While not ground zero, the Pillowtex closing in 2003 and the loss of 450 jobs was a devastating event to Eden, which was clearly still more dependent on the textile industry during that time period than was Concord. Eden had experienced other significant plant closings in the past, including the closure in 2001 of Spray Cotton Mill, the city's 105-year-old yarn-making company, but these were less of an economic shock because there were other mills operating that could absorb the labor and frequently new owners purchased the operations. Until the Pillowtex closure, mill workers believed that layoffs were temporary conditions. The psychological impact of the Pillowtex plant closure on the community cannot be overstated. It was the community's identity. Or as one resident put it, "it was part of our soul." When we interviewed residents in 2012, the emotions were still raw. They referred to the closing as a death and meetings as funerals: "Everyone was in shock. Everything they ever knew was gone." The residents in Eden we interviewed also brought up the loss of human capital associated with the loss of Pillowtex. The community lost many of its civic leaders and a major investor in the community. As one person said, "it was a brain drain."

In Eden, the closing of a local Hanesbrands plant in December 2008–February 2009 (720 jobs were lost) was also cited as a significant economic shock. At the time of its closure, it was a major employer, and residents considered it a key to their economic survival. It was the company's last large knit-fabric textile plant in the United States, and it closed earlier than expected. The Winston-Salem-based company announced in September 2008 that it was closing nine plants in Central America and the United States, resulting in jobs losses for 8,100 workers. The company planned to move production to Asia ("Hanesbrands Closing" 2008). When Hanes left town, Eden lost $3 million a year in tax revenue. Hanes left behind a vacant 900,000 square foot building on the edge of town with few prospects for redevelopment. As a local economic developer noted, its low ceiling height did not fit the demands of new manufacturing options.

Relative Recoveries

In this section, we analyze the degree to which Concord and Eden have been able to recover and return to their 1990 social and economic states and growth paths.

Concord

As expected, given our hypothesis outlined above, Concord seems to have made a full recovery from both economic shocks analyzed in this chapter. While a lack of data makes it impossible to calculate income growth trajectories in either Concord or Eden, a casual visual analysis suggests that Concord is closer to its 1990 economic growth path than Eden (Figure 6.3). In both cases, one also needs to account for the impact of the recession, which would have changed economic growth paths irrespective of any independent industry shocks. In 2010, real median household income was about $10,000 higher than in 1990. Real per capita income grew modestly, and the poverty rate declined. This recovery is even more remarkable given the recession of 2007–2009. The unemployment rate, however, more than doubled during this period, reflecting the state and nation's high unemployment.

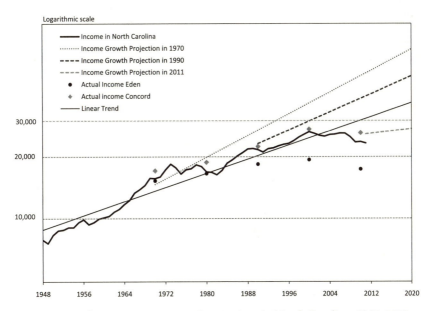

Figure 6.3. Real per capita income and projections in North Carolina, 1948–2020. U.S. Census Bureau, Bureau of Economic Analytics/Haver Analytics.

Concord continues to develop its tourism industry, building on its early investments in a regional airport and the Charlotte Motor Speedway. In 1990, Concord residents voted to reverse a long-standing ban on allowing restaurants to serve alcohol. The reversal of the liquor ban spurred the expansion of restaurants into Concord, particularly those affiliated with national chains. Concord Mills, a large outdoor shopping destination, was developed in 1999. Today it is the number-one tourist destination in the state and features more than 200 stores. The Speedway also attracts major NASCAR races throughout the year. As the mayor noted, two of the races are the equivalent of hosting a Super Bowl twice a year. The top three employers in Concord employ more than 10,000 people and represent a diverse set of public employers and private industries. Carolinas Medical Center Northeast and Concord Mills Mall are the largest employers, each employing 4,000 local people.

The population of Concord has nearly tripled, although much of the growth is due to annexation, and overall educational attainment has increased. The only negative trend is the declining percentage of the population with a high school diploma. Concord has become more diverse and older. A greater percentage of the population in 2010 was born in a different state or was foreign born. The median age of housing dropped nearly a decade during 2000–2010, which is most likely due to the annexation of new housing developments.

In Kannapolis, the mills have been torn down, and the site is now home to the North Carolina Research Campus (NCRC), a $1.5 billion joint effort between six of North Carolina's state public universities, Duke University, and Dole Foods. In 2006, six million square feet of antiquated textile buildings were imploded or demolished to make way for the new research campus. In September of that year, Rowan Cabarrus Community College announced the development and implementation of its R3 (Refocus, Retrain, Reemploy) Center at the NCRC, designed to train a local workforce for opportunities at the NCRC (North Carolina Research Campus n.d.: 2–3).

Eden

Also as expected, given our hypothesis above, Eden has made a slower recovery, and it has not yet regained its 1990 economic state or growth path. In 2010, real median household income was about $5,000 lower than in 1990. In addition, real per capita income declined by $1,000, the poverty rate increased by approximately 8 percentage points (to nearly 25 percent), and the unemployment rate more than doubled. Clearly, Eden was also impacted by the recession, but the comparison with Concord suggests that other factors were also at play. As the textile industry declined, it left Eden dependent on only a few major employers. The largest employer in Eden is Morehead Hospital with just over 1,000 employees. A Miller Coors manufacturing facility employs 600 and is the second largest employer. All the major employers except the hospital are manufacturing or transportation companies.

Eden's population has remained essentially constant, increasing by less than 300 people between 1990 and 2010. However, as residents told us, this is the first generation that cannot find a "good job" in the area, and many youth are leaving. "Some have left because their parents left when the textile mills closed. They don't have any homes to come back to." Educational attainment has also stayed relatively the same across all categories. The residents we interviewed cited low education and the lack of the general population's concern over it as a major barrier to future growth. Eden has the highest dropout rate in the county. As with Concord, Eden has also become more diverse and older. A greater percentage of the population in 2010 was foreign born, although, unlike Concord, the percentage of population born in a different state declined slightly. Not surprisingly given the lack of population growth, the community does not seem to be building many new homes. The median age of housing declined by only one year between 2000 and 2010.

A tour of the town and our interviews with residents suggest a stable community with a lot of civic pride. Karastan spun off from Fieldcrest in the 1920s, still using the same mill in which it was originally established in 1926. Although it has laid off workers, Karastan continues to weave rugs in Eden (Karastan Rug News 2009). As one economic developer summed it up, "you have two choices, you can either fold up the tent or reinvent yourself. We are doing the latter." Eden has some redevelopment in the old textile mills on the waterfront, and the old Fieldcrest lab is now used as Eden's city hall. However, it struggles to find alternative uses for the very large, abandoned plants scattered around the community. Rockingham County, in which Eden is located, is one of the most distressed counties in the state.

The Pillowtex purchase of Fieldcrest helped spur the city to plan for its declining textile base. By 2003, Eden had hired a new, experienced city manager; renovated some old mills; and developed several new initiatives to boost tourism and improve quality of life in town. These included a new city park, a Greenway project, and an annual pottery festival. Eden also actively pursued a traditional, but aggressive, business attraction and retention policy. The city has also continued to develop a professional development staff. There are two full-time staff, which is rare for small towns.

Conclusion

This chapter compares the economic recovery of two small manufacturing-dependent towns in North Carolina to both the chronic decline of the textile industry between 1990 and 2000 and the same local plant closure on a single day in 2003. Our analysis contributes to the understanding of redevelopment and revitalization by a comparative analysis and focusing on small cities.

Eden illustrates the challenges of creating a resilient economy in small, rural communities. Even without the textile shocks, Eden would not be on the same growth trajectory as Concord in large part because of its relative isolation. Concord's proximity to Charlotte is a key factor in its growth and resilience. Concord also took advantage of annexation opportunities, which increased the town's population and afforded it new strategic development opportunities (the regional airport, speedway, and land for a business park). Given its rural location, Eden simply did not have similar annexation opportunities, and, in some cases, its location has constrained its revitalization efforts. Eden's natural resource endowments (two major rivers) lured textile companies to the region and fostered a dependence on the textile industry. In contrast, Concord's scarce water resources forced the town to diversify its economic base.

Our comparative case study also highlights the importance of leadership to economic redevelopment and revitalization and the transitory state of resiliency. Concord's leaders realized the risk of a textile-based economy decades before the leaders of Eden and aggressively pursued alternative development strategies. The capacities of local actors to effect change matter. The success of some of these strategies in Concord may, however, have brought it back to a single-industry dependency (motorsports). Conversely, the near total collapse of the textile industry eventually forced Concord to pursue other development strategies aggressively and increase its general economic resilience. As Concord and Eden demonstrate, a community's resiliency can change over time through intentional and unintentional actions, and drivers of growth do not necessarily drive resiliency.

CHAPTER 7

Parallel Histories, Diverging Trajectories: Resilience in Small Industrial Cities

Alan Mallach

The transformation of the United States from an agrarian nation to the world's leading industrial economy during the nineteenth century began in the small cities of the northeastern United States such as Reading, Pennsylvania, or Lowell, Massachusetts. Many of these places remained important manufacturing centers even after the growth of larger industrial hubs like Detroit or Pittsburgh. All of them, however, lost most of their industrial base in the decades following the end of World War II and have struggled since to find a new postindustrial identity and identify new economic drivers to replace their lost manufacturing base and to address changing social and demographic conditions. Many have lost much of the population they once had, which, in most cases, peaked between 1920 and 1950.

These cities' similarities today, however, appear less notable than the variation between them. In recent decades, some have become major immigrant destinations and have reversed their population decline, while others show signs of significant resilience and rebound, with or without population growth. Still others show massive concentrations of poverty and abandoned buildings and offer little hope of revival in the foreseeable future. This chapter draws upon a study of thirteen such cities in the extended Philadelphia region of southern New Jersey, eastern Pennsylvania, and Delaware (Table 7.1).[1] After a brief historic overview, I will define what I consider the salient features that reflect urban vitality, present a typology of these cities based on those features, and suggest some of the underlying

Table 7.1. Thirteen Cities: Population by City from Peak to 2010 (peak year highlighted)

City	Pre-1950*	1950	1960	1970	1980	1990	2000	2010
Allentown		106757	108347	109527	103758	105473	106632	118032
Altoona	82054	77177	69407	6 2900	57078	51881	49523	46320
Bethlehem		66340	75408	72686	70419	71855	71329	74982
Camden		124555	117159	102551	84910	87460	79904	77344
Chester		66039	63658	56331	45794	41973	36854	33972
Harrisburg		89544	79697	68061	53264	51964	48950	49528
Lancaster		63744	61055	57690	54725	55720	56348	59322
Reading	111171	109320	98177	87643	78686	77864	81207	88082
Scranton	143433	125404	111443	103564	88117	81914	76415	76089
Trenton		128009	114167	104638	92124	88549	85403	84913
Wilkes–Barre	86626	76826	63551	58856	51551	49653	43123	41498
Wilmington	112504	110356	95827	80386	70195	71526	72664	70851
York		59953	54504	50335	44619	42205	40862	43718
TOTAL	NA	1204024	1112400	1015168	895240	878037	849214	864655

U.S. Census of Population.
*Cities that reached their population peak prior to 1950.

factors that appear to be associated with resilience and revitalization in some of these cities.

Origins and Growth

These thirteen cities include some of the oldest cities in the United States.[2] While some, like Reading, Pennsylvania, were ironworking centers even before the Revolutionary War, others were industrialized as they were connected by the canals built in the 1830s and the railroads that followed soon thereafter. After the middle of the nineteenth century, these cities grew rapidly; Reading nearly doubled its population between 1860 and 1880 and again between 1880 and 1900. Much of this growth was fueled by immigration. Irish and Eastern European immigrants flocked to the coal country of northeastern Pennsylvania, while large Italian and Polish communities emerged in Trenton.

Although industrialization was a common theme, each city grew differently, developing a unique industrial mix. That mix often changed over time, as old industries lost ground and new ones took their place. Allentown, Pennsylvania, emerged as a steel and iron center in the mid-nineteenth century; as those sectors declined at the end of the century, silk and textile industries began to emerge. Scranton, Pennsylvania, was the first home of Lackawanna Steel; after that company moved to Buffalo in 1901,[3] the city remained the center of the anthracite coal[4] industry, while developing a subsidiary sector in textiles and becoming a major center in a minor industry, phonograph record manufacturing.

Resilience, in the sense of the ability to rebound from setbacks and find new economic sectors to exploit, was characteristic of these cities, reflecting the strength of their locally based entrepreneurial or capitalist structures. Local or civic capitalism, "individual entrepreneurs who mastered new methods of production and marketing and who mobilized the labor needed to make their machines productive" (Cumbler 1989: 3), dominated local and regional economies. These entrepreneurs were firmly grounded in their city and its civic structures and formed close-knit elite networks. They also underwrote many of the features that were considered hallmarks of a beautiful and prosperous city, founding colleges and universities, art museums and symphony orchestras, and building impressive city halls and other public buildings.

The story of these cities, however, is not only one of beauty and prosperity but also one of substandard, overcrowded living conditions, rampant air and water pollution, and recurrent labor strife. The gap between rich and poor in all these cities was often great, although job opportunities and the growth of public education meant that the second and third generations often lived lives very different from those of their parents or grandparents.

In 1950, these cities were still the economic centers of their respective regions, although forces of urban decline had been gathering steam since the 1920s and they were living, in a sense, on borrowed time.[5] In most of the cities, household incomes and housing costs in the 1950s were equal to or higher than in their suburbs. The thirteen cities had strong economies, heavily oriented toward manufacturing, while their downtowns were their regions' retail and service centers, boasting large department stores and numerous movie theaters. Seven had over 40 percent of their workforce engaged in manufacturing, while over one-third of Altoona, Pennsylvania's workers were engaged in railroad maintenance and repair. Most had unemployment rates below the national average. Even then, however, Chester, Pennsylvania, and Camden, New Jersey, which were more industrial satellites of Philadelphia than independent cities, had higher unemployment rates and lower incomes, both by comparison to the other cities and to the nation as a whole. The 1950s, though, were the end of an era; over the course of the next decade, the forces that would send these cities into long-term decline would become clearly visible.

The Course of Decline

Since the 1950s, these cities have been transformed by the three forces affecting nearly all older American cities: suburbanization, regional population movement, and deindustrialization. Although all declined during the first decades of this period, their trajectories have significantly diverged since the 1980s. Since the broad course of urban decline is well known, I will only briefly sketch the outlines of the story as it applies to these cities.[6]

As with other older cities, these cities became smaller, both in absolute numbers and as a share of their county or metro population; poorer; and more greatly populated by people of color. By 2010, nine of the thirteen cities were "majority-minority" cities, in which the combined Black and Latino population made up a clear majority of the city's residents. While most cities' Black populations are now stable or declining, their Latino communities have grown sharply in recent years. Between 1990 and 2010, the Latino population share grew from 12 to 43 percent in Allentown and from 18 to 58 percent in Reading. Although immigration has led some of these cities' populations to rebound in recent years, they remain below their historic peak population today, Allentown being the sole exception.

The movement of the retail sector to the suburbs beginning in the 1960s was heralded by the opening in 1961 of the Cherry Hill Mall, the first enclosed suburban shopping center east of the Mississippi, only five miles from downtown Camden. While suburbanization led to a rapid decline in these cities' role as regional centers, manufacturing was their lifeblood. While some cities began to lose parts of their industrial base as early as the 1950s, others maintained it largely intact well into the 1970s. By that point, though, all of the region's small manufacturing cities were seeing significant declines in manufacturing activity. The number of manufacturing jobs in these thirteen cities has declined by 84 percent since the 1950s. While far smaller than at its historic peak, manufacturing still remains a significant economic sector in these thirteen cities, with 1,000 firms and more than 40,000 primary workers.

Loss of population and economic activity led to far-reaching changes in the physical fabric of these cities. Most cities saw declines in the number of households and level of homeownership and increases in housing vacancies. Deterioration and deferred maintenance—reflecting both greater poverty and an increase in absentee ownership—became widespread, affecting both modest working-class areas and once-affluent neighborhoods rich in historic and architectural character. Similar disinvestment took place at the same time among industrial and commercial properties. As manufacturing concerns closed their doors, some industrial buildings were reused for other purposes, such as the VF Outlet Village in Reading,[7] but many sat empty and were often ultimately abandoned. Similar fates befell many retail and office buildings, both in downtowns and in traditional neighborhood retail corridors.

Challenges and Responses

Cities responded to the challenges posed by suburbanization and deindustrialization. Many used the federal urban renewal program, enacted in 1949, often focusing initially on revitalizing downtown areas that had lost ground to suburbanization. Trenton and Reading both made unsuccessful efforts to create downtown shopping malls, clearing land that was later used for other purposes.[8] Lancaster built a downtown shopping mall, but it failed as a vehicle for downtown revitalization (Schuyler 2002).

The end of federal urban renewal funds did not mean the end of urban revitalization efforts. Public-private partnerships such as the Harristown Development Corporation (HDC), created by the city of Harrisburg in 1974 to revitalize its downtown, emerged in the 1970s. Cities used other tools to jump-start redevelopment, such as tax-increment financing, tax-exempt debt, and targeted state initiatives, such as those that have spearheaded Wilmington's revitalization.[9]

Since the 1990s, urban redevelopment activity in these cities has been an eclectic mix of initiatives. Arts, entertainment, and creation of visitor destinations have been popular strategies; Wilmington, Lancaster, and Bethlehem, among others, have worked to craft distinctive images for themselves based on history, arts, and tourism. Ten of the thirteen cities have constructed minor league baseball stadiums, while a number have built multipurpose arenas.[10]

Residential and neighborhood strategies have also evolved. During the 1950s and 1960s, large-scale demolition was widespread, reflecting the availability of relatively large amounts of federal money for acquisition, relocation, and demolition. Most new housing took the shape of subsidized, means-tested projects, particularly after enactment of the Section 235 and 236 programs in 1968. Recent trends toward market-driven development reflect the recognition that healthy housing markets are important to a city's vitality, as well as public officials' desire to draw more middle- and upper-income residents into cities that have become disproportionately poor and service-dependent. Both objectives are reflected in the number of market-rate housing developments within and close to these cities' downtowns, often built with tax abatements or other public sector assistance.

Each city's condition today reflects both the effects of the underlying forces driving change as well as the mixed results of its efforts to influence those forces over the past sixty years. Despite those efforts, however, these cities are, for the most part, in worse condition than they were in 1950, beset by many challenges in rebuilding their physical infrastructure, creating new economic bases, fostering stronger housing markets, and finding a path to fiscal solvency.

For all the many similarities between these cities, however, the differences are equally important. Some cities are clearly faring better than others, while others are falling behind. Bethlehem, Pennsylvania, Wilmington, Delaware, and, to a somewhat lesser degree, Lancaster, Pennsylvania, appear to be rebounding strongly from the loss of their historic manufacturing base, while others, Camden and Chester in particular, are not. Before comparing these cities' distinct outcomes in more detail, I will outline what I consider to be the salient features of urban vitality, in order to provide a common framework for evaluating these cities' relative success or failure in responding to their common challenges.

What Does Urban Vitality Mean?

Cities can be viewed through many lenses. They are government entities as well as defined spatial entities containing buildings and land, and they are also social and economic entities, serving as frames for economic activity and accommodating their populations. In defining what constitutes vitality in such a framework, one must look at three distinct elements: the social and economic well-being of the city's residents, the health of the city's neighborhoods and housing market, and the extent to which the city has been able to recreate an export-driven economy to replace its lost economic base.

Social and Economic Well-Being

A successful city is not one without poor people (Glaeser 2011). A successful, vital city provides opportunity to its poor, while containing a healthy mix of lower-, middle- and upper-income households. If a city's residents are mired in chronic poverty and unemployment, revitalization of a downtown or waterfront represents at most a partial success and arguably a hollow one.

Poverty and income distribution are clearly one measure of well-being. Other measures include the unemployment rate and the level of educational attainment. Extensive research has documented the relationship between educational attainment and economic growth (Kodrzycki 2002; Glaeser and Shapiro 2001; Edward Glaeser's chapter in this volume, among others), while, within the spectrum of educational attainment, the most significant measure appears to be the percentage of adults who hold a BA/BS or higher degree.[11] I use the following metrics to measure social and economic well-being:

(1) Median household income.
(2) Household economic dependency ratio, defined as the ratio be-
    tween the number of people in households below the poverty level
    and the number in households with incomes more than double the
    poverty level.[12]
(3) Unemployment rate.
(4) Percentage of adults with BA/BS or higher degree.

The thirteen cities vary widely on all these measures. The share of the
population in poverty in these cities ranges from a high of over 38 percent in
Camden to a low of 15 percent, close to the national average, in Bethlehem.
Three cities contain particularly high concentrations of poverty and proportionately few nonpoor households: Camden, Chester, and Reading, while York
is not far behind.

Only in Wilmington and Bethlehem is the share of the population over
twenty-five with a BA/BS or higher degree close to the 2010 national level.
After those two cities, percentages drop off sharply; in Camden, barely 6
percent of adults have a college degree, while over 40 percent lack even a
high school diploma.[13]

Labor force participation rates are lowest in Camden and Chester, which
also have the highest unemployment rates. The lowest unemployment rates,
outside relatively prosperous Bethlehem, are in the three most isolated
cities—Altoona, Scranton, and Wilkes-Barre—which have seen little immigration and have experienced the greatest population losses of any of the
cities studied, other than Chester. It appears that these cities' workforce is
shrinking in parallel with the decline in employment opportunities, suggesting relatively successful adaptation to sustained population decline. By
contrast, Camden, Chester, and Reading all have unemployment rates in
excess of 15 percent.

Housing and Neighborhood Health

Strong housing markets increase property values and municipal revenues
and are an all-but-essential condition for healthy neighborhoods, which are,
in turn, the foundation of a vital city. Neighborhood health is strongly
driven by consumer choices, reflected in decisions to stay in or buy a home
in a neighborhood (Brophy and Burnett 2003; also see Brophy's chapter in

this volume). Reflecting this, neighborhood revitalization strategies have been increasingly grounded in strategies designed to build stronger housing markets (Boehlke 2004; Mallach 2008). Cities have also widely recognized that building housing demand is an effective revitalization strategy for underutilized downtowns or industrial loft areas (Leinberger 2005).

With rare exceptions, housing market and neighborhood strength are far more driven by home buying than by decisions by either tenants or absentee investors. Homeowner decisions are much more sensitive to neighborhood conditions than renter or investor decisions, which tend to be driven by narrower, more short-term economic considerations. A strong homeownership base is powerfully associated with neighborhood social benefits (Galster 1987; and others) and increased property values (Colson, Hwang, and Imai 2002, 2003).[14] Value, homeownership, and vacancy trends measure the extent to which a city or neighborhood is effectively competing for regional housing market share and are thus strong indicators of neighborhood health. The following metrics are used to measure housing market and neighborhood strength:

(1) Median sales price.
(2) Homebuyer ratio, defined as the ratio of total sales to home purchase mortgages.[15]
(3) Vacancy rate.

Bethlehem has the strongest housing market of any of the cities. House prices are highest, vacancy rates are low, and the city is strongly competitive with its surrounding county. Prices in Bethlehem, moreover, stayed relatively stable between 2007 and 2009, in contrast to most of the nation. Four other cities—Allentown, Lancaster, Scranton, and Wilmington—are at least moderately competitive, while others are far less so. Dramatic declines in prices since 2007 in Camden, Chester, and Trenton reflect not only current market weakness but also the extent to which prices in those cities were pushed upward during the bubble years by the lethal combination of speculative buying and subprime lending.

Most of these cities have seen a steady erosion of homeownership since the 1950s. The exceptions are the three cities of Altoona, Scranton, and Wilkes-Barre, where growth in the homeownership rate is consistent with the "stability in decline" pattern that appears to characterize those three cities. In some cases, as in Bethlehem or Wilmington, the decline in homeownership has been modest, while in others—most notably Trenton, Camden, and Reading—it has been precipitous.

Bethlehem, Lancaster, Scranton, and Wilmington are currently experiencing strong homebuyer demand, with ownership levels in Wilmington and Lancaster potentially rebounding from earlier declines. At the other end, housing markets in Camden, Trenton, Reading, and, in particular, Chester are dominated by investors. House prices are low enough in Chester, and in many parts of the other three cities, for an investor to buy a house, pocket the rental income for a few years while putting little or no money into the property, and walk away from the house with a profit realized entirely from cash flow (Mallach 2010).

Local Economy

The extent to which a city as a geographic entity is economically productive is distinct from the extent to which it may be accommodating and providing opportunity to a socially and economically successful population.[16] The economic productivity of a city as a geographic entity can be studied through indicators such as the number of jobs and business establishments and the level of activity in various economic sectors. The two metrics used here are as follows:[17]

(1) City/county population/jobs location quotient. A location quotient over 1.0 indicates that the city has a greater share of the county's jobs than of its population.
(2) Per capita retail sales.

The presence of a strong job base within a city may or may not benefit residents, as, in most cities, most local jobs are filled by commuters, while most employed local residents work in the suburbs. This raises difficult questions. First, it suggests that creating jobs in the city, by itself, may have only a limited effect on workforce opportunities for city residents; that, in turn, raises the question whether the most effective strategies to increase workforce participation and reduce unemployment in a city are to maximize access to suburban job opportunities, create additional jobs within the city and try to connect city residents to those jobs, or increase the access of city residents to jobs already in the city as they become available through turnover. This demands a better understanding of why so few local jobs are held by local residents—whether it is a matter of preference, access, job/skill mismatch, or some combination of all three.

Further questions arise when one compares performance on economic activity measures with performance on the measures of neighborhood health or social and economic well-being. While variables measuring neighborhood health and social and economic well-being correlate strongly with one another, there is little relationship between any of those variables and each city's level of local economic activity. Correlations between the variables are shown in Table 7.2.

These data suggest that the well-being of a city's population and the strength of its housing market and neighborhoods are likely to be driven more by the extent to which the city is effectively integrated into the regional economy than by the level of economic activity inside the city; that depends, in turn, on the extent to which its residents are competitive in the regional labor market and its housing stock is competitive in the regional housing market. This is likely to be particularly true with respect to small cities, where the suburbs are close by and where there is little difference in accessibility between city and suburb.

Most of these cities' economies are driven by a combination of what are known as "eds and meds," social services, and government. In ten of the cities, health care and social services employ more than one-third of the local private sector workforce, and in Trenton and Camden they employ over half the private sector workforce. The apparent strength of those sectors is both an asset and a risk, arguably more indicative of weakness in other sectors than of true vitality.[18] While health care has grown significantly in recent years and offers jobs at many skill levels, it is heavily dependent on transfer payments and susceptible to public policy changes, as are social services and education. Local government, particularly in cities with constrained and often shrinking fiscal resource bases, has been shrinking in recent years, and public workforces in many of these cities have experienced substantial reductions.[19]

This highlights the importance of building an export-driven economy. That can mean many things, from producing goods for export to drawing short- or long-term visitors who spend money earned elsewhere in the city. Lancaster's growing tourist-oriented economy is as much an export industry as are Reading's remaining manufacturing plants. While import substitution may play some role in local economic development, efforts to foster municipal-level autarchy are likely to be doomed to failure.

In theory, however, in light of the integration of many cities' workforce with regional economies, one might argue that a city could prosper by being

Table 7.2. Correlation between Measures of Economic Vitality

	Social and economic condition of the population				Housing market strength			Local economic activity	
	HH INCOME	DEP RATIO	UNEMP	COLL GRAD %	MORT	SALES PRICE	VACANCY RATE	JOB LQ	RET SALES
HH INCOME		−0.826	−0.641	0.843	−0.642	0.897	0.643	0.234	0.013
DEP RATIO	−0.826		0.9	−0.814	0.598	−0.677	0.525	0.233	−0.436
UNEMP	−0.641	0.9		−0.849	0.572	−0.602	0.487	−0.247	−0.575
COLL GRAD %	0.843	−0.814	−0.849		−0.541	0.849	−0.645	−0.418	0.207
MORT	−0.642	0.598	0.572	−0.541		−0.65	0.573	0.412	−0.244
SALES	0.897	−0.677	−0.602	0.849	−0.65		−0.808	−0.509	0.05
VACANCY RATE	0.643	0.525	0.487	−0.645	0.573	−0.808		0.391	0.034
JOB LQ	0.234	0.233	−0.247	−0.418	0.412	−0.509	0.391		0.328
RET SALES	0.013	−0.436	−0.575	0.207	−0.244	0.05	0.034	0.328	

NOTE: Correlations highlighted in dark gray are significant at the 90 percent level, while correlations highlighted in light gray are significant at the 95 percent or stronger level.

an attractive dormitory for people who work throughout the region, along the lines of the post-World War II communities that Dolores Hayden has called the "sitcom suburbs" (Hayden 2003). For a city to remain vital *as a city*, however, is a different matter. I would argue that a vital city, as distinct from an arguably vital suburb, needs to have a central economic function. That function must be export-driven, both because only such economies are capable of creating the multipliers that can foster sustainable growth and because only such economies can foster the regional relationships on which the city's ultimate vitality depends.

A strong export-driven economy, particularly one that draws the regional population into the city as workers or visitors, serves a further function, helping to change perceptions and reknit regional connections that have deteriorated, as these cities have become smaller, poorer, and less economically significant vis-à-vis the rest of their metropolitan areas. Cultural or artistic venues, such as those that have emerged in recent years in Wilmington and Lancaster, can play an important role in such a process.

Diverging Trajectories and Future Challenges

The most striking conclusion from an assessment of these thirteen cities' respective urban vitality is not their similarity but their differences. Wilmington and Bethlehem are in an entirely different economic realm than Chester or Camden, while Altoona, Scranton, and Wilkes-Barre are following a very different path, but not necessarily a less successful one, from the other cities in the region. It is difficult to tell, of course, whether those variations reflect differences in intentional strategies, the effectiveness of political and civic leaders, the level of civic capacity, baseline conditions, regional location and other external factors, or simply good or bad luck (Reese and Ye 2011). While, in all likelihood, many or all of these factors are involved, some important elements that appear to be relevant to the trajectories of the more successful cities can be identified.

A Typology of Small Industrial Cities

In order to compare the thirteen cities, I have ranked in Table 7.3 the thirteen cities on the nine measures of urban vitality described above, based

Table 7.3. Comparison of Thirteen Cities on Nine Measures of Economic Vitality

	Resident Social and Economic Condition				Housing Market Condition			City Economic Activity			
	Median household income	Household economic dependency ratio (note 1)	Unemployment rate	Percentage of college graduates	Mortgage ratio (note 2)	Median sales price	Vacancy rate	Private sector job location quotient	Per capita retail sales	Composite score	Composite rank
Bethlehem	1	1	2	2	5	1	1	4	8	25	1
Wilmington	2	4	7	1	2	3	8	2	4	33	2
Scranton	5	3	1	3	3	5	5	7	5	37	3
Altoona	6	2	4	7	1	6	4	5	2	37	3
Lancaster	7	8	8	5	4	4	2	3	3	44	5
Allentown	3	6	5	6	5	2	3	12	7	49	6
Wilkes-Barre	10	5	3	8	6	9	11	6	1	59	7
York	9	10	9	10	7	7	6	9	10	69	8
Harrisburg	8	9	6	4	8	8	12	9	6	70	9
Trenton	4	7	10	9	10	10	9	13	11	83	10
Reading	11	12	11	12	11	12	7	8	9	93	11
Camden	12	13	13	13	12	11	10	10	12	106	12
Chester	13	11	12	11	13	13	13	11	13	110	13

Cities in the top four on any measure are highlighted

NOTES

(1) Ratio between households below the poverty level and households with incomes more than twice the poverty level.

(2) Ratio between total sales and purchase mortgages. This is an indicator of the relative weight of owner-occupant and absentee buyers in the marketplace.

U.S. Bureau of the Census (2010 Census, American Community Survey, On the Map Application, Census of Retail Trade); Boxwood Means from PolicyMap; Home Mortgage Disclosure Act (HMDA).

on the rankings in the table, these thirteen cities fall into four distinct categories.

REBOUNDING CITIES: BETHLEHEM, WILMINGTON, AND LANCASTER

These three cities are rebounding strongly from deindustrialization and appear to be building a strong postindustrial future. This is particularly true for Bethlehem and Wilmington, although their progress may be partial and the benefits of progress unevenly distributed. Lancaster's progress, while significant, is less clear cut at this point. It appears to be building strongly on its assets, although it lacks some of the other two cities' locational advantages and the economic well-being of its residents lags behind its progress in economic and housing market activity.

All three cities have important locational advantages. All three are in relatively healthy regions. Wilmington has capitalized on its position in the New York-Washington corridor and the unique conditions that have made Delaware an attractive location for financial service firms. Bethlehem is located in a strong subregion and benefits from proximity to New York and northern New Jersey. Lancaster's principal locational advantage is its position in the heart of the major tourist destination known as Amish country. While Lehigh University is important to Bethlehem, Lancaster has effectively leveraged the more modest asset represented by Franklin and Marshall College.

All three cities have shown effective political or civic leadership, pursued long-term, sustained, and focused redevelopment strategies, including the multifaceted reuse of the Bethlehem Steel Works, Lancaster's arts- and tourism-driven strategy, and Wilmington's downtown and riverfront revitalization. Few similar cities, among these thirteen or elsewhere, can point to comparable sustained efforts.

DECLINING BUT STABLE CITIES: ALTOONA, SCRANTON, AND WILKES-BARRE

Strong associations have been found between sustained population loss and high levels of poverty and unemployment (Vey 2007; Brachman and Mallach 2010). Cities such as Detroit or Youngstown, with highly elevated poverty rates and devastated housing markets, are widely seen as the paradigms of shrinking cities. Altoona, Scranton, and to a lesser extent Wilkes-Barre may offer a different model of the shrinking city, in which long-term population

loss may be taking place without similarly dire social and economic consequences. All three cities have lost over 40 percent of their peak population.
Despite this, these cities, particularly Scranton and Altoona, are performing
well compared to most of their regional peers; Scranton, whose population
may be stabilizing, may come to be seen before long as a rebounding city.

While these cities have seen considerable declines in economic activity,
the declines have been paralleled by changes in population and aging out of
their workforce; as a result, it appears that these cities have maintained a
higher level of social and economic equilibrium during their decline. They
have experienced neither the massive flight of the middle class nor the collapse of the retail sector that took place in cities like Trenton or Reading and
have retained greater regional population and retail activity shares. Their
relative vitality stands as a strong argument against simplistic associations
of population growth and decline with urban vitality or weakness.[20]

One should neither minimize the importance of the efforts these cities
are making to foster revitalization nor suggest that they lack serious social
and economic problems. They have many problems, but they also have valuable assets, including clusters of higher education institutions, waterfronts,
and historic districts. Other shrinking cities, however, that exhibit far more
serious economic problems also have similar assets. The reasons underlying
the relative vitality of these three cities demand further study.

COPING CITIES: HARRISBURG, ALLENTOWN, AND YORK

These three cities occupy a middle ground. Although they have not shown
signs of revival comparable to Wilmington or Bethlehem, economic growth
and revitalization would appear to be achievable goals over the coming
years. All three cities retain relatively strong downtowns, although downtown Allentown, the historic retail center of the Lehigh Valley, has lost
ground to Bethlehem in recent years.

Downtown Harrisburg has benefited from the efforts of the Harristown
Development Corporation and most probably from the state government
presence. York has seen a growing number of small-scale redevelopment
efforts in and around downtown. Given the city's rich historic texture, effective leadership to harness the energy of local entrepreneurs could lead to
changes in York's future.

In other respects, the three cities have little in common. Harrisburg is a
shrinking city, although showing a slight gain between 2000 and 2010, while
Allentown is at its peak population today as a result of sustained Latino in-

migration. While the integration of the newly arriving Latino population is straining Allentown's social fabric today, it may well become a source of future strength.

The remaining four cities all show deeper distress and fewer signs of revival than those described above. Trenton appears to be underperforming relative to its potential; it is located in an economically strong region, with strong regional rail connections, and is New Jersey's state capital. Despite a long history of efforts at revival, however, Trenton's progress appears stalled today, while the current political and civic leadership offers no cause for near-term optimism (Manahan 2012).

Largely because of the greater economic well-being of its population, reflecting the strength of its region's economy, Trenton stands out modestly from the other cities in this category and might be considered a borderline case between "coping" and "struggling" cities. Camden, Chester, and Reading fall into a distinct and troubling category of cities exhibiting particularly severe levels of poverty and disinvestment, with few resources or assets to address what appear to be overwhelming problems. In contrast to many of the other cities, which show a mix of positive and negative features, these three cities show consistent weakness on all of the measures of urban vitality.

Camden, in particular, would appear to have assets capable of spurring change. It is close to Philadelphia and has a substantial university, a major regional medical center, good highway and transit connections, and an impressive cluster of waterfront visitor destinations. Chester has a university of similar size, as well as commuter rail service to Philadelphia. Trenton, however, has neither a resident college nor a medical center of more than local importance, while a highway cuts off its downtown from the Delaware River. These assets appear to have done little to affect these cities' conditions. Philadelphia's economic growth does not appear to be strong enough to spill over in the form of significant benefits to nearby cities, while the hundreds of millions spent by the State of New Jersey to build waterfront destinations in Camden have had little impact; they are isolated from the rest of the city and create few economic spillovers, in contrast to visitor destinations in Lancaster or Bethlehem, which are better integrated into those cities' fabric.

During the preceding decade, indeed, the State of New Jersey has lavished a remarkable level of money and attention on Camden, but its expenditures appear to have led to little or no change in Camden's current realities or underlying conditions.[21] Poverty, unemployment, and abandonment are endemic, while public services remain seriously inadequate. Recent declines in state aid have forced Camden to make drastic cuts to public services, with severe effects on the level of police services and potentially on criminal activity (Goldstein 2011).[22]

Chester's profile is not unlike that of Camden. Waterfront development has taken place, but its impact on the rest of the city remains uncertain. In recent years, a growing civic commitment by Widener University has led to the university's taking the lead in developing a mixed-use development adjacent to the campus including a hotel, housing and retail facilities, and the University Technology Park, a twenty-acre planned technology campus.

Reading appears to have retained more economic assets than either Chester or Camden, including a stronger downtown economic base and some competitive neighborhoods such as Center Square. It is hindered, however, by being in a relatively weak economic subregion; it faces the need to integrate an influx of Latino households without the economic base to offer them adequate economic opportunities. Although Reading has gained population since the early 1990s, it has continued to fall behind economically, to the point that it was recently proclaimed the "poorest city in the country," in terms of its percentage of residents living below the poverty level (Tavernise 2011).[23]

These four cities share a similar bind. The combination of poverty, lack of economic opportunity, housing market collapse, and insufficient fiscal resources makes the prospect of regeneration from within appear remote. Some years ago, David Rusk argued that certain cities reach a "point of no return," based on population loss, minority population share, and suburban-urban income disparity (1993). While Rusk's metrics are questionable,[24] his principle is sound; beyond some level of cumulative decline in wealth, income, and opportunity, a community's ability to rebound without substantial outside support, if at all, becomes doubtful. The implications of this have yet to be fully assimilated by policymakers, either state or federal government.

The Roots of Resilience: What Fosters Urban Vitality?

The variation in each of these thirteen cities' relative vitality appears to reflect a mixture of exogenous factors largely outside the individual city's control and endogenous factors that the city may be able to control to some degree. While seemingly obvious, it is important to stress this in light of tendencies to portray cities as masters of their destinies and at fault if they fail to thrive or, alternatively, as purely passive victims or beneficiaries of larger trends and forces.

"Place luck," as Reese and Ye (2011) call it, clearly plays an important role. As noted, the three cities I consider resilient cities share strong locational advantages. What constitutes place luck, however, is not always clear. I would argue, perhaps counterintuitively, that the proximity of Camden and Chester to Philadelphia may have actually affected those cities negatively; rather than representing a locational asset, the gravitational pull of that far larger city has effectively stifled the growth of independent economic activities and social institutions in its industrial satellites, in contrast to the far greater economic strength of New York, which has created spillovers that benefit its satellites like Hoboken and Jersey City.

A second important factor is the mix of unique assets with which each city is endowed. The presence of a major university, or a geographic asset such as a riverfront, clearly has some bearing on the opportunities available to a city. A policy, such as the Delaware statutes that make the state particularly attractive as a financial sector location, can also be an asset. Such assets, however, represent potential alone; they do not in themselves foster either resilience or vitality. Franklin & Marshall College, although a small undergraduate institution, has contributed more to Lancaster's regeneration than has Rutgers to Camden, despite the latter's graduate schools and far greater size. Similarly, Delaware's statutes would have had less effect on Wilmington without an active, receptive climate and leadership in that city. The manner in which assets are leveraged is significant as well; the redevelopment of Wilmington's riverfront appears to have had far more impact on the course of that city than the redevelopment of the Camden riverfront, despite the massive public sector investment in the latter, reflecting both the mix of facilities and the connections between the riverfront and other parts of the city.

This, in turn, points to the importance of what might be considered cultural factors, three of which seem to be particularly salient to the experience of the thirteen cities: leadership, vision, and continuity. The importance of strong leadership and effective partnerships as a driving force for change has been widely recognized (Reese 1997; Briggs 2008; also see chapters by Yolanda K. Kodrzycki and Ana Patricia Muñoz and by Kimberly Zeuli in this volume). Clearly, having a strong, effective mayor such as Christopher

Doherty in Scranton or Richard Gray in Lancaster is important. While leadership can also come from outside the political system, including the business and nonprofit worlds, it must emerge from within and be rooted in the city.

Arguably more important than the role of any single leader or partnership entity, however, may be the quality of the city's vision of the future and the continuity and consistency with which it pursues it. "Vision," as I use it, is something very different from a vision statement or a generalized (usually unrealistic) statement of aspirations for the city's future. It is a coherent body of aspirations, grounded in reality, for the city or for a part of it, capable of being translated into a concrete plan or strategy; Bethlehem's vision for the future of the Bethlehem Steel Works or Lancaster's vision of the city as a center for arts, history, and tourism are examples.

Realizing any such vision is a long-term process. Implementing even modest strategies takes years, and major efforts are likely to take decades. Successful regeneration, moreover, is rarely the result of a single megaproject, but is far more likely to emerge through the cumulative effect of smaller initiatives. Continuity, in the sense of sustaining the effort year after year and maintaining a consistent, coherent strategy over many years, is the sine qua non of successful regeneration. Arguably, the ability to frame a usable vision and maintain that sort of continuity may be the litmus test of a city's resilience. That ability, more than the high-profile presence of a single individual, may be the strongest evidence that effective leadership is present.

Finally, whatever the vision, it must be one of a city integrated into and interdependent with its region. Autarchy is a dead end. No city can thrive by recycling its own limited resources. Its assets become genuine assets for regeneration only to the extent that they can leverage regional, or even national or global, resources, whether in the form of a college drawing a worldwide student body, a collection of destinations drawing visitors from across the nation, or a workforce capable of competing for jobs in globally competitive firms. No one today *has to* buy a home, locate a business, shop, or visit in Allentown, Lancaster, or Scranton. People will do so only to the extent the city offers regionally competitive reasons for them to do so.

Conclusion

These thirteen cities will face daunting challenges over the coming years. Even the most successful may find it difficult to maintain their momentum in the face of sluggish economic growth and weak housing demand, while those that have lagged may find it even more difficult to advance in a challenging economic climate. To do so, they will have to pursue sustained, coherent strategies for change, build stronger regional partnerships, and more effectively leverage their assets. Beyond this, these cities face a further challenge: the need to integrate diverse and often fractured communities and foster the conditions that can reduce their large, and in some cases growing, social and economic disparities.

Those cities, such as Reading or Allentown, that are major migrant destinations will have to overcome strains between their Latino and non-Latino residents, build economic opportunities for new arrivals, and ensure that the new generation of Latino children emerging in these cities find educational and employment opportunities. While the Latino population is widely growing, African American populations are stable or declining, particularly in cities with historically large African American communities.[25] These communities are steadily losing economic ground as large numbers of better educated and more affluent African Americans move to the suburbs, leaving behind an increasingly marginalized and impoverished community. In cities like Harrisburg and Wilmington, the economic divide between white and black, always large, is widening into a chasm.

For all of these thirteen cities, and particularly those that have already demonstrated their resilience, turning their regained vitality into meaningful opportunity for all their citizens may be the greatest challenge of all.

PART III

Land and Neighborhood Policy

CHAPTER 8

A Market-Oriented Approach to
Neighborhoods

Paul C. Brophy

Asking a group of city planning students for measures of neighborhood health usually produces a good list of textbook answers: crime, school quality, poverty rate, number of vacant structures, price trends, and so forth.

Ask that same group of students why they choose to live where they do and another kind of answer emerges: "I like my neighborhood because it's diverse," "I want to be near the bar scene," "I want a place with a yard for my dog," "I need quiet, so I live in a neighborhood that's mostly older people," "I want to live near my extended family." These answers come from students as *consumers* of neighborhoods, not as planners of neighborhoods.

This exercise demonstrates that we are all consumers of neighborhoods—that there is a market in which neighborhoods exist—and that neighborhoods compete with each other in a city or metro area for residents, businesses, and investment. Some neighborhoods have broader appeal, attracting large numbers of people. These neighborhoods have the highest home prices and rents because the law of supply and demand applies as much to neighborhoods as it does to anything else. And, like product differentiation in other spheres (think autos), personal preferences help determine where people choose to live, as does their income and whether they are a homebuyer or a renter. When people as consumers cannot afford the neighborhood they really want, they will find the best substitute. Of course, neighborhood differences are more complex than differences among automobiles; the product is less standardized, so imperfect knowledge of neighborhoods can distort choices. A neighborhood consumer cannot pick up a *Consumer Reports* rating on the long-term performance of the neighborhood, making the neighborhood's future something of an educated guess.[1]

Yet policymakers trying to improve city neighborhoods have seldom factored in market dynamics and consumer preferences in formulating approaches to neighborhood improvement. Current federal neighborhood programs continue to target the most distressed neighborhoods, keeping with the federal program tradition described below. These distressed neighborhoods require dramatic and costly interventions to hold their current populations and to attract newcomers. Other approaches, described at the end of this chapter, may be helpful to the people living in these distressed places that can facilitate personal and family upward mobility; these approaches are more focused on helping people than on improving place.

There is another category of neighborhoods that have largely been ignored by federal programs—neighborhoods that can become stronger and more desirable with relatively modest assistance.

Cities need strong, vibrant neighborhoods, places where people want to live because the neighborhoods are pleasant, good places to raise children, accessible to jobs, and, from a homebuyer's perspective, are likely to see appreciation in home values. Cities also need these neighborhoods because these stable places are an important source of property and wage taxes—revenues essential to cities to support adequate services for all.

Thriving cities are filled with people who have a love for the place and contribute their energies toward making it work and who want to be in the city and neighborhoods because of the amenities present—including good neighbors, parks, entertainment, good retail, and good schools.

More practically, strong neighborhoods help cities thrive because these neighborhoods typically have had steady or rising property values, which means that cities dependent on property taxes have the tax revenue from these neighborhoods to provide essential city services. The recent dip in property values and the accompanying loss of property taxes underscore the importance of the long-term trend that the solid tax income coming from these neighborhoods provides revenue to city governments equipping them in providing safe streets, good schools, attractive parks, and many other local services. Cities with thriving neighborhoods and a correspondingly strong tax base can afford to provide better services. In some cities, where population has declined and, along with it, tax revenues, city governments are financially strapped, making it difficult and sometimes impossible for the local government to provide the services needed to keep neighborhoods functioning and pleasant. While many cities in the United States are thriving, many other cities, especially smaller cities and older industrial cities, are caught in this vicious cycle, where reductions in city services lead to neighborhood decline, causing people to move out, prices to decline, and taxes to fall farther.

This chapter argues that, in addition to programs that seek to help low-income people grow out of poverty, those who work to improve neighborhoods have been taking too narrow an approach to neighborhood improvement, especially in these older industrial cities, sometimes called "legacy cities" (American Assembly 2011). This chapter describes more balanced neighborhood improvement strategies that show genuine promise in helping cities improve a category of neighborhoods—middle neighborhoods—that have largely been taken for granted.

This chapter also provides a brief history of federal neighborhood policy; explores the current challenge to population-losing cities in setting neighborhood policy; offers some remarkable tools that are being used to understand neighborhood market conditions; and recommends significant shifts in how policymakers think and act on neighborhood improvement.

Looking Back

When World War II ended, America's cities needed renewal. The Great Depression and World War II years curtailed construction in downtowns for a generation, and many cities had slums that we now forget existed—places that were unsanitary (some houses lacked plumbing) and overcrowded and viewed as causes of juvenile delinquency, disease, crime, and other social ills.

The movement to improve housing for low-wage workers began in part with the passage of the federal public housing program just before World War II; after the war, cities clamored for federal help in clearing slums and building public housing, some of which was the best housing available to workers at the time. Through congressional action in the late 1940s and early 1950s, the federal government created the Urban Renewal Program, beginning a three-decade-long local-federal partnership to clear slums with the intention of creating better neighborhoods.

Some of this urban renewal and public housing development worked very well, but, overall, the program is now seen as a major federal program failure—it disrupted neighborhoods that, while problematic, had character and were loved; it often targeted low-income minority neighborhoods; it misread markets, moving people out and demolishing neighborhoods only to see the vacant land sit idle for years (Jacobs 2011; Anderson 1967). One author reports that urban renewal "bulldozed" 2,500 neighborhoods in 993 cities between 1949 and 1973 (Fullilove 2004). Overall, the programs seem to have had a negative effect on a broad range of people.

Along with the disruptive urban renewal program came the National Interstate and Defense Highway Act in 1954, which allied the federal government and state highway departments to build the nation's interstate system. When built in cities, the highways often devastated neighborhoods, both directly by taking out blocks of occupied residential and commercial areas and indirectly by bisecting neighborhoods.

Along with these physical change efforts, the civil rights movement was forcing the nation to deal with long-deferred issues of race and racial segregation. As the urban renewal and highway programs affected minority neighborhoods, the grass-roots reactions were often along racial lines, adding fuel to an already tense situation in many cities. Blockbusting and white flight, when added to this programmatic mix, led to radical changes in racial mix in many cities.[2]

These large federal interventions created massive opposition. In many cities, smart citizen organizations stopped urban renewal or moved planned interstates, but, in many places, neighborhoods were devastated by urban renewal and the interstate system.

In this milieu, the federal government also developed programs to fight poverty. The Economic Opportunity Act of 1964 began Lyndon Johnson's War on Poverty; its requirement for "maximum feasible participation" of the poor in the planning and execution of the program led to an increase in organized low-income groups in cities. Then, in 1966, the high-water mark of these federal efforts, Congress enacted the Model Cities program. President Johnson described its aspirational goals: "The dream is of cities of promise, cities of hope, where it could truly be said, to every man his chance, to every man, regardless of his birth, his shining golden opportunity, to every man the right to live and work and to be himself and to become whatever thing his manhood and his vision can combine to make him" (Pritchett 2008: 284–85).

These programs—public housing, urban renewal, highways, poverty reduction, and model cities—are the origins of the de facto neighborhood policy that has been promulgated by the federal government from then until now. The goals are laudable. Yet, the roots of neighborhood improvement programs at the federal level intertwine two different urban policies: policies to improve city neighborhoods and policies to alleviate poverty and racial segregation. The vast bulk of the federal programs have focused on improving cities' most distressed areas because these areas are connected with issues of poverty and race.

The federal intervention programs that followed the programs of the 1970s and 1980s continued this approach. For example, the Clinton administration's Empowerment Zone program focused on job creation in targeted distressed areas, using a combination of federal appropriations and tax credits to stimulate jobs and neighborhood improvement (HUD 2012). Choice Neighborhoods and Promise Neighborhoods, two contemporary programs, are both aimed at distressed neighborhoods as well. Compared to the Model Cities program, which had a starting budget of almost $1 billion ($19 billion in today's dollars) targeted to it, today's programs are far smaller. The Choice Neighborhood program, for example, is underway in only five neighborhoods, and the amount of funding for each place ($10–30 million) may be insufficient to dramatically improve these very distressed places. In 2011, the program had an overall budget of $250 million.

Some important exceptions to this federal pattern of focusing on distressed neighborhoods exist, however. First, the Federally Assisted Code Enforcement Program (FACE), a long-forgotten HUD program from the 1970s, worked to stabilize neighborhoods that were not yet deteriorated. The FACE program combined local targeted code enforcement with grants and low-interest loans to property owners to make housing repairs. The program worked in some places but failed in others for many reasons, but, in part, the results were mixed because the techniques of understanding neighborhood market conditions were undeveloped and some FACE programs were targeted to neighborhoods where markets were too weak for the intervention. Faced with the requirement to improve their properties, many landlords in these settings walked away from their properties, even when financial help was available (Simmons 1981). The program was one of many folded into the Community Development Block Grant program begun in 1974.

The second exception occurred during the Carter presidency when Monsignor Geno Baroni headed up the Office of Neighborhoods, Voluntary Associations, and Consumer Protection. Baroni, a civil rights activist and long-time advocate for neighborhood growth from the bottom up, used a $25 million appropriation from Congress to fund the Neighborhood Self-Help Development Program, which provided encouragement, grant assistance, and technical assistance to community-based groups in a range of neighborhoods, many of them working-class ethnic neighborhoods in cities. This program was terminated when the Reagan administration came into office, as part of a broad shift in focus from neighborhoods to housing.

Secretary Henry Cisneros initiated the third exception through the HOPE VI program, which emphasized the deconcentration of poverty through a transformation of public housing, placing low-income people in mixed-income communities, an approach based on the assumption that mixed-income communities are more likely to produce a better environment for low-income people than neighborhoods with only low-income residents (Cisneros and Engdahl 2009). The HOPE VI program stimulated local housing authorities to create better housing communities for their low-income residents. Between 1993 and 2010, there were 254 HOPE VI revitalization grants awarded to 132 housing authorities, totaling more than $6.1 billion. While not all these developments were mixed-income, a substantial portion did take the mixed-income approach.[3]

The fourth, and enduring, exception is what is now NeighborWorks America, a congressionally chartered corporation born from a working agreement between HUD and the Federal Home Loan Board in the mid-1970s. The Neighborhood Reinvestment Task Force, as it was first called, was formed to promote the principles and actions of the Neighborhood Housing Services Program, which originated in Pittsburgh. That program grew from grass-roots efforts to promote reinvestment in Pittsburgh neighborhoods harmed by urban renewal. An innovative partnership among neighborhood leaders, lenders, foundations, and city government, the model sought to increase investment in "middle" neighborhoods—areas still healthy enough that, with increased availability of mortgage and home improvement loans, and neighborhood self-help and city government investment, could be stabilized and put on a path toward a normalized market (Ahlbrandt and Brophy 1975).

As NeighborWorks America evolved, its emphasis broadened to focus also on affordable homeownership, housing counseling, neighborhood success measures, training and other housing and neighborhood-related activities.[4] While its mission still references communities—"NeighborWorks America creates opportunities for people to live in affordable homes, improve their lives and strengthen their communities"—its original thrust to improve middle neighborhoods is now interwoven with its focus on home-ownership and, more recently, foreclosure relief.

As a result of this historic emphasis on distressed neighborhoods and affordable housing, local governments, policymakers, and neighborhood leaders have been conditioned to focus on very distressed neighborhoods, so they lack the orientation and tools to strengthen neighborhoods with mar-ket conditions capable of retaining residents and attracting newcomers—strategies essential to healthy cities.

Promising Contemporary Approaches

A growing body of literature and experience indicates that, in addition to seeking to improve distressed neighborhoods, cities need to embrace a broader range of neighborhood strategies—strategies that match neighbor-hood market conditions. The approach of strengthening middle neighbor-hoods is important in cities that are struggling to hold their populations and their tax base. These middle neighborhoods are neither distressed nor com-pletely healthy and stable. They are typically neighborhoods that house working people. They could become stable over time if market forces work in their favor, or they could decline significantly if their market competi-tiveness declines because they are viewed as an undesirable place to locate and buy a home since their future trajectory is uncertain.[5]

One important aspect of viewing these neighborhoods as part of a larger market is that they sometimes have more market strength than meets the eye. Michael Porter and his colleagues at the Institute for a Competitive Inner City have furthered the understanding of neighborhoods a great deal. The Colum-bia University-based American Assembly issued a 1997 report called *Commu-nity Capitalism: Rediscovering the Markets of America's Urban Neighborhoods* that sought to help inner-city neighborhoods compete and understand them as market opportunities. This work helped change thinking about neighbor-hoods from deficit-ridden places to places with hidden assets.

Advocates and practitioners working to strengthen neighborhoods are now able to use new sophisticated techniques to understand the market con-ditions in neighborhoods. These techniques use up-to-date data sources and contemporary data analysis to gauge the relative market strengths of neigh-borhoods and the direction of their markets and to permit neighborhood improvement strategists to fit intervention strategies to neighborhood market conditions. These intervention strategies are meant to maintain market strength where it exists and build it where it is tentative or weak. A related technique gauges buying power in central city neighborhoods more accurately than in the past, something of major importance for retail location decisions.

A leading example is the Philadelphia-based Reinvestment Fund's approach called Market Value Analysis. Initially developed to assist mayor John Street develop neighborhood strategies in the early 2000s, the technique has been used in ten cities to describe neighborhood market conditions (for an overview of the MVA, see Goldstein 2011).

The MVA uses a neighborhood market index based on a composite of neighborhood market indicators, including sales prices, foreclosures, availability of commercial space, vacant housing, volume of building permits, and others. The technique combines block groups with similar characteristics and categorizes neighborhood markets into strong, transitional, and distressed categories.

The typology permits planners, policymakers, and neighborhood leaders to understand neighborhoods by their residential market strength or weakness.[6] The categories also suggest broad remedies, as described in Table 8.1, which vary by neighborhood market type. For example, acquisition and repositioning of vacant properties is a strategy needed in distressed neighborhoods where the housing market is very weak, but is unnecessary in stronger market settings, where enforcement of codes related to maintenance of vacant land and buildings is typically sufficient to cause an owner to sell a vacant property or bring it into code compliance.

The results of the Market Value Analysis work indicates the different neighborhood market conditions in these cities, and gives some very preliminary evidence of the types of markets that exist there and maybe elsewhere. Categorizing neighborhoods by market type shows that the percentage of middle neighborhoods varies by city (see Table 8.2). In the cities studied to date, the percentage comprised of middle neighborhoods is quite substantial: from a low of 31 percent in Newark to a high of 54 percent in Wilmington. To state this in shorthand fashion, in the cities studied to date by the Reinvestment Fund, middle neighborhoods make up one-third to one-half of these cities' residential geography; the remaining neighborhoods in these cities are in either the healthy or distressed categories. The cities self-selected for the MVA and are obviously not a cross section of cities in the nation—but

Table 8.1. Housing Market Descriptions

Regional Choice

Neighborhoods in the Regional Choice market category represent competitive housing markets with high owner-occupancy rates and high property values in comparison to all other market types. Foreclosure, vacancy, and abandonment rates are low. Substantial market interventions are not necessary in the Regional Choice market. Basic municipal services such as street maintenance are essential to maintaining these markets.

Middle Market Choice

Neighborhoods in the Middle Market Choice category have housing prices above the city's average with strong ownership rates and low vacancies, but with slightly increased foreclosure rates. Modest incentives and strong neighborhood marketing should keep these communities healthy, with the potential for growth.

Middle Market

Neighborhoods in the Middle Market category have median sales values of $91,000 (above the city's average of $65,000) as well as high homeownership rates. These markets experienced higher foreclosure rates when compared to higher value markets, with slight population loss. Neighborhood stabilization and aggressive marketing of vacant houses should be considered in this category. Diligent housing code enforcement is also essential to maintain the existing housing stock.

Middle Market Stressed

Neighborhoods in this category have slightly lower home sale values than the city's average, and have not shown significant sales price appreciation. Vacancies and foreclosure rates are high, and the rate of population loss has increased in this market type, according to 2010 Census data. Based on these market conditions, intervention strategies should support homeowners who may be facing economic hardships due to the national economy.

Distressed Market

These neighborhoods have experienced significant deterioration of the housing stock. This market category contains the highest vacancy rates and lowest homeownership rates, compared to the other market types. It also has experienced some of the most substantial population losses in the city during the past decade. Comprehensive housing market inventions should be targeted in this market category, including site assembly, tax increment financing, and concentrated demolitions to create potential for greater public safety and new green amenities.

Table 8.2. Percentage of Housing Units Located in
Middle Neighborhoods in Selected Cities, Based on
Analysis in Various Years from 2008–2011

City	Middle neighborhoods as percent of city
Baltimore	32
Philadelphia	36
Pittsburgh	44
San Antonio	48
Trenton/Mercer County	44
Wilmington	42
Newark	51

Reinvestment Fund, Market Value Analyses for each city.

these preliminary data indicate that a substantial portion of U.S. cities may
have large portions of their housing stock and neighborhoods in these middle market categories—portions of cities for which there are no federal tools
that local governments can use to keep these areas stable.

Separately, RW-Ventures, in conjunction with Living Cities, developed a
similar market approach. "Dynamic Neighborhoods" examines drivers and
patterns of neighborhood change in different types of neighborhoods, as
well as the relationship of neighborhood and regional change, based on
analysis of hundreds of variables over twenty years in four diverse regions.
Using the most important characteristics of neighborhoods revealed in the
analysis, the study creates a comprehensive "neighborhood taxonomy" using hierarchical clustering techniques. This analysis identifies nine distinct
neighborhood types and over thirty subtypes based on neighborhood market conditions and examines how different neighborhoods tend to change
over time between types. RW-Ventures' neighborhood types are the Truly
Disadvantaged; Transient Under-Developed; Stable Low Income; Port of Entry; Urban Tapestry; Coming Attractions; No Place like Home; Close, Cool,
Commercial; and Fortune 100.

As the RW-Ventures work indicates, neighborhoods are complex and
constantly changing places. Neighborhoods

- Arise from the interaction of economic, social and political systems with place.

- Create capacity and opportunity for their residents by connecting them to the larger systems.
- Enable transactions that deploy their real estate and business assets in the context of regional markets.
- Are integral to healthy and prosperous regions.[7]

A third approach to understanding neighborhood markets has been developed by Social Compact, a nonprofit, nonpartisan organization formed by a coalition of business leaders from across the country committed to promoting successful investment in lower-income communities. Working in close partnership with community and corporate leaders over the past decade and a half, Social Compact has pioneered the DrillDown™, a methodology to analyze inner-city retail markets and create accurate, business-oriented profiles of "emerging" neighborhood markets. Drawing on business disciplines and community strength, these drilldowns have a strong track record of catalyzing sustainable, private investment, benefiting communities and businesses alike.

Social Compact has performed its DrillDown™ analysis in more than 400 diverse neighborhoods across the country in twenty cities. The result of this work has shown that more people, households, and buying power exist in these neighborhoods than was previously understood. Social Compact reports that, in these 400 neighborhoods, there is an informal economy worth over $16 billion; that aggregate household income is over $35 billion; that there are an estimated 360,000 more households than census trend projections; and that there are an estimated 1,250,000 more residents than census trend projections.

This analysis is important in understanding neighborhood retail markets and particularly the buying power in these neighborhoods that might be underestimated as retail establishments make locational decisions.

What is the policy and strategic value of this new market information about neighborhoods? Not much public or philanthropic action needs to be taken to help the neighborhoods in the strongest market neighborhood types compete favorably. These regionally competitive neighborhoods have solid reputations, are promoted by real estate agents, and are attractive to many market segments. House prices in these neighborhoods reflect their market strength. Provision of high quality city services may be all that is needed to keep these neighborhoods competitive.

Neighborhoods in the distressed category, especially those in cities los-ing population, are unlikely to maintain their current population or attract newcomers. These neighborhoods have lost population because they are undesirable to most market segments and are, therefore, typically where the cities' vacant housing is located. They have lost in the regional neighbor-hood competition.[8] Residents often leave these neighborhoods when they are financially able to do so, while others remain and do their best to cope with challenging living conditions. These neighborhoods need radical intervention—very expensive and potentially disruptive investments to make enough change to affect their market conditions. The combination of today's overall housing market conditions and financial constraints at all levels of government means that it is unlikely that public funds will be available for the kinds of market-affecting interventions that are needed. Rather, ap-proaches to help the people in these neighborhoods and unconventional place-based interventions, described below, may be the more appropriate approach.

The middle neighborhoods in many cities are often the major over-looked places that are capable of holding their populations and attracting newcomers if strategic interventions are successful and if these neighbor-hoods are actively promoted as desirable places to live.

But local governments are challenged to help these middle neighbor-hoods, in part because they cannot use federal income-restricted funds to improve them. Since the goal in these middle neighborhoods is to hold and attract middle-income families and to normalize the market, using funds aimed at those who need income-restricted affordable housing is not practi-cal or desirable, as the presence of these kinds of subsidy dollars may signal to the market that the neighborhood is no longer viable and needs federal help to sustain itself. To be helpful, city government needs to find funds that are not income restricted, which typically means tapping very scarce city funds, so it can target programs that are aimed at stabilizing these areas and holding and attracting middle-income households.

Baltimore's Efforts to Strengthen Middle Neighborhoods

Baltimore is a good example of a city that is improving middle neighbor-hoods as a strategy to increase the city's population and overall well-being.[9]

As the mayor of the only major East Coast city to lose population in the 2000s, Mayor Stephanie Rollings-Blake has committed her administration to increasing the city's population by 10,000 households over the next ten years. While there are many reasons particular households may choose to live in Baltimore or elsewhere, the MVA for Baltimore suggests that, to attract new households, neighborhood policy should aim at improving those neighborhoods in the "middle market" categories. Helping these neighborhoods maintain their fabric and attractiveness and helping them compete better in the market can help Baltimore hold residents and attract newcomers.

This middle market approach is now a decade old in Baltimore. The population of Baltimore has been falling since the 1950s; in the 1990s, the city lost a larger percentage of its population than any other major American city. To cope with this situation, policymakers sought new approaches to stem population loss. In 2001, the Goldseker Foundation, a local private foundation with a program emphasis on neighborhood improvement, published a paper authored by a specialist on neighborhood recovery, David Boehlke, that called for crafting an approach to neighborhood improvement by working on those neighborhoods that were still in a normal market situation, but that were most in peril of decline (Boehlke 2001). The Healthy Neighborhoods Program, begun by the Baltimore Community Foundation in 2000, targeted these "middle neighborhoods." The neighborhoods selected by Healthy Neighborhoods typically have homeownership of 50 percent or higher; steady house values, but not much appreciation; a limited number of vacant structures; a strong neighborhood organization; and some fraying around the neighborhoods' edges.

The approach was and is remarkably simple and entirely consistent with the 1970s Neighborhood Housing Services Program begun in Pittsburgh and promulgated in the earlier days of NeighborWorks America. The program is based on four simple elements of neighborhood stability that Boehlke described in a subsequent report. These are "a positive image, a viable real estate market, good physical conditions and strong social connections (Boehlke 2004: 8).

As the Healthy Neighborhoods Program evolved, it developed the following organizational and programmatic elements:

1. It is governed by a nonprofit organization, Healthy Neighborhoods Inc., with a board composed of a coalition of city government, local

foundations, and lenders who work in partnership with neighborhood residents to strengthen neighborhoods.

2. It has chosen neighborhoods that have enough fabric that, with modest help, can become stronger competitors for investment by residents
   and businesses.
3. It works to change the investment psychology in neighborhoods so
   that residents and businesses see a promising future for their neighborhoods.
4. It intervenes by working on and near the strongest areas in a neighborhood first and then builds from that strength to the weaker areas.
5. It helps residents organize themselves to bring stronger social connections in the neighborhood and helps them become advocates for living in their neighborhoods.
6. It funds modest neighborhood improvements to bolster an upbeat
   investment psychology.
7. It makes it easier for homeowners to improve their homes and for interested newcomers to buy a home in the neighborhoods.
8. It markets the neighborhoods to prospective residents.
9. It finds assets in the neighborhoods, such as schools that are performing well, and promotes them to existing residents and newcomers.

The program has some compelling features that may make it an attractive model. First, the program is relatively efficient and leverages its resources well. The annual budget for the core operations of the program is
approximately $1.3 million, about half of which goes directly to neighbor-
hood groups for marketing, organizing and for community improvements.
Lenders have formed loan pools twice to provide mortgage and home improvement loans in the neighborhoods, totaling $63 million. The first pool
of mortgage loans allowed loans up to 120 percent of appraised value so
that rehab could add value to the home and neighborhood. Three foundations and the Maryland Housing Fund guaranteed a portion of the mortgages. Of 230 loans made, only three had gone into foreclosure by the end
of 2011. Loans are 1 percent below market and hover around 4 percent
with no mortgage insurance. In addition, public funding is limited. Although no full evaluation has been done to date, all involved in the Healthy
Neighborhoods Program assume that the additional property tax revenues to the city surpass the amount of funds directly invested in the program.

Second, data from the 2010 census indicate that the Healthy Neighborhoods Program model is having promising results:

- *The middle neighborhoods saw more housing improvements than the city as a whole.* On average, there were consistently more permits in these neighborhood clusters than citywide during the 2000s. This shows a higher-than-average rate of reinvestment, and an investment psychology that may, in fact, be improving in many of these neighborhoods.
- *Overall, the middle neighborhoods in Baltimore held their populations better than the city as a whole.* Population in these middle neighborhoods declined only by 1 percent overall compared to the city's loss of 4.6 percent. This provides some evidence that interventions in some of these neighborhoods add stability. Neighborhood performance varied considerably, which indicates that interventions like this program are only one variable in the equation.
- *The program is stabilizing neighborhoods, not gentrifying them.* The median family income in these middle neighborhoods increased in the decade at a rate slightly higher than the city as a whole. Only two neighborhoods adjacent to very strong market neighborhoods showed dramatic increases in incomes; these neighborhoods were able to attract some higher-income buyers because of the nearby strength. Overall, the Healthy Neighborhoods program is not gentrifying neighborhoods; instead, it is helping neighborhoods attract and hold people of modest incomes who might otherwise find a suburban home.
- *Housing prices generally increased relative to citywide trends.* Housing prices in Baltimore city rose 110 percent during the 2000s, which was widely distributed among neighborhoods (some saw prices rise by over 400 percent while others dropped by 45 percent). Housing prices also increased in these middle neighborhoods (only one middle neighborhood showed a loss). These value increases are essential to the future marketability of these neighborhoods. Buyers must feel that there it is likely that property values will increase over time, the mark of a stable, attractive neighborhood. This is how—until the recent real estate crash—most American households built wealth.

A second major initiative to increase Baltimore's population is aggressive marketing of neighborhoods led by Live Baltimore. This small, energetic nonprofit's mission is to market Baltimore as a good place to live.[10] To this end, Live Baltimore works closely with neighborhood groups, real estate agents, lenders, developers, employers, and apartment owners. Commercial partners, city government foundations,[11] companies, and individual donors support the program financially. Marketing comes in many forms, including semi-annual neighborhood bus tours (Buy into Baltimore) that provide financial incentives to prospects to buy homes in designated sections of the city.

The numerical effects—how many people move to Baltimore as the result of Live Baltimore's work—is impossible to gauge accurately, but the number of web site visits is high, and the city's population grew in the young and working-age population, the population segments Live Baltimore has targeted.

A More Balanced Approach

These two Baltimore programs aimed at middle neighborhoods are unable to use federal funds. Why? Largely because no federal programs exist that are aimed at helping cities like Baltimore become stronger by growing their populations and tax bases.

America's cities would benefit from an approach from the federal government that adds approaches to assist cities hold and attract middle-income people.

What would such an approach look like?

Philanthropic and public neighborhood policy needs to factor in market conditions when shaping programs. Currently, policies, incentives, and the overall orientation are aimed at affordable housing and distressed communities, with subtle, but important, repercussions:

- The IRS's charitable purpose language that guides foundation giving in neighborhoods focuses on charitable benefit as defined by income—affordable housing is more easily connected to "charitable purpose" than is attracting middle-income households into neighborhoods in cities that need these residents. While mixed-income housing can qualify depending on the amount of affordable housing in the development, a more balanced policy would incent affordable housing wherever it gets built and developed, including affordable housing in job-rich areas; and would also incent programs that hold and attract middle-income people into cities and suburbs that are experiencing population loss, so that their tax bases can be rebuilt, making these cities healthier fiscally and socially. A city that is more fiscally sound has more capacity to provide services to those in need than cities that are financially impoverished. The revenues to help those who need help come from a robust economy and sound tax base.

- The Community Reinvestment Act (CRA) encourages regulated financial institutions to invest in local communities, especially in low- and moderate-income areas and to low- and moderate-income borrowers. Banks receive exam credit for such lending and investing, but do not get the same credit for lending or investing in *middle*-income neighborhoods—yet such activities strengthen these crucial middle-income areas, which are often squeezed between a low- and moderate-income area area and a higher-growth neighborhood. Amending CRA, or providing education for banks, could help direct more capital to middle-income areas.

- Congress and the Executive branch of the federal government should examine what changes are needed in the CDBG program to make this tool more pliable so that local governments can use it to bolster activity and market strength in these middle neighborhoods.

In addition, the urban research community should look more closely at the middle neighborhoods in cities—particularly cities that have been losing population—to analyze fully the relationship between middle neighborhoods and urban growth and to determine what approaches in addition to the Baltimore Healthy Neighborhoods Program should be undertaken to strengthen markets in these neighborhoods.

What about the distressed communities? In focusing on distressed places—those where there is little or no market demand—intervention strategies need to be differentiated between place and people. A recent American Assembly report lays out some basic principles on how to treat the *physical condition* in these distressed areas (American Assembly 2011). These include (1) get land under public control so its future use can be guided by local government, not speculators; (2) incentivize responsible property stewardship through code enforcement and other local legal tools; (3) encourage alternative land uses, such as urban farming; and (4) encourage relocation where appropriate.

In addition to these place-oriented strategies, there are *people-oriented* approaches that are equally important. These include improving and developing cradle-to-career programs to help children succeed and/or school enrollment policies that permit children from distressed areas to attend schools in other neighborhoods.[12] Well-orchestrated workforce training and placement programs using effective workforce intermediaries can help residents in distressed areas improve their incomes and upward mobility (American Assembly 2003). Helping people in these distressed neighborhoods be safe through effective policing is essential. Delivering needed social services in a user-friendly way continues to be a challenge but one that must be overcome to help families, children, and seniors in these types of neighborhoods. These people-oriented approaches are critical to the lives of low-income people living in the nation's most distressed communities.

There is another quite different people-oriented strategy that the federal government has been promulgating—encouraging low-income households in these distressed areas to "move to opportunity" (MTO) through the creative use of the Section 8 voucher program. Begun by HUD in 1994, this demonstration in Baltimore, Boston, Chicago, Los Angeles, and New York targeted families living in some of the nation's poorest, highest-crime communities and used housing subsidies to offer them a chance to move to lower-poverty neighborhoods. The Urban Institute and others have reported that this strategy has many nuances but that it has helped many families improve educational and employment outcomes (Ferryman et al. 2008; Cove et al. 2008).

Good neighborhoods are essential to a city's overall well-being. The soul of the city lives in these places—in the day-to-day interactions between children on a city block, parents visiting at a playground, dog-lovers sharing time in a dog park, runners enjoying a jaunt through city streets, neighbors chatting in a corner tavern, or seniors tending to a shared vegetable garden. These planned and spontaneous intersections make neighborhoods distinct.

Helping middle neighborhoods get stronger, holding and attracting middle-income people, and helping home values normalize and increase are sound policies to helping cities become better places to live and work and, financially, to building stronger public corporations, able to provide improved services to residents and businesses.

CHAPTER 9

Transformation Is Messy Work: The Complex Challenge of Spatial Reconfiguration in America's Legacy Cities

Alan Mallach

As America's older industrial cities like Detroit, Cleveland, or Pittsburgh grew during the nineteenth and early twentieth centuries, their spatial configuration followed a common path shared by most Western cities of that or earlier periods. Within the constraints imposed by water bodies or topography, their growth followed the classic density gradient model of urban form (Muth 1969), in which the highest densities were in the center, and gradually diminished with distance from the center. As the cities filled out their boundaries, or in some cases expanded them, they grew in a continuous fashion, in which nearly every property was improved in ways linked to the urban economy. By the middle of the twentieth century, little if any land remained within these cities' borders that was not being purposefully used for an urban activity.

While growth slowed after 1930, almost all of these cities grew steadily through 1950 or 1960. At that point, however, a process of sustained population and job loss began, which in many cases has continued to the present. By 2010, "legacy cities" like Cleveland, St. Louis, and Pittsburgh had lost well over half of their peak population, as well as the overwhelming majority of the factories and manufacturing jobs that had once sustained their growth and prosperity.[1] Large-scale property abandonment followed on the heels of population and job loss; while cities demolished thousands of abandoned, blighted buildings, others took their place. By the end of the century, large parts of these cities had become derelict landscapes dominated by abandoned buildings and vacant lots, turning their historic density gradient nearly on its head.

Although some prescient observers had called attention to these trends as early as the 1970s, by the end of the century, it had become widely apparent that these cities had a vast and growing surplus of land and buildings relative to both present and likely future demand (Mallach 2012a). It was also widely understood that the abandonment and underutilization of their built environments was a product of systemic rather than cyclic low demand and was, therefore, not likely to be remedied by future redevelopment. As the Youngstown 2010 plan put it, "[the city of Youngstown] has been described as a size 40 man wearing a size 60 suit. There are too many abandoned properties and too many underutilized sites" (Youngstown 2005: 18). Although one should not dismiss the possibility of new industries reviving these cities' fortunes, it is hard to imagine any new economic engine likely either to absorb a city's vacant property surplus or restore its peak population, within any time frame relevant to the planning process.

In view of these conditions, the idea of reconfiguring these legacy cities to reflect their significantly smaller populations and built footprints, in the sense of converting large parts of these cities into green or essentially nonurban use, while concentrating urban resources in the city's remaining areas, began to emerge as a subject of interest to those engaged in addressing the future of these cities. A number of both scholars and practitioners have begun to look closely at this question, including exploring its implications for urban agriculture (Hodgson, Campbell, and Bailkey 2011), stormwater management, and reconfiguration of infrastructure systems (Hoornbeek and Schwarz 2009; Schilling and Logan 2008). More recent work has increasingly looked at this question in a larger context, reflected in a volume of essays covering a wide range of strategic issues affecting legacy cities (Mallach 2012c) and another publication addressing the role of planners and the nature of planning practice in these and similar cities (Schilling and Mallach 2012).[2]

While the issue of spatial reconfiguration, or "right-sizing" as it has been widely but inappropriately called,[3] of cities has drawn growing attention, change has been slow to emerge on the ground. It is clearly one thing to design a conceptual framework for the large-scale spatial reconfiguration of older cities but a very different matter to transform that framework into reality, beyond the modest scale of scattered community gardens and other idiosyncratic ventures that have long taken place at the interstices of redevelopment activity.

A growing number of cities, however, have begun to recognize the value of physical reconfiguration as a powerful way of thinking about the city's future and a way of organizing their planning efforts. As halting but potentially important efforts are initiated, important questions are beginning to emerge. The first is the role of plans and planning in the process and the extent to which large-scale spatial reconfiguration demands large-scale planning. The second is whether large-scale, comprehensive reconfiguration strategies as visualized in the emerging literature are, in fact, plausible on the ground, however strong their appeal from the 30,000-foot perspective beloved of planners and urbanists, and whether alternative strategies, more incremental in nature, may be worth exploring in their stead. There may be, indeed, an inherent tension between the scale of these issues and the seeming need for comprehensive strategies and the extent to which the systems, capacities, and resources of urban America can address them.

These questions are central to the larger issue of the future of America's legacy cities. While spatial reconfiguration is far from the only strategy that is central to their future, it is hard to imagine how these cities can evolve into healthier, albeit smaller, postindustrial cities without it being successfully addressed. If we are to be serious about these cities' futures, we need to approach the issue in a substantially more hard-headed and realistic fashion than has characterized much of the conversation up to this point, with greater recognition of the very real obstacles to change and less wishful thinking about how change might come about.

Make No Small Plans?

Daniel Burnham famously said, "Make no small plans; they have no magic to stir men's blood."[4] The argument for big plans and ambitious visions would seem particularly compelling in the context of legacy cities, where decades of job and population loss have left these cities in profound ways little more than shells of their one-time glory. One could reasonably argue that big plans might not only stir men's (and women's) blood but serve an important intangible purpose in such settings: to create a framework through which the residents of a city can rethink the nature of their community in fundamental ways and envision a future of their city that is not simply an extrapolation of the decline of the preceding decades (Morrison and Dewar 2012).

The need for such a fundamental rethinking in many cities is hard to dispute. Detroit and Youngstown, to pick two of the harder cases, each contain today less than 40 percent of the population they had during their heyday. Despite steady demolition activity, the number of vacant and abandoned houses continues to increase. With little of the ongoing demolition leading to replacement, the number of vacant lots also increases, and large areas have emerged in which vacant land is the dominant land use. Today, it is estimated that there are over 100,000 vacant lots and over 40,000 vacant structures in Detroit.

Demand for houses in these areas, even when they sell for less than the price of a good used car, has all but vanished (Mallach 2011a, 2012a).[5] In the meantime, these cities are saddled with the cost of maintaining an infrastructure designed to accommodate a far larger population and physical inventory than exists today (Hoornbeek and Schwarz 2009; Mallach 2011b). Detroit and Youngstown, along with most similarly situated cities, moreover, are located in regions of the United States where future growth is likely to be slow and incremental at best and unlikely to trigger enough short-term in-migration to resolve this condition (Longworth 2008).

In this context, planners, political leaders, and others are faced with difficult choices. To begin, they can either remain in a state of denial derived from, as Morrison and Dewar (2012: 120) write, "the widely-held American belief that growth equates with 'success' and population decline equates with 'failure'," while perpetuating policies and practices based on patently unrealistic assumptions; or they can acknowledge the reality of their condition and begin envisioning a future for their city that, while growing out of the reality of their smaller population and built footprint, is qualitatively different and offers at least the potential of the city becoming a healthier or stronger city, albeit one much smaller than in the city's past. Such a vision is not antithetical to growth but recognizes that the future, whatever it may hold, must be grounded in the economic and demographic realities of the present, not of the past.

Many questions, however, flow from that choice, not least of which is what such a process entails. Does a vision of a different future for a city call for a "big plan," à la Burnham, or does the idea of a big plan in this context raise more questions than it resolves? A vision and a plan are two very different things. Without some animating vision to drive people's thinking, and arguably stir their blood, it is hard to see how a city's potential could be realized; in the context of today's realities, however, the question is whether such a vision can be translated into a plan—in the sense of a concrete, comprehensive road map of actions—that has a realistic chance of being realized or whether the effort to craft a large, comprehensive plan raises the specter of creating unrealizable, chimerical goals, which may undo the credibility of, and ultimately render more difficult or even impossible, the realization of the vision? I will return to this central question after looking at what spatial reconfiguration might actually mean and how it has been conceived in some of the planning efforts up to this point.

Spatial Reconfiguration as Urban Transformation

In cities with large amounts of surplus land and buildings and weak housing market conditions, spatial or physical reconfiguration has come to be widely seen as a productive framework through which the city's present reality can be acknowledged and through which the physical parameters of a future city that offers its residents, workers, and visitors a good quality of life can potentially be realized. Reconfiguration includes not only a recognition that some areas may have to be reprogrammed for nonurban uses such as agriculture and green infrastructure, but that other areas need to be strengthened and enhanced and that demand and investment must be directed toward those areas, to preserve viable but at-risk residential neighborhoods, industrial zones that may serve to attract economic activity, and mixed-use areas such as downtowns that offer particular promise for future revitalization. Two prototypical comprehensive visions that have been put forth for spatial reconfiguration are the Youngstown 2010 Plan (Youngstown 2005), and the 2008 report *Leaner, Greener Detroit,* prepared by an AIA Sustainable Development Assessment Team (SDAT) (American Institute of Architects 2008).[6] To my knowledge, these two documents were the first published efforts seriously to grapple from a planning perspective with the issues of spatial reconfiguration in specific cities.

The Youngstown 2010 Plan identified four "Plan Themes" to drive the detailed plan and its future implementation:

1. Green Network
2. Competitive Industrial Districts
3. Viable Neighborhoods
4. Vibrant Core

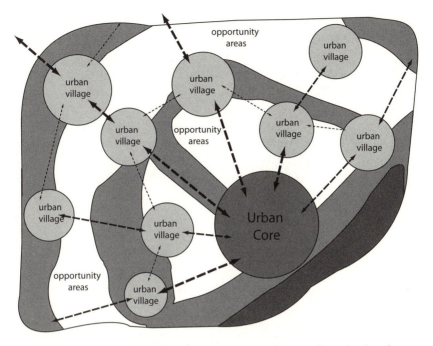

Figure 9.1. Relationship between the three elements of a reconfigured urban form. AIA Center for Communities by Design, from American Institute of Architects 2008: 23.

The SDAT report, although addressing economic development extensively, did not explicitly distinguish industrial activity as a separate spatial element in its highly generalized framework.[7] Otherwise, however, it produced a model that parallels the Youngstown themes:

1. Urban Core (vibrant core)
2. Urban Villages (viable neighborhoods)
3. Opportunity Areas (green network)

The schematic diagram developed for the SDAT report shows the relationship between these three elements of a reconfigured urban form, as shown in Figure 9.1.[8] The features of the three elements, and the role each plays in the reconfigured city, are discussed below.

The vision of spatial reconfiguration assumes a change to a discontinuous form, in which large parts of the city no longer share the continuous urban texture and may even be removed from the city's integrated infrastructure network. This process of deconstruction, as it were, represents a radical reconceptualization of the traditional city form.

The core is the heart of the economic city, the mixed-use area that contains the central functions and most important assets of the city, such as government offices, universities, and medical centers. In most cities, it represents the area with the greatest potential for the creation of new economic engines and transformative developments. It is also the symbolic heart of the city; as Mayor Christopher Doherty of Scranton said, "if we're going to succeed as a city, we need a strong downtown."[9] Core areas, particularly downtowns, are also a form of "urban glue"; without a vital core to link the disparate elements of a city's social and physical fabric, the city may not be able to function as a coherent urban entity, provide common ground for an economically and racially diverse population, or offer the features that are associated with a distinctively *urban* quality of life. It may be narrowly defined as the city's traditional downtown or, as in Detroit, seen as an "extended downtown," which takes in adjacent areas to the north, east, and west. Cleveland has two cores: the traditional downtown, which functions as the business and government center, and the University Circle area, which houses most of the city's major educational, health care, and cultural institutions.

Viable neighborhoods or urban villages are the city's largely residential neighborhoods where the fabric that enables them to function as vital communities remains intact. Many, however, are showing disinvestment and are, to varying degrees, at risk of decline and loss of vitality; all are in need of increased public and private investment to build greater market demand and maintain neighborhood stability. Strong neighborhoods are arguably at least as important to a city as a strong core: it is doubtful that a city's downtown could retain or regain its vitality or sustain itself economically and fiscally if surrounded by a mass of visibly disinvested, deteriorated areas encompassing all or most of the rest of the city. In many cities, however, without effective intervention to direct public investment and channel private investment into a discrete number of neighborhoods, the effect of weak aggregate market demand being spread too thinly across all the city's neighborhoods may lead to an incremental process of deterioration and decline spreading across most of the city's remaining neighborhoods (Mallach 2012a).[10]

Green areas, which have also been called opportunity areas, reclamation areas, or areas of land use change,[11] are the remaining areas where the greater part of each city's population loss and abandonment has taken and continues to take place and where a disproportionate share of the city's vacant land and buildings are located. They may represent one-third or more of Detroit's land area. Over time, some of these areas may reconstitute as viable lower density neighborhoods, while others will gradually lose what remaining population they have; in their present state, however, they act as a drag on any effort to strengthen either the core or the city's still-viable neighborhoods. As they continue to lose population, their vacant land is no longer needed or suitable for redevelopment but can potentially be used for other purposes consistent with a low population density, which can not only be productive in themselves but create a physical environment consistent with improved quality of life, including urban agriculture or a succession forest, that is, plantings designed gradually to bring about the creation of a mature woodland.

In practice, of course, no city divides as neatly into these three elements as Figure 9.1 might suggest. Cities are messy things; not only do areas fall along a continuum with extensive variation at scales too small to represent on a single citywide map rather than fitting into neat categories but, even within the most disinvested areas, some population remains and is likely to remain for the foreseeable future. Detroit is not likely ever to resemble an English rural scene of picturesque compact villages surrounded by landscapes of fields, woods, and pastures; it is no more likely, however, to resemble the fully developed, continuous Detroit of 1950 with its classic density gradient.[12] While recognizing that its ideal form does not exist, this tripartite division of the legacy city nonetheless represents a useful starting point for thinking about the future of these cities.

Youngstown, Cleveland, Dayton, Rochester, and Saginaw, among others, are pursuing planning strategies grounded in the principle of physical reconfiguration of their built environment.[13] Dayton has developed a "Green and Gold" investment strategy, in which "the green portion . . . focuses on rebuilding and sustaining an improved quality of life, while the gold section focuses on asset-based investments. . . . With vacancies a major issue, a central theme [of the green plan] is reimaging[14] high-vacancy communities through various means such as strategic demolition, property acquisition and land banking, coupled with greening schemes such as, community gardens and agriculture" (Schilling and Mallach 2012: 47). Saginaw, a small industrial city of roughly 50,000 about 100 miles north of Detroit, has designated 344 acres (roughly one-half square mile) of the city as a "Green

Zone"; as characterized by one observer, "The Green Zone is a heavily de-populated area north of the city that is the central focus of Saginaw's right-sizing efforts. As properties there become vacant, they are purchased and demolished by the Saginaw County Land Bank. Eventually the streets, wa-ter, electric and gas lines will be removed and the area will be allowed to return to nature, left for future redevelopment" (Moloney 2011).

What is instructive about these approaches, however, is that, with the possible exception of Youngstown, none of them are grounded in what Burn-ham might consider a big plan. Indeed, as I will discuss in the next section, there are compelling reasons to argue that big plans in this context are prob-lematic, in all likelihood unrealizable, and arguably counterproductive.

Can a Legacy City Carry Out a Big Plan?

John Lennon, not a disciple of Burnham, famously said "life is what happens to you while you're busy making other plans."[15] Lennon's rule applies to cities as well as people, and never more so when the goal of a plan is to realize a vi-sion of a fundamental change in the city's trajectory rather than an enhance-ment of the status quo. This is true more of strategies that seek to reconfigure largely disinvested areas than of efforts to revitalize at-risk neighborhoods or foster downtown redevelopment, although those are not without their chal-lenges. While the latter two can reasonably be perceived as efforts to restore the status quo ante although in changed form, transformation of disinvested areas into green zones or the equivalent is inherently a radical departure from it. The many practical and political obstacles standing in the way of such a transformation are combined with more fundamental obstacles, which I would suggest can be understood through the prism of path depen-dence, as I discuss below. These obstacles, it is important to stress, are not barriers to the reuse or reconfiguration of any individual site; they are, in-stead, barriers to the large-scale, comprehensive, reconfiguration of large land areas that would be the goal of a Burnhamite big plan.

Practical Barriers

The practical barriers to realization of a plan for spatial reconfiguration might well be more than enough in themselves to scuttle any such plan.

Most cities are under severe fiscal stress at present (Muro and Hoene 2009); legacy cities are particularly hard hit, as they suffer from structural fiscal problems that constrain their ability to maintain public services, let alone invest in change (Mallach and Scorsone 2011). Harrisburg and Reading, Pennsylvania, are under state financial supervision, while Camden, New Jersey, and Springfield, Massachusetts, have only recently emerged from state control.[16] Flint, Benton Harbor, and Pontiac, all in Michigan, have been run for some time by state-appointed emergency financial managers, while a financial manager was appointed by the governor for Detroit in March 2013.

Activities associated with physical reconfiguration such as demolition and relocation are wildly expensive. The cost to demolish only the most clearly unsalvageable abandoned properties in Cleveland over the next five years has been conservatively estimated at $105 million.[17] The ballpark cost to relocate the remaining homeowners from only the most heavily abandoned blocks in Detroit has been estimated at $750 million,[18] while the daunting political obstacles to such a step would arguably make it unrealizable in any event. The cost of remediating environmentally contaminated sites, which are widespread in the disinvested sections of legacy cities and which may be necessary for many prospective reuses of these sites, is likely to be in the billions. No plausible source of funds currently exists, nor is any likely to emerge in the foreseeable future at any level of government or any private source at a scale capable of implementing a large-scale physical reconfiguration plan in any of the cities in which it might be seen as an appropriate strategy. Moreover, given the many competing demands facing cities, if funds of such magnitude were available, it is hard to argue that these activities should be the highest priority.

If the resources to mount large-scale physical reconfiguration strategies are lacking, many of the direct fiscal or economic benefits may well be overstated. While it is easy enough to speak of the inefficiency of an infrastructure and service delivery system designed for a far larger population than it now serves, a remedy for that problem is not readily available. Hoornbeek and Schwarz (2009) make a strong case that the feasibility as well as the desirability of decommissioning large amounts of a city's fixed network of sewer and water lines are both doubtful and the savings most probably illusory. Most such cities have already cut services drastically in response to their fiscal problems, making draconian reductions to municipal service delivery such as police and fire personnel and eliminating capital expenditures or street lighting.[19] Public schools and firehouses have been closed, often not without controversy, while some cities have engaged in a form of triage, cutting back public services and de facto decommissioning streets in largely depopulated areas by severely curtailing maintenance and repair. The results have been widespread deterioration in the quality of public service and the physical environment, without offering long-term relief to the overwhelming fiscal problems.

Fostering practical, large-scale reuse strategies is equally problematic. No city fully controls the inventory of vacant and underutilized land whose reuse is a condition of reconfiguration; in Detroit, speculators have aggressively acquired strategic parcels in areas potentially slated for reconfiguration (MacDonald 2011). With the exercise of eminent domain for anything other than traditional public uses largely barred under Michigan law, Detroit has little recourse against such speculators.[20] As a result, public holdings are largely fragmented and scattered; according to a 2010 study, 96 percent of the parcels in public ownership in Detroit were 10,000 square feet or less in area.[21] With the possible exception of the Genesee County Land Bank in Flint, Michigan, no local entity has even contemplated, let alone attempted, to gain control of that inventory; despite ten years of systematic effort, however, the Land Bank does not control the entirety of a single city block in Flint.[22] Even where appropriate legal tools exist, political and practical obstacles, including the very real reluctance of local officials to take responsibility for hundreds or even thousands of vacant properties and remove them from the tax rolls, make large-scale assembly often impracticable.[23] Land assembly as a response to a specific development proposal or community initiative may take place, but land assembly *as a comprehensive strategy* appears stillborn.

Even if land assembly were less of an obstacle, large-scale reuse would still be problematic. While urban agriculture is practiced on a small scale in many legacy cities, no city has been able to expand it to a scale where it could absorb more than a minute fraction of the available land, while the obstacles to doing so, including environmentally contaminated soils, access to markets, and the short growing season characteristic of most legacy city regions, are substantial. While urban agriculture offers a variety of real benefits (Hodgson, Campbell, and Bailkey 2011), its potential as a tool for large-scale urban reconfiguration is uncertain and may turn out to be very limited. The use of vacant land in largely disinvested areas for stormwater management, and as a way of diverting stormwater from combined storm and sanitary sewers, may have more promise as a large-scale strategy but remains largely untested.[24]

Political Obstacles

Over and above the practical obstacles, the political barriers to carrying out large-scale reconfiguration appear equally daunting. Although an area may appear to the planner to have lost its viability as a community, the remaining people who live there may not share that perspective. The Detroit homeowner in the last occupied home on her desolate block who told a reporter "I refuse to move unless the Lord says so" (Hackney 2009) is not alone; the following account summarizes subsequent developments in that city:

> On February 24, 2010, prompted by the release of a citywide residential parcel survey, Mayor Bing announced his plans to rightsize Detroit. Citing the need to balance the enormity of vacant land and the city's $300 million budget deficit, Bing said that the city administration "can't support every neighborhood in the city" and that relocation programs would be imminent, thereby creating "winners and losers." This prompted a firestorm with community activists railing against the ever-present specter of eminent domain, which now seemed very real.[25] *The Michigan Citizen*, which proclaims itself "America's most progressive community newspaper," unleashed a series of articles deriding the mayor, calling any effort to shrink Detroit "a modern-day trail of tears" whose goal was to abet a "land grab" for "special interests." Other progressive newspapers followed suit. (Butler 2012)

As the newspaper articles cited by Butler suggest, reconfiguration carries with it powerful negative associations that can override seemingly practical considerations. Pronouncements from public officials about which neighborhoods will "win" and which will "lose" bring back the specter of urban renewal, creating a vocal backlash among those who perceive the city as writing them off (Yeoman 2012).

Although the federal urban renewal program was formally abolished almost forty years ago, it still resonates in hundreds of urban neighborhoods,

particularly African American ones (Fullilove 2004). While physical reconfiguration may be racially neutral in intent, the reality is that the residents of
areas most likely to be seen as candidates for reconfiguration in most cities
are disproportionately African American. My own analysis of Youngstown
found that 56 percent of the city's African American residents lived in areas
where a market effectively no longer existed for the houses of the area and
thus are the most likely candidate areas for reconfiguration, compared to
only one-quarter of the city's white residents.

The racial divide continues to be central to the political reality of nearly
all legacy cities, which are typically divided between white and African
American populations and where the latter are usually both disproportionately poor and disproportionately underrepresented in the city's circles
of power.[26] Even where much of the visible political leadership may be
African American, the nongovernmental leadership forming the civic
infrastructure—the remaining economic actors, the heads of major institutions, and the leaders of powerful citywide organizations—is often largely
white. As I have written elsewhere, "In an already fragmented polity, any
public action that can be read in overtly racial terms—as is likely to be true
of land reconfiguration—when the action will in fact disproportionately affect African-Americans, is at risk of being interpreted as such, whatever its
intent" (Mallach 2011a: 1878).

The Problem of Resource Allocation

As noted earlier, the fiscal environment of America's legacy cities is one of
severe scarcity. However public officials may try to cushion the blow, allocating resources in such an environment is almost always a zero-sum game.
If a city rebuilds one street, it puts off rebuilding another; if one house is rehabilitated or demolished, another is left to the mercy of the elements. This
reality is particularly relevant to the question of stabilizing and regenerating
"vulnerable, undervalued and transitional neighborhoods" (Youngstown
Neighborhood Development Corporation 2012). Not only are the fiscal and
organizational resources that might be used to tackle these neighborhoods'
problems severely limited, but, even more important, aggregate market demand for the type of largely single-family housing that these neighborhoods
offer is extremely limited, and almost certainly inadequate, even under the

best circumstances, to ensure that demand exists for all of the homes in all of the neighborhoods that still remain at least potentially viable.

Moreover, to the extent that discretionary resources are used to pursue reconfiguration strategies designed to turn heavily disinvested areas into green environments, such as the relocation of remaining residents, demolition of remaining houses, or reconfiguration of infrastructure, those activities demand discretionary resources that might otherwise be used to sustain viable but severely at-risk neighborhoods.

That, coupled with the limited public sector financial and technical resources available, raises the central question: Should public resources and market demand be intentionally channeled into some neighborhoods and not others in order to ensure that the critical mass of resources and demand are available in at least a few areas? While such a policy means that some areas may thrive and others wither, failure to do so is likely to result in more, or even all, of the city's remaining neighborhoods deteriorating and ultimately being added to the city's inventory of heavily abandoned and disinvested areas through lack of sustainable market demand.

This is a variation on Philippa Foot's famous trolley problem (Foot 1967), in which a bystander has the opportunity to flip a switch and divert a runaway trolley to a line where it will kill one, rather than five, people.[27] From a strictly utilitarian perspective, it is considered appropriate for the bystander to flip the switch. The governance of cities, however, is not driven by utilitarian principles but by a delicate balancing of personal, political, ideological, and practical considerations.[28] It is doubtful whether the realities of the political balancing process would ever permit a city to adopt such a utilitarian strategy.

Path Dependence

As commonly used in the literature, "path dependence means that current and future states, actions, or decisions depend on the path of previous states, actions, or decisions" (Page 2006: 88). As such, path dependence stresses the extent to which the decisions being made in the future are constrained by those made in the past. There are few arenas where the evidence for path dependence is stronger than in the case of legacy cities; behaviors and attitudes that were formed in the years of these cities' industrial strength continued to dominate for decades afterward, during which time it was not only impossible to act on the basis of the obvious changes that were taking place to the cities' fabric but all but impossible even to discuss them in a rational fashion. The polemics that followed Roger Starr's 1976 article calling for the "planned shrinkage" of parts of New York City (Starr 1976; Wallace 1990) or the ridicule with which the Detroit city ombudsman's call for "mothballing" severely blighted areas in 1993 was received (Bonham, Spilka, and Rastorfer 2002; Butler 2012) reflected not only the political sensitivity of these issues but also the effect of path dependence on the culture of these cities.

The shift in attitudes that began in the past decade reflected the cumulative effect of decades of decline and the emergence of a generation of political, civic, and business leaders who had come of age since the trajectory of decline had begun. What this often meant, however, was that, rather than a readiness to confront these issues, a new structure of path dependence, based on assumptions of continued decline and grounded in behaviors associated with mitigating the visible effects of decline rather than fostering change, emerged to replace the predecline model. While those who have experienced nothing but decline may be willing to acknowledge its existence, they may also have difficulty even conceptualizing a different reality. Although the discourse may have changed, the political and institutional systems that drive decision making have changed less, if at all, in most cities.[29]

Path dependence is facilitated by the institutional status quo in legacy cities, which continues to provide significant benefits for those who participate in the system and perpetuate the spatial status quo. This can be financial, in the sense of the salaries and perks for mayors and city council members[30] or the flow of subsidy funds for construction of new housing in areas that already have a vast surplus of existing low-cost housing; or can be measured in terms of status and prestige, whether that of elected officials or of civic leaders. In such systems, allocation of public resources tends to be driven by past practices, however irrelevant or wasteful they may have become; or, as with the federal Community Development Block Grant (CDBG) program, tends to become a form of benign patronage, spreading funds thinly across the community with no strategic focus or direction. These policies can be seen as a form of what is known as "lock in" in path dependence, where an inferior outcome is pursued even "where superior alternatives exist, are known, and where the costs of switching are not high" (Leibowitz and

Margolis 1999: 982). As Jeremy Nowak, former president of the William Penn Foundation, has said, "the past has a well-organized constituency, but the future does not."[31]

This behavior is not necessarily driven by base or inappropriate interests. For a political leader who does not truly believe that a significant change in her city's trajectory is realistically possible and who is well aware of the political and practical constraints discussed above, there is no credible reason for her to risk her political resources or the city's fiscal resources on actions that, from her perspective, are unlikely to have any productive outcomes. As Page (2006) points out, "Any constraint, be it a budget constraint, a spatial constraint or a time constraint, imposes negative externalities" (90), which reinforce path dependence. The larger and more ambitious the effort, the greater the difficulty in overcoming the constraints, the greater the perceived risk, and the more remote any likely beneficial return, in terms of either positive community outcomes or personal political benefit.

To carry out a big plan in the face of these constraints is not only all but impossible, to try to do so could be seen as perverse. Moreover, trying to do so could easily lead to a paralysis that impedes the community's ability to take smaller steps; while the Youngstown 2010 Plan may have changed the way people perceived their community, it led to little or no change in the way the city made its decisions or allocated its resources. Path dependence forms the fourth link in the argument against the big plan.

Toward Strategic Incrementalism

If the above analysis is sound, it leads to a seeming conundrum. While the realities of legacy cities call for fundamentally rethinking their future and for taking ambitious and far-reaching steps toward transforming them into cities very different from what they once were, a host of obstacles dictates that an ambitious and comprehensive plan for transformation is unlikely to lead to any such outcomes. Is there a way, then, to square the circle?

I would suggest that two steps are necessary. First, planners and policymakers in legacy cities should scale back their ambitions to reflect reality and avoid big plans along with grandiose pronouncements at odds with that reality; second, they should focus more clearly on the distinction between vision, plan, and action. A vision is needed: without one, as the Bible says, the people perish (Proverbs 29:18). This maxim is nowhere more valid than in legacy cities. Without a shared sense that their city can be a better place and that its seemingly inexorable downward trajectory can be halted and reversed, no body of local officials or civic leaders will find the will to break loose of path dependence and make decisions that go beyond perpetuating the status quo and, at best, cushioning the path of decline.

Framing a vision does not require that it be embodied in a formal plan or implementation document. While a plan can appear to be a powerful embodiment of a vision, it can equally become a diversion or an impediment. The actions that a city can realistically take to pursue its vision are modest, incremental ones: a revitalization strategy for a particular neighborhood or a green reuse of a handful of parcels or a city block. Over time, if pursued consistently, those incremental actions may become transformational.

The revitalization strategy may stabilize a neighborhood that was at imminent risk of collapse, while the cumulative effect of green reuse projects in a particular area may create an environment that enhances the city's quality of life and that may further important concrete objectives such as stormwater management or food security.

Cities, even those with limited resources, take incremental actions all the time. Streets are resurfaced, parks improved, houses rehabilitated with HOME funds, Low Income Tax Credit projects built, and CDBG funds funneled into neighborhood improvement projects. In most cities, however, those actions and the choice of whether to pursue them and where they take place are not animated by any larger strategy or overall vision. In some cases, they may be driven by political considerations; in others, as suggested earlier, by path dependence. Successful developers, in the narrow sense that their previous projects were completed more or less on time and on budget, are rewarded with more public funding and land to build projects that may or may not serve any useful purpose for the city's future. Similarly, funds continue to flow to certain neighborhoods or community development corporations (CDC) for no better reason than that they have received such funds in the past.

A vision can replace such haphazard and often wasteful approaches by animating a series of strategies that can, in turn, guide specific decisions. For example, the vision for the city's neighborhoods may be no more complex than to make those neighborhoods, or some of them, neighborhoods of choice: that is, neighborhoods with the features that attract homebuyers who have enough income to choose between multiple neighborhoods within the regional housing market (Boehlke 2012; Mallach 2008). That, in turn, can prompt a series of actions designed to build a stronger market in that neighborhood, to draw new homebuyers, or to convince existing homeowners that it is in their interest to stay.

Similarly, an understanding of which areas are losing population and should ultimately become "green" areas—but without adopting a hard-line map that becomes a lightning rod for conflict—can serve as a guide for opportunistic efforts such as those being pursued in Dayton or small-scale bottom-up initiatives such as the Re-Imagining Cleveland pilot projects. This last is an example of how strategic incrementalism can work in practice; as described by one of its organizers, it is grounded in a coherent vision:

> The purpose of the Re-Imagining Cleveland initiative is to create new urban landscapes that better serve communities. These landscapes are envisioned to be made up of sustainable, distinctive neighborhoods with more efficient and valuable housing surrounded by repurposed land providing community benefit. (Reichtell 2012)

A series of incremental steps driven by that vision have been jointly pursued by the city's Planning Department in partnership with Neighborhood Progress Inc. (a local community development funding intermediary), and the Cleveland Urban Design Center of the Kent State University School of Architecture. This led to the creation of a series of publications, including a land use decision matrix for evaluating appropriate reuses of vacant land and a pattern book of specific reuse options. That, in turn, led to a pilot project, using $500,000 in public funds to provide small grants to over fifty individuals, organizations, and institutions to undertake small-scale demonstration or pilot projects on vacant land sites around the city. Specific land reutilization strategies include the following:

- Greening small parks and walking paths
- Urban agriculture, including community gardens, urban farms, vineyards and orchards
- Side yard expansions and lot splits between neighbors
- Stormwater management, including rain gardens and bio-swales

- Off-street parking with pervious paving
- Remediation of polluted sites through bio- and phyto-remediation techniques

As Reichtell (2012: 187) points out, this initiative has led to significant local policy changes:

> The City's Land Bank program ... has crafted policy and adminis-trative changes to streamline vacant lot disposition. The City's Water Department is crafting new policies and fee structures for water us-age to accommodate community and entrepreneurial vacant land reuse projects. The City Planning Commission and Cleveland City Council have adopted zoning changes and legislation that protect gardens and farms through garden district zoning and allow for easier use of land for agricultural purposes. ... To foster local food entrepreneurs, the Cleveland Economic Development Department offers a small start-up grant and low-interest loan program for mar-ket gardens and urban farms.

Another instructive example comes from Youngstown. Little action fol-lowed adoption of the Youngstown 2010 plan in 2005 (Kutner 2009).[32] Things began to change in 2009, when a local foundation created a citywide non-profit CDC (the Youngstown Neighborhood Development Corporation or YNDC) to carry out incremental strategies consistent with the vision em-bodied in the plan. This was a critical distinction; the YNDC was not cre-ated to implement (nor did it attempt to implement) the plan itself but to pursue independent, incremental actions consistent with the underlying vision, focusing on "transform(ing) neighborhoods into meaningful places where people invest time, money and energy into their homes and neigh-borhoods; where neighbors have the capacity to manage day-to-day issues; and where neighbors feel confident about the future of their neighborhood" (YNDC 2013).

Based on assessments that combined hard data on such issues as owner occupancy, foreclosures, and vacant properties with more qualitative assess-ment of community assets such as parks, schools, and cultural institutions, and resident organizational strength and capacity, the YNDC has begun to engage with three neighborhoods, with its greatest efforts focused on the Idora neighborhood in the city's southwest. A central part of their effort was the Lots of Green strategy, which "seeks to repurpose all land in a target area, transforming the physical fabric of strategic neighborhoods" (YNDC 2012). There were some 120 vacant lots in the relatively small Idora neighborhood, making up a substantial part of the area's land inventory. Almost all of them have been reused, including expansion of an adjacent regional park, community gardens, native planting sites, pocket parks, small community orchards, a 1.5-acre urban farm and training center, and side yard expansions.

It is worth noting that the YNDC has focused its resources not on the parts of Youngstown that contain the most vacant land, but on relatively small neighborhoods that, although troubled, are at least potentially capable of regeneration. While this was clearly driven by the organization's mission, there is a compelling broader case to be made for concentrating public and private resources in those areas, rather than on attempts to pursue large-scale reconfiguration of heavily abandoned areas. Legacy cities like Youngstown are seeing large-scale destabilization of neighborhoods that were until recently relatively stable working-class or middle-class communities, to the point where, absent concerted efforts to reverse this trend, some such cities may be left with few if any viable neighborhoods outside their downtown and near-downtown cores. This is a matter of far more urgency for the future health, or even survival, of these cities than reuse of land in largely vacant areas. The truly difficult question, however, is whether, even with concerted effort, all or even most of those neighborhoods can indeed be salvaged and restored to stability.

Conclusion

Incremental models such as Re-Imagining Cleveland and the YNDC neighborhood strategies offer a far better model for addressing the realities of physical change in legacy cities than large-scale or long-term comprehensive planning efforts. They represent ways of grappling with those realities that, however much they may fall short of radical transformation, are realistic and feasible and offer the potential of leading to a transformative process made up of a series of small, cumulative steps.

It remains to be determined, however, whether it is realistic to expect that incremental steps will, in fact, add up to more than the sum of their parts or, following Lennon's rule, just happen. If not animated by a coherent vision, incremental steps may end up being nothing more than a patchwork with little or no cumulative impact; the question arises, then, whether it is possible to frame a vision that is compelling—and credible—enough to drive individual incremental activities, without triggering the obstacles that are likely to block implementation of a comprehensive plan. It will be important to watch those cities like Cleveland or Dayton or nonprofit organizations like the Youngstown Neighborhood Development Corporation that have implicitly or explicitly adopted the course of strategic incrementalism as they pursue that course over the coming years.

CHAPTER 10

Tactical Options for Stable Properties

Frank S. Alexander

All cities face a constant challenge of confronting deterioration of vacant, abandoned, and substandard properties. The costs of neglect—promulgated by these vacant, abandoned, substandard, or tax-delinquent properties—are real; while these burdens have long been apparent, in recent years the costs of neglect have been empirically demonstrated and verified, and they are large. To stabilize a city's real property, these external costs must be internalized. This problem is complex, and no single approach will solve it. Each city needs a range of options tailored to its specific inventory of neglected real property.

In addressing the costs of abandoned properties and the possibilities of rebuilding communities, state and local governments have begun to use five tactical options. Each takes a slightly different approach, and each is based upon differing assessments of the local government capacity, the market dynamics, and the structural barriers. The five options are (1) property tax foreclosure reform, (2) housing and building code enforcement, (3) vacant property registration ordinances, (4) vacant property receiverships, and (5) mortgage foreclosure reforms. Land banks and land banking programs are additional structural options that, when used, can and should be closely tied to one or more of these five tactical options (Alexander and Powell 2011). This chapter discusses these options.

The Problem Properties

To design an effective solution, the problem must be clearly understood. Vacant, abandoned, and foreclosed properties are "problem properties" for most neighborhoods and local governments—but those neighborhoods and governments may find the properties problematic for different reasons. Years before the Great Recession took hold, Paul Brophy and Jennifer Vey identified the ten key steps to urban land reform; at the top of this list is the importance of knowing the inventory (Brophy and Vey 2002). If an inventory of property is imposing external costs on a local government, what are those costs, and why are they tolerated? Properties that are significantly delinquent in the payment of property taxes impose the most obvious and direct public cost in the form of lost tax revenues. This may well be due to the complexity of a nineteenth-century tax foreclosure system that makes little legal or economic sense in the twenty-first century (Alexander 2000b). However, not all vacant properties impose external costs, as not all vacant properties are tax delinquent. But when "vacancy" refers to deteriorated or substandard structures, then external costs become evident in the form of negative effects on adjacent property values (GAO 2011). The demolition of substandard structures may well represent the single greatest return on the investment of public dollars (Norris and Griswold 2007). Properties that are vacant, abandoned, *and* foreclosed result in a decline of almost 10 percent in the market value of all properties within 500 feet (Whitaker and Fitzpatrick 2011).

To know the inventory is to know more than that problem properties impose significant costs and liabilities: it is to know why they exist (Brophy and Vey 2002). It requires an evaluation of the legal impediments (such as the inadequacies of the tax foreclosure system or the code enforcement system) and the economic and social trends that contribute to the abandonment (declines in employment and population) (Accordino and Johnson 2000). In an otherwise strong real estate market, all that may be necessary is a highly focused tactical approach addressing one specific intervention or one subset of the properties. In a weak market that has been declining for years, no single tactical option will suffice, and long-term land banking of excess inventory may be critical. The relative geographical and spatial concentration of such properties may indicate the abandonment of a particular neighborhood, but it could also be an indicator of conflicts between the jurisdiction of overlapping political subdivisions, such as conflicts between cities and counties.

The Overall Strategy

Identifying the appropriate tactical options for any given community pre-supposes an overarching strategy. For present purposes, both chronically weak market communities and stronger communities facing temporary or geographically concentrated abandonment share the same essential strategy: adopt policies and programs that compel the owners of problem properties to internalize the costs imposed by their properties on neighbors and neighborhoods, communities and governments (Alexander 2000a). The strategic goal is to let every owner of real property know that neglect and abandonment are not options since the rest of the community pays the price (Community Research Partners 2008). This strategy has three components. First, governments must establish clear minimum standards for property conditions and property ownership and issue clear instructions to bring the property into compliance—"Fix it up." Second, the public sector must undertake enforcement of liens for public receivables (property taxes) or public expenditures (code enforcement liens)—"Pay it up." When neither of these meets with success, the third component comes into play: to compel a transfer of ownership through foreclosure enforcement proceedings—"Give it up." *Fix It Up; Pay It Up; or Give It Up.*

By adopting *Fix It Up; Pay It Up; or Give It Up* policies, the public sector will eliminate or reform the systems and structures that permit or even encourage the presence of real property as liabilities for the community at large, an essential foundation for building a resilient city. Unless and until they are removed, the costs of neglect will undermine any and all plans for the future of a city.

Option No. 1: Property Tax Foreclosure Reform

When problem properties are characterized primarily by delinquent property taxes, there are four possible consequences. First and most directly, general revenues available to fund local government are lost. However, when property taxes are ultimately paid, including the applicable penalties and interest, the local government will not lose revenue and may actually receive a surplus, given the relationship of penalties and interest to public borrowing rates. Second, those communities that sell or transfer property tax liens to third party investors gain an immediate cash contribution equivalent to the delinquency; however, those communities lose control of and accountability over the tax enforcement process, and any cash flow reflected in penalties and interest goes to the private investor. Third, if the delinquency is never paid and a tax sale is conducted, the property may be transferred to a new owner. Such a transfer, however, is commonly a multiyear process at best, due to postsale redemption rights. The constitutional inadequacy of most property tax foreclosure procedures means that marketable and insurable title is unavailable for properties transferred at tax sales. Fourth, if state law specifies a minimum bid at a tax sale equal to all taxes, penalties, interest, and costs and the fair market value of the property has declined below the minimum bid, the property is essentially stuck in a state of uncertainty.

The tactical option that solves this indecipherable maze of state property tax laws is relatively simple: revise the tax foreclosure laws to provide adequate notice once to all parties, and, if the taxes are not paid, then sell the property to the highest bidder or convey it to a public entity. The problem is complex; the solution is not. Local governments should resist the temptation to sell or transfer tax liens to private investors and should instead retain the authority and responsibility to collect the taxes—and thereby also retain the positive cash flow from delinquent payments—that are made before the sale of the property.

Reform of a broken property tax enforcement system must lead to the creation of a new approach that is efficient, effective, and equitable (National Consumer Law Center 2012). An efficient tax enforcement statute clearly states the priority of the lien, the amount of the lien, and the time frames for payment in a manner consistent with local government budget and revenue processes. Most jurisdictions are clear that property taxes have "superpriority" status as liens, taking precedence each year over all preexisting mortgages, judgments, and encumbrances. They are not necessarily as clear with respect to the relative priority of older tax liens relative to more recent tax liens or to competing tax claims among overlapping local governments (such as cities and counties). Existing property tax enforcement systems also are inefficient simply because of the tendency—over the past two hundred years—to extend, and then extend again, the deadlines for payment before the property is transferred. Lengthy time periods before the sale and multiple years of postsale rights of redemption serve primarily to increase the costs of abandonment on the community at large, rather than to protect individual property rights. Eliminating postsale redemption rights and shortening the presale enforcement period will increase the efficiency of all tax foreclosure systems.

An effective tax enforcement statute will yield maximum tax payments prior to deterioration and abandonment and will culminate, in the event of nonpayment, in the transfer to a new responsible owner of a title that is insurable and marketable. The most important component of any tax foreclosure system is the provision of constitutionally adequate notice to all interested parties.[1] Federal constitutional standards evolved during the latter quarter of the twentieth century, leaving most state and local systems out of compliance with constitutional minimums (Alexander 2000b). The tax enforcement systems that developed during the first half of the twentieth century often created numerous events that require notices to owners by local governments or require multiple different forms of notice. Yet these systems do not necessarily constitute with constitutionally adequate notice, with the simple consequence that very few property tax foreclosure sales result in title that is insurable and marketable. Designing an effective system requires providing maximum constitutionally adequate notice once to all interested parties (not providing constitutionally inadequate notice multiple times).[2]

An equitable tax enforcement system is premised on a fair assessment system. Though state requirements regarding uniformity in property taxation vary, virtually all states treat residential property differently from commercial and agricultural property, and many jurisdictions recognize exemptions based on the property's value or the owner's income. Public policies designed to accomplish equity in property taxation should focus on assessment rather than enforcement. Even in the context of enforcement proceedings, however, equitable treatment of low-income owners may require providing some form of a "hardship" repayment plans to avoid the foreclosure sale.

Option No. 2: Housing and Building Code Enforcement

When the primary characteristic of the inventory is not delinquent taxes but the presence of significant violations of local housing and building codes, the best tactical option is to confront directly the efficiency and effectiveness of code enforcement procedures. As is the case in property tax enforcement, many existing state and local procedures are a complex set of laws designed in the middle of the twentieth century (Schilling 2009). Unfortunately, existing code enforcement procedures tend to (i) be characterized by criminal sanctions, which dramatically increase the procedural and enforcement hurdles, (ii) understate the actual costs to the local governments of expenditures on code compliance activities, (iii) provide that a code enforcement lien is a subordinate lien of little practical value, and (iv) fail to provide a final enforcement remedy that results in a transfer of the property with marketable and insurable title (Lind 2012).

When a housing code is grounded in criminal enforcement, it expresses the community's moral outrage toward those who own seriously deteriorated structures. Such outrage, however, runs quickly into legal hurdles related to criminal jurisdiction and criminal convictions; and, when the defendant property owner is a single-asset shell corporation, a threat of jail time accomplishes little. Defining the *property* as the actor causing harm and imposing sanctions as liens on the property are far more effective approaches. Referred to as an *in rem* proceeding, such an approach has the advantage of working within legal standards (of process and of jurisdiction) that are easier to meet than are criminal standards. Fines and penalties are imposed upon the property as liens and not as personal liability judgments against the owners.

If the actual costs of code enforcement are not placed on the owner or on the property, then any and all such enforcement quickly becomes counterproductive. Instead of achieving the goal of requiring owners to *Fix It Up*, local governments become burdened with the costs of doing the owners' work, as the governmental claims and liens are functionally unenforceable. For the local government to charge $25 for mowing the grass on privately owned property or $250 for boarding and securing all windows and doors simply makes no sense when the actual costs to the government of such activities are far greater. Code enforcement should include explicit charges for inspections and for every violation; these should reflect the full cost to government, including personnel and administration costs. Sanctions should also include the fully loaded costs of administration of hearings, provision of notice, and research to identify owners. When the local government expends public funds to remedy code violations (whether cutting grass or demolishing structures), the full amount of such expenditures should be assessed against the owner or the property.

This tactical option of efficient and effective code enforcement works, but only if a lien for the full amount of the code enforcement activity is placed on the property. The lien has little value, however, unless the code enforcement lien is expressly granted, as a matter of state law, a superpriority status similar to that of property tax liens. The code enforcement lien, as a lien for public expenditures, should take priority over all other liens, mortgages, and encumbrances against the property, with the sole exception of property taxes.[3] Some states allow local governments periodically to provide the property tax collector with a list of such liens so that they may be collected through the property tax collection system. Other jurisdictions, particularly those with a split of authority between a county taxing authority and a municipal code enforcement program, specify a separate but parallel procedure for enforcement of code liens.

Option No. 3: Vacant Property Registration Ordinances

Finding the owner or manager of real property that is unoccupied and in danger of deteriorating is often difficult. When owners of residential, commercial, or industrial properties no longer have any net equity in a property and the costs of maintenance, rehabilitation, and repair exceed its fair market value, the economic incentive is to walk away. When title to the property is encumbered by one or more mortgages in various stages of default, delinquency, or foreclosure, lenders and mortgage-servicing companies are reluctant to maintain or improve the property prior to the final event of a foreclosure sale transferring ownership. The lenders and mortgage-servicing companies also tend systemically to overvalue the properties by undervaluing the costs of maintenance and remediation of substandard conditions (Fitzpatrick and Whitaker 2012).

The need for accurate ownership information about vacant, abandoned, substandard, and foreclosed properties predates the Great Recession, but it was less of a problem with residential properties and far more of a problem with commercial properties (including small multifamily residential facilities) owned by a single asset corporation that has functionally become defunct. The Great Recession profoundly altered the challenge by exponentially increasing residential foreclosures, causing owners to depart from their properties, and uncovering the highly fragmented secondary mortgage market and the multiplicity of roles of mortgage servicers and subordinate mortgagees.

Over 700 local governments across the United States have—in response to this challenge of finding owners and responsible parties—created Vacant

Property Registration (VPR) ordinances (Davis 2012). These VPRs take a range of forms but share a common objective: to require a person or entity with authority to manage and maintain a property to file his or her contact information with the local government (Martin 2010).

Any VPR must begin by defining the subject property (Davis 2012). What "vacant" property is subject to the ordinance? Some jurisdictions may define it as property that is not lawfully occupied for a specific period of time.[4] Others define it as property that is not lawfully occupied and that has terminated utility service, such as electricity, gas, or water. Yet others define the property as that with one or more serious housing or building code violations.

The simplicity of VPRs masks the complexity of the problem and often leads to greater confusion and resistance than is anticipated or necessary. To the extent that the strategy is identification and the tactical option is a VPR, the ordinance can serve an important role, but it will be inefficient, as it is likely to be both underinclusive and overinclusive at the same time. It will be underinclusive in that an owner who has walked away from a tract will have little incentive to comply with a VPR but often have incentives to ignore it. If a VPR requires all mortgagees to provide the identity of the mortgage servicer, it will likely be overinclusive in that the majority of mortgages, including residential mortgages, are not in default and are neither vacant nor substandard. When a VPR is designed to apply only to owners and to the mortgagees who become owners at foreclosure sales, the identification function is relatively consistent and straightforward as long as the statute requires that foreclosure deeds are publicly recorded within a short period of time following the sale.

When a VPR is intended to impose legal and financial liability—rather than simply identifying owners and responsible parties—it becomes far more difficult to design well. Not only is it more difficult to create an efficient and effective VPR with this function, but it is also far more difficult to engage in comparison of VPRs across states and even within states.

Imposing legal and financial liability for substandard properties is most clear and direct when enforcing housing and building code violations.[5] This liability is triggered by a property inspection that finds violations, and it should make little difference whether the owner is a long-term owner or a recent purchaser at a mortgage foreclosure sale (which would include the mortgagee as purchaser, commonly classified as Real Estate Owned or "REO"). Though there may be confusion in the mortgage servicing industry about the precise identity of the REO purchaser at the foreclosure sale, such confusion should make little difference to the local government in enforcement of its lien for violations of the housing and building code. How much federal agencies—as owners of REOs—can avoid local government imposition of liability by virtue of the federal constitutional supremacy clause remains an open question, however.

When the strategic goal of a VPR is not identification of parties but liability for conditions, key differences arise among the states; these differences depend on whether the state requires foreclosure of mortgages through judicial process or permits nonjudicial mortgage foreclosure.[6] A judicial foreclosure state presents strong and clear opportunity not just for identification information to be presented to the local government at the commencement of foreclosure but also for a judicial determination of whether the property is occupied or vacant and for a local government inspection if the property is vacant.

Judicial process also clearly and directly solves the problem of legal and financial liability for remediation of substandard conditions that affect the property. The mortgage-servicing industry has strong reservations about any ordinance or statute that imposes obligations or liability during the pendency of a foreclosure proceeding, as compared with owner of an REO postsale. Every mortgagee, however, has the right—as a matter of common law and in the standard form mortgage documents—to take such actions as necessary to preserve and protect the underlying security. To the extent that a mortgage servicer has concerns about the indeterminate nature of liability from becoming a mortgagee in possession, the presence of judicial process affords a venue for seeking the appointment of a judicial receiver to manage and remediate the property.

With the rapid increase in the number of local governments enacting VPRs in recent years, more states have enacted new legislation designed to modify the authority of local governments to create a VPR. Usually enacted in the name of statewide standardization of VPRs and backed by the mortgage industry's desire to minimize differences in local government approaches, the state VPR legislation usually has one overriding characteristic, the preemption of all local government authority to create standards or requirements that go beyond the parameters of the state legislation.[7] Whether a VPR remains a viable tactical option for local governments in the future will depend in large measure on the form and substance of any such state preemption legislation.

Option No. 4: Vacant Property Receiverships

Of all the tactical options for dealing with the externalities of vacant, abandoned, and foreclosed properties, the possibility of judicial receivership proceedings has the deepest history in Western common law. For over 400 years the law has recognized the inherent power of courts, grounded in equity, to appoint a disinterested third party to manage real property (Clark 1959). In its simplest form, a receivership action requests a court to appoint a receiver to manage, preserve, and protect property where the owner or owners cannot or will not do so.

While states diverge in the procedures and standards for receivership actions, the basic requirement is that the request for a receivership must be initiated either by a party with an interest in the property or by the local government. The petitioner must be able to demonstrate that the property is at risk of deteriorating or sustaining damage if a receiver is not appointed. In general, a receiver is granted full control to manage the property, though without authority to divest interests in the property. Receiverships in the context of vacant and abandoned properties can meet easily the deterioration threshold. To be judicially appointed, the receiver must meet qualifications, which usually include applicable property management experience; the petitioner seeking a receivership as well as other parties with an interest in the property may recommend a list of potential receivers, which may be private entities, nongovernmental not-for-profit entities, or special purpose governmental entities.

To be effective, the judicial receivership tactical option must overcome two obstacles. First, funds to manage, repair, or rehabilitate the property must be available. Costs and expenses (including management fees) of receivership are normally accorded first priority claim against the property, subject only to governmental liens.[8] Thus, to the extent that the underlying property has market value, after payment of the receiver's lien, the property's equity can be available to pay for management and remediation. When the costs of management and remediation exceed the resale value, a judicial receivership action will not be viable without supplemental funding.

Second, it must be possible to obtain judicial authorization to sell the property free and clear of all liens and encumbrances. A judicial decision to appoint a third party receiver to manage a parcel of property does not usually include the power to sell the property and divest all prior interests in the property. Such authorization requires a separate hearing and judicial ruling.

Local governments with growing inventories of vacant, abandoned, and foreclosed properties have only recently begun to turn to receivership actions as tactical options (Kelly 2004), yet these may be one of the most effective options when the dominant cause of vacancy and abandonment is the division of ownership among a range of fractured title claims, including multiple mortgages, judgments, tax liens, defunct corporations, and lack of probate proceedings.[9] Ironically, every commercial and residential mortgagee, because it has an interest in the real property, has standing to petition for a judicially appointed receiver to manage and protect the property. Only very rarely, however, have residential mortgagees exercised this power.

Option No. 5: Mortgage Foreclosure Reforms

For decades, communities with declining economies and population losses have found vacant and abandoned properties a challenge. The Great Recession has effectively shared this challenge with communities throughout the United States. Record-high foreclosures—heavily concentrated in some communities and spread across a range of neighborhoods in other communities—have exacerbated the problem and increased its complexity. Single-family mortgage foreclosures (including 1–4-family structures) can result in significant economic costs to adjoining properties that are just as devastating as vacancy and abandonment from any other cause (Immergluck and Smith 2006). The federal Neighborhood Stabilization Program was an attempt at direct intervention in the sharply increasing supply of low-value foreclosed properties, partially in recognition of the increasing costs being sustained by local governments as a result of the mortgage foreclosure crisis (Immergluck 2012).

There is no doubt about the connection between the collapse of the housing market, the rise of mortgage foreclosures, and the prevalence of vacant and abandoned properties. The nature and extent of the causal connections between mortgage foreclosure and deteriorating vacant properties are heavily contested, however (Furman Center 2009).

Many identify the length of time it takes to conduct a mortgage foreclosure as the biggest factor contributing to the increase in vacant and abandoned properties, arguing that the longer that a property remains tied up in a foreclosure proceeding the greater the likelihood of vacancy, vandalism, and deterioration. The average length of the foreclosure process varies widely across the United States, with slightly more than half the states permitting a nonjudicial foreclosure, which requires two to six months, and the remaining states requiring some form of judicial oversight, which takes from six to twenty months. During the depths of the housing collapse, many states considered, and some enacted, statutory reforms to foreclosure procedures (Alexander et al. 2012), but the effect of such change is difficult to identify and quantify. Other studies have shown that the mortgagee's tendency to overvalue the property during the foreclosure proceedings dampens the willingness to engage in more economically rational alternatives such as loan modifications or short sales (Fitzpatrick and Whitaker 2012).

Creating an expedited process for foreclosure on abandoned properties is the tactical option suggested most frequently in the context of mortgage foreclosure reform. For those jurisdictions that already use nonjudicial foreclosure procedures with relatively short time frames, the suggestion makes little sense and will not likely result in any change. But for those jurisdictions with protracted timeframes for residential foreclosures, such a suggestion may be appropriate if tailored carefully to both the existing statutory procedures and the applicable property. To the extent that a residential foreclosure procedure is considered overly lengthy because of the presence of a postforeclosure sale right of redemption, shortening or terminating such postsale redemption rights may be appropriate—if there is a judicial termination, prior to sale, that the property meets specified criteria of being unoccupied and subject to deterioration. To the extent that existing foreclosure procedures are lengthy for other reasons—such as congested trial calendars, multiple hearings related to default, the possibility of loan modifications, or the standing of the plaintiff to conduct a foreclosure—any expedited foreclosure process would be misplaced.

The most plausible mortgage foreclosure reform designed to address vacant and substandard conditions involves two elements: (i) a determination of when the property actually becomes vacant and (ii) the assignment of responsibility for maintaining the property in accordance with local standards. If, in a judicial foreclosure state, the property is unoccupied when the foreclosure proceeding begins (as determined by the mortgagee and confirmed by the court and by evidence of termination of utility services), an expedited schedule for a foreclosure sale, along with shortened or eliminated postsale rights of redemption, should be possible but only if the mortgagee takes responsibility for securing and maintaining the property pending the transfer of ownership at the foreclosure sale.

Mortgage foreclosure reforms almost invariably need to occur at the state legislative level, as such procedures are not within the discretion of local governments. Local governments can, however, make the case to the state legislature that—with respect to certain narrowly defined categories of properties that are harming neighborhoods—an expedited process for transferring control and ownership of the property is equitable and efficient. This should occur only when the borrower has factually or legally disclaimed the property and when the mortgagee is willing to acquire and quickly transfer the property or otherwise assume full legal responsibility for ensuring the property is in compliance with applicable housing and building codes.

Land Banks and Land Banking

Land banks are government entities that acquire, manage, and dispose of vacant, abandoned, tax-delinquent, and foreclosed properties (Alexander 2011). They target properties that, in their current form, are liabilities that impose external costs. They focus particularly on properties that are inaccessible to the private market because of structural impediments (such as tax foreclosure proceedings that require five to seven years to complete) or that have low or negative value. Land banking is the process or policy by which local governments acquire surplus properties and convert them into productive use. Land banks are public authorities or special purpose not-for-profit corporations that specialize in land bank activities.

A land banking program is a potential option for local governments to use that overlays all five tactical options available to local governments discussed above: property tax foreclosure reform, housing and building code enforcement, vacant property registration ordinances, vacant property receiverships, and mortgage foreclosure. In the absence of one or more of these five tactical options, a land bank is likely to accomplish very little in the stabilization of properties.

When the problem properties are characterized primarily by ineffective and inefficient property tax foreclosure procedures, a land bank can be authorized by statute to engage in earlier acquisition of the properties, to acquire the properties at tax sales, or to acquire the tax liens themselves—all as measures designed to ensure public accountability for and responsibility for the management and reuse of such properties. In parallel, a strong code enforcement system can provide that—in the event that the owners and other interested parties fail to *Fix It Up* and *Pay it Up*—a public entity, not only third party investors or speculators, can become the new owner of the property; this helps keep the property from cycling through the process again if the new owners do not make the necessary investments in subsequent years.

Land banks and land banking programs originated over forty years ago and have undergone several generations of growth and development. Originally, they focused solely on properties stuck in an antiquated tax foreclosure system, but the "third generation" of land bank statutes has recently been enacted in New York (2011),[10] Georgia (2012),[11] Missouri (2012),[12] and Pennsylvania (2012).[13] The third generation of land banks and land banking builds upon the lessons learned from the first two generations by focusing on new roles and new powers. Recent land bank statutes permit a far broader range of intergovernmental cooperation and regional collaboration. Multiple municipalities within a given county may elect to participate in a single land bank, and multiple counties may join to create a regional land bank or to achieve economies of scale in intergovernmental contracts for land bank operations.

The newest land bank statutes also provide for the possibility of internal financing of land bank operations so that a land bank does not require annual appropriations of local government general revenues. Recognizing that a land bank focuses primarily on those properties that are delinquent in property taxes, thus yielding no revenue to local governments while simultaneously imposing costs, the statutes permit local governments to dedicate to the land bank for a limited period of time a portion of the property tax revenues that are generated by the property once it returns to the tax rolls.

The Great Recession has prompted a deeper and broader vision for land banks and land banking. First recognized in federal law in the Housing and Economic Recovery Act of 2008, land banking played a key role in the application of Neighborhood Stabilization Funds to acquire the excess inventory of foreclosed properties. With the continued decline of property conditions and property values, the Federal Reserve Board identified land banks as a key option for consideration by the mortgage industry in the context of low value assets (Federal Reserve Board 2012).

Land banks do not displace a functioning private market. They are designed to address, in combination with the five tactical options, barriers to a functioning market or the complete absence of any market. They are local government entities with a high degree of flexibility and adaptability to local conditions. The priorities on disposition and reuse of properties are locally determined and range from the provision of new public parks and green spaces, to the provision of affordable housing, to catalyzing new retail and commercial development.

*   *   *

Revitalizing America's cities cannot occur without strategic commitments to confront substandard properties and tactical options appropriate for both the market conditions and the panoply of state and local laws. Revitalizing a city requires identifying the structures and systems that allow real property to be liabilities rather than assets. It requires the selection of tactical options appropriate to those barriers and to the possibilities for new uses. Most important, a city needs to have the power and the vision to shift the costs of property abandonment back to the owners and to ensure that owners *Fix It Up, Pay It Up*, or *Give It Up*. Some of the tactical options are likely to be with the existing authority of a city (housing and building code enforcement, vacant property registration ordinances, and vacant property receiverships), while others are likely to require reforms at the state legislative level (property tax foreclosure reform and mortgage foreclosure reforms). Land banks and land banking programs are likely to be structural options needed by cities not just to acquire excess inventories of abandoned properties but also to manage them and to hold them pending adaptive reuse.

PART IV

The New Economy and Cities

CHAPTER 11

Anchor Institutions in the Northeast Megaregion: An Important But Not Fully Realized Resource

Eugenie L. Birch

As former manufacturing cities in the United States seek to reinvent their economies, they have engaged in several types of revitalization strategies to use their key asset, land, to attract investment in new industries. Land is a critical ingredient for revitalization because it supports activities that generate income for both the public and private sectors, which, in turn, generate additional municipal revenues by the entity occupying the land.

To attract income-producing land uses, municipalities employ such economic development incentives as accelerated zoning code approvals and/or amenity or infrastructure improvements, including open space (parks, gardens), transportation (highways, bike lanes, parking), or services (schools, police stations). In recent decades, cities have sought to attract or retain private corporations but have given much less attention to nurturing another type of important land holder: the anchor institution, usually defined as universities, medical centers, performing arts centers, museums, sports facilities, and libraries. Local officials' failure to appreciate fully the potential role of "eds and meds" in urban revitalization stems from a number of factors. For example, planners often fail to conceptualize these entities as "industry clusters," budget directors do not appreciate these institutions' contributions to municipal budgets since, as nonprofits, the nature of their contributions differs from those of for-profit entities, and many elected officials, often tainted by a history of insensitive urban renewal activities, are reluctant to engage with anchors in the face of community opposition to institutional expansion. In addition, anchor institution leaders tend to shy from or resist undertaking the strong civic leadership roles in their communities that their corporate counterparts once provided because they have not traditionally taken on this type of role.

In many cities, especially those in the Northeast Megaregion, anchor institutions are important, relatively stable landowners. They are committed to their city locations because of their real estate holdings, their missions, the attraction of their locations to their audiences, or the presence of other economic activities that support their work and sometimes their location at the center of a network of satellite operations. While the Northeast Megaregion is well endowed with prestigious universities and hospitals, many of which date from America's colonial era, it also has a great number of less prominent institutions, often invented in the late Industrial Era to meet the needs of the nation's rapidly growing economy and fast-urbanizing places.

The anchor presence, especially high-performing universities and medical centers, is important to local economies and to central city resilience. By examining the role of universities and their associated medical centers in the Northeast Megaregion, this chapter explores urban revitalization strategies and how anchors, in general, fit into them. It begins with a broad discussion of anchors' role in urban revitalization and follows with a review of eds and meds as a regional industry cluster using the Northeast Megaregion as an example. (While analyses for other megaregions would demonstrate some similarities, the details would change in different historical and demographic contexts.) It briefly profiles three relatively large cities—Boston, Baltimore, and Washington—that have a strong anchor presence, including some common and some different land use arrangements related to each one's eds and meds. It also reviews the presence and effects of smaller-scale anchors in three less populous cities—Bethlehem, Providence, and Hartford.

Of the six cities examined, five were once among the nation's largest industrial producers. Boston was known for garment production, leather goods, and machinery industries; Baltimore for men's clothing, foundry and machine shop products, cars, and tobacco; Bethlehem for steel; Providence for metals, machinery, textiles, jewelry, and silverware; and Hartford for firearms, precision manufacturing (clocks), bicycles, and nails. While the loss of these sectors has been a challenge, the agglomeration of university (or college) and hospital (or medical center) operations has provided an important source of economic energy that is fueling these cities' revitalization. The chapter concludes with suggestions for further study to maximize the positive economic impact of anchor institutions in the local and megaregional contexts.

Types and Benefits of Land-Based Urban Revitalization

Once articulated as economic base theory, the "importing" of new capital into a city through the judicious use of land creates a virtuous cycle of economic growth, with initial influxes multiplying as residents and business or anchors recirculate that money through their purchases and other expenditures (Tiebout 1962; Klosterman 1990; Isserman 2000; Wang and Vam Hofe 2007). The effects of revitalization decisions on these income patterns have short-term and long-term consequences, depending on the different approaches chosen by the institutions and their cities.

Like any industry, anchor institutions attract external dollars by exporting their product. In this case, the product is knowledge, expertise, or experience; and the "factories" are the individual anchor institutions. For example, art museums mount "blockbuster" exhibitions that bring in viewers from the suburbs and neighboring states. In 2012, the Philadelphia Museum of Art's fourteen-week Van Gogh show attracted 150,000 visitors from forty-four countries and forty-eight states. They came to the City of Brotherly Love, spent a few hours in the museum (after paying a hefty admission fee) and perhaps remained longer to have a meal or take in other sites in this heavily tourist-dependent city (Philadelphia Museum of Art 2012: 1). High-performing universities exhibit similar drawing power, attracting national or international students who bring in tuition dollars and spending capacity. They also garner external dollars from the faculty research or service activities and receive contributions from appreciative alumni and others. For example, in 2010 the University of Pennsylvania and its associated medical center reported income of $711 million in tuition revenue; $1 billion in research funding, including over $300 million in private gifts, grants and contracts; and $90 million or more in Medicaid payments. Fees for clinical services were in the hundreds of millions of dollars, and students spent an estimated $200 million (with another $18 million added by their visitors or those attending Penn events) (University of Pennsylvania 2011; Birch 2012).

Urban Revitalization: From Catalytic
to Project-Oriented Approaches

Urban revitalization strategies focus directly or indirectly on enhancing the return on land within a city's political boundaries. They fall into four categories: catalytic, downtown, neighborhood, and project-focused (Birch 2007). In each of these categories, anchor institutions, especially universities and associated medical centers, can play important roles.

Catalytic strategies encompass bold moves, affecting large amounts of land and/or coordinated, large-scale projects, engaging public and private leaders, involving significant economic and political resources. They include nonconstruction efforts (annexation, consolidation, zoning changes, and municipal service [schools, crime] reform) and construction projects (major infrastructure linked to highways or mass transit; improvement in the public realm, large-scale conversion of obsolete sites [rail yards, industrial waterfronts] and associated brownfield clean-ups, and linkage programs harnessing market rate development to city-wide improvements). Typical involvement of anchor institutions in catalytic strategies includes a university assisting with school reform campaigns or occupying a site in a large-scale redevelopment project. For example, while any number of universities provides technical assistance and staff for primary and secondary schools in their cities, the work of the City University of New York is exemplary. Expansion into reclaimed sites has also occurred in many cities; the salvaging of Providence's 360-acre former Jewelry District has provided space for Brown, Johnson and Wales and others; San Francisco's 303-acre Mission Bay project supplied a 43-acre site for the University of California San Francisco Medical Center; and in Boston, Harvard University is deeply engaged in the revitalization of part of the Allston neighborhood, a former industrial area.

Downtown strategies entail reviving old and inventing new downtowns. Older cities build on a long-standing tradition to strengthen centrally located business districts but recognize that the era of office use domination is past. Smaller suburban cities, having lost retail and other business to the mall, fashion specialized "Main Street" functions. Residential suburbs-turned-cities delineate new central business districts, sometimes called "faux downtowns." Overall, downtowns, as "super" neighborhoods, adapt to contemporary changes in business and hospitality practices by supporting mixed office, hospitality, residential, and commercial uses; adding residential office, loft, or new construction; recruiting anchor institutions in higher education, health, arts and culture, and entertainment; providing major open-space amenities; and improving pedestrian and vehicular mobility. Anchors are particularly active in downtown revitalization strategies. In Providence, for example, the Rhode Island School of Design has adapted Class B and C office buildings into spectacular studios, dormitories, and other academic space, and similar projects exist in Boston (by Emerson College) and Lower Manhattan (by NYU). Another example is Pace University, which is headquartered in Lower Manhattan and has placed its Graduate Center in the White Plains financial district, adjacent to the regional (Metro North) rail station. In Philadelphia, eds and meds supply 35 percent of downtown private sector employment; enroll 85,000 students; and, between 2008 and 2012, attracted $4.3 billion in research funds (Center City District 2012: 15).

Neighborhood strategies focus on improving deteriorated residential districts and associated commercial corridors. While these kinds of programs date from the late nineteenth century, today's corrections aim to reduce concentrated poverty by enhancing low-income residents' life chances and attracting middle-income households. They include identifying a specific residential district or districts and then upgrading and increasing the supply of affordable housing, energizing retail corridors, providing better schools and neighborhood centers, improving streetscapes and public space, cleaning up brownfields, and greening vacant lots. Other improvements center on offering better social services and transportation links to the surrounding region's jobs. Agents of neighborhood development can be community development corporations, intermediaries (Local Initiative Support Corporation and Enterprise), specialized private developers (McCormack Baron), and anchor institutions (universities, hospitals, performing arts centers, libraries, sports facilities, and others). Among the best-known work in revitalizing older neighborhoods is that of the University of Chicago in Hyde Park/Kenwood; University of Pennsylvania in West Philadelphia; University of Southern California in Los Angeles; Portland State University; University of Baltimore; University of Illinois, Chicago; Illinois Institute of Technology in Chicago; Cleveland State University; and Wayne State University in Detroit (Rodin 2007; Perry and Wiewel 2005). Other anchor complexes like Cleveland State, University of Illinois, Chicago Circle, and Wayne

State are now the centerpieces of multianchor, multiuse neighborhood creation strategies (Haar 2011; Perry and Wiewel 2005). Notably, eds and meds have a long history in the neighborhood revitalization arena, dating from urban renewal programs that, in the 1950s, permitted university and medical center expansion activities. The redevelopment of Boston's West End featuring facilities for Massachusetts General is one of the most widely publicized examples, although once considered a huge mistake (Gans 1962). Today, Mass General is the city's largest employer (23,000) and second largest PILOT contributor ($2.2 million) (Business Journals 2012; Kenyon and Langley 2012).

Project-focused strategies concentrate on a single project—these tend to be expensive, large facilities ranging from convention centers to performing arts venues to sports stadia or research parks. They have precise site-location demands related to their spatial requirements and need for highway access or parking. They require massive financing packages and often inspire considerable controversy due to their expense or location. Again, anchors, often stadiums and performing arts centers but also universities and hospitals, are involved in these kinds of projects. For universities, the redevelopment efforts extend over a long period. For example, in the years 2004–2012, the University of Pennsylvania bought two large parcels (twenty-four and twenty-three acres) of underutilized commercial/industrial land in Philadelphia but does not expect to use this land for many years. Penn—serving as a land bank and as an owner—has to steward the sites for reputational and liability reasons, sometimes subletting them, making sure they are clean, ridding them of derelict or dangerous properties, or placing temporary uses on them.

Public and Private Sector Benefits of Urban Revitalization

Calculating the monetary outcomes to the public sector of enhancing land use through urban revitalization strategies includes counting "direct" taxes, like property taxes, that reflect higher values generated by the investments on the land and/or "indirect" taxes, like wage or sales taxes or payments in lieu of taxes (PILOT). These funds flow into the municipal budget to pay for existing or enhanced public services, service debt, and such other municipal liabilities as pensions.

In the case of anchor institutions (as nonprofit, tax-exempt entities), direct public contributions are less likely to come in the form of property taxes except when the institutions spin off for-profit activities (as might occur with the ownership of a hotel or apartment building rented to the public). In many cities, anchors contribute PILOTs, but, in general, these payments are relatively small and their impact limited. Boston provides an excellent example. While 51 percent of the city's land is owned by nonprofits, those land holdings represent only 8 percent of the assessed value of the city's real property (Kenyon and Langley 2012: 8; Lima 2011: 1). Of the land held by tax-exempt entities, the lion's share is owned by the state (26 percent) and the city (14 percent) and very little (2 percent) by eds and meds. (Lima 2011: 1). Further, Boston has one of the strongest PILOT programs in the nation, yet, in 2009, it yielded only $15.7 million ($14.9 million contributed by the eds and meds) or 0.66 percent of municipal revenues. Baltimore, New Haven, and Providence have similar programs, yielding 0.33 percent, 1.2 percent, and 0.56 percent respectively of those cities' municipal revenues (Kenyon and Langley 2012: 21–22).

Anchor institution indirect contributions to municipal revenues are far more significant (and somewhat difficult to calculate), especially in cities like Philadelphia where the property tax constitutes only 11 percent of municipal revenues and where the tax base generated by manufacturing, finance, and other traditional sources of income has declined precipitously. Anchor payrolls, purchases, and capital expenditures generate income, wage, sales, entertainment, hospitality, and corporate or business excise taxes collected by the city or state that then returns some portion to the municipality. Much of the effect derives from private sector vendors (products, jobs, business profit). Depending on the location of these vendors, the dollars have a multiplier effect as the funds are recirculated through their spending on other activities in the city and region.

Anchors regularly contract with specialized consulting firms to report these impacts, which are often estimated to be quite large. Regardless whether the exact amount reported is absolutely correct in every case, the scale and breadth of anchor contributions, especially the eds and meds, are important to any municipality. For example, in 2010, the University of Pennsylvania, the largest private employer in Philadelphia (32,000 employees), had a $4 billion payroll, total operating expenditures of $8.4 billion, and capital investments of $683 million. That year, Penn students and visitors

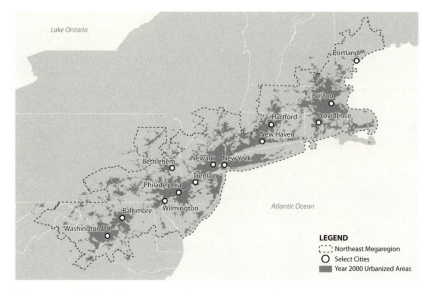

Figure 11.1. The Northeast megaregion.

spent another $325 million in the city. At a minimum, Penn's presence in Philadelphia generated $172 million in local taxes (University of Pennsylvania 2011).

Eds and Meds as an Industry Cluster in the Northeast Megaregion

The Northeast Megaregion extends from southern New England to northern Virginia (see Figure 11.1). It encompasses twelve states and 142 counties and has a large number of anchor institutions. Its major cities and metropolitan areas are Boston, New York, Philadelphia, Baltimore, and Washington D.C.; smaller places include Bethlehem, Providence, Hartford, New Haven, White Plains, Newark, Trenton, and Wilmington. Its population of 52.3 million (projected to increase to 70 million by 2050) supports a $2.92 trillion economy, represents 17 percent of the U.S. population, and generates 20 percent of the nation's GDP. Relatively dense land use characterizes the region that encompasses 2 percent of the nation's land area (America 2050 n.d.).

Bolstering the megaregion's economy are the important sectors of finance, pharmaceuticals, food, technology, communications, education, and health. Anchors are leading employers in the area's five major metro areas. Within the political boundaries of this area's cities, the eds and meds lead the mix of dominant nongovernment employers. For example, in Philadelphia and Washington, four of the top employers are eds or meds; in Boston and New York three of five, and in Baltimore one of five. Adding public universities to the list puts ed and meds in the top five in Boston and Baltimore. In Providence, eds and meds occupy four of the top five spots (Business Journals 2012; Crain's 2012).

A look at the actual numbers of employees in the top one or two nongovernmental employers in several of the cities gives a sense of the scale of these labor forces in individual firms or institutions in 2010. In the larger cities where the number of workers among the largest employers ranged from 17,000 to 48,000, eds and meds dominate as the top employers in Baltimore (with Johns Hopkins having 48,000 employees) in Philadelphia (with the University of Pennsylvania having 32,000 employees and Jefferson Medical School, 19,000) and in Boston (with Massachusetts General Hospital having 23,000 employees). In the smaller cities, a similar pattern prevails as exemplified by Providence's top two employers: Rhode Island Hospital with 6,910 employees and Brown University with 4,800 (Business Journals 2012; Crain's 2012). In New York, eds and meds fill the third and fourth spots.

In the entire Northeast Megaregion, universities and their associated medical centers generate a substantial number of jobs, have multi-million and in some cases multi-billion-dollar operating and capital budgets, attract billions of dollars in government-sponsored research, private donations, and federal funds in the form of Medicare payments or student loans, and stimulate local spending through their own purchases and spending by visitors and students. While a precise accounting of these impacts is beyond the scope of this chapter, data from national databases (U.S. Departments of Education and Treasury) yield a rough estimate of these megaregional impacts. In 2010, major eds and meds anchors collectively employed nearly a million people, had aggregated operating budgets of nearly $100 billion, attracted $28 billion in sponsored programs, gifts, and contracts ($23 billion from government grants and contracts, a minimum of $5 billion in Medicare payments), and brought in upward of one and a half million students (Birch 2012). While these institutions attract highly skilled and highly paid

Table 11.1. Top Employers in the Larger Megaregional Cities

Employer	Industry	Employees	City
Johns Hopkins	Education/health	48,000	Baltimore
University of Pennsylvania	Education/health	32,000	Philadelphia
Columbia University/ NY Presbyterian	Education/health	32,000	New York
New York University	Education/health	31,000	New York
JP Morgan Chase	Finance	25,000	New York
Citibank	Finance	24,000	New York
Massachusetts General Hospital	Education/health	23,000	Boston
Stop and Shop	Food	23,000	Boston
North Shore JIJ Health System	Health/education	20,000	New York
Jefferson Health System	Health/education	19,000	Philadelphia
Mount Sinai Medical Center	Health/education	18,000	New York
Continuum Health Partners	Health/education	19,000	New York
New York-Presyterian Hospital	Health/education	19,000	New York
Harvard University	Education/health	17,000	Boston
Northrup Grumman	Defense/technology	17,000	Washington

knowledge workers, they also have well-defined job ladders for entry and movement from unskilled to medium-skilled work. Salaries at the top exceed national averages. Although faculty are less than 10 percent of the total workforce in these anchors, their average salary of $85,000 is double the nation's per capita average income. Finally, these anchors capture a disproportionate share of government research dollars—in 2010 they received some 25–35 percent of the total (Webber 2012).

Due to historic and economic reasons, an important locus of action among the megaregion's eds and meds is in its five major cities. In the data cited above, Boston, New York, Philadelphia, Baltimore, and Washington were responsible for 59 percent of sponsored programs, gifts, and contracts, 73 percent of aggregated operating budgets, 65 percent of all employees, and 49 percent of all students. (Remarkably, even in New York City, known for the dominance of the Finance, Insurance, and Real Estate (FIRE) industries, eds and meds are important. For example, the city's student population in higher education is higher than the entire populations of Boston, Denver, or Seattle.) High shares of aggregated budgets and employees may be attributed to the large staffs of the university/medical centers that tend to be in cities. For example, Johns Hopkins, University of Pennsylvania, Columbia, and NYU have labor forces ranging from 32,000 to 48,000. The relatively low proportion of students may be accounted for by the fact that the flagship, highly populated campuses of state universities with student populations of 20,000–30,000 tend to locate outside large cities.

This higher ed agglomeration is even more pronounced when traced beyond a city's boundaries. For example, the eleven-county Greater Philadelphia area has 101 colleges and universities that, in 2010, supported 91,000 jobs, attracted 295,000 full-time-equivalent students, and contributed $15 billion to the regional economy (CEO Council for Growth 2010: 3–7). Drilling down to eds and meds in small and medium-sized cities in the Northeast Megaregion—as in Providence, Hartford, Middletown, New London, New Haven, Bethlehem, Easton, Allentown, Newark, Wilmington, Towson, and their suburbs—reveals the different types of eds and meds, which, like firms in any industrial cluster, vary in size and resources. While the numbers of students and other resources in small and medium-sized cities are less important to the megaregion than are the larger cities, they are quite significant in the cities in which they are located, where they are important employers and city builders. Notably, within the megaregion (and beyond), important synergies exist among the institutions' research and instructional arms, creating an intricate, networked economic ecology. Research teams often work across institutional boundaries, with a grant-recipient university subcontracting parts of a given project to others. Or students may study in a program sponsored by a partner institution. For example, in 2009, Lehigh University made substantial payments to thirty institutions, including Carnegie Mellon, Children's Hospital of Philadelphia, Cornell, Johns Hopkins, MIT, NYU/Polytechnic, Dartmouth, and Widener College, for research and other services (Lehigh University 2009).

Eds and Meds in Boston, Baltimore, and Washington

Boston, Baltimore, and Washington—each having abundant supplies of anchor institutions, especially eds and meds—not only have shared histories but also similar physical and socioeconomic profiles currently. All were founded more than 200 years ago, are small in terms of geography and population, and have suffered severe economic (and subsequent population)

Table 11.2. Eds and Meds as an Industry Cluster in the Northeast Megaregion's Five Major Cities

City	Sponsored programs, gifts, contracts ($000)	Government grants and contracts ($000)	Operating budget ($000)	Number of staff	Number of faculty	Average faculty salary ($)	Number of students
Boston	2,758,299	409,010	14,909,972	144,477	14,870	71,515	140,686
New York	4,682,554	2,076,118	29,631,319	222,492	32,247	88,587	359,386
Philadelphia	1,888,853	1,096,471	11,870,709	101,839	8,236	71,781	119,781
Baltimore	2,601,310	1,494,168	8,895,544	68,042	7,640	77,564	76,945
Washington	1,440,285	428,010	5,890,272	68,821	5,149	84,474	85,230
Total	13,371,301	5,503,777	71,197,816	605,671	68,142	78,706	782,028
% of megaregion	59	47	73	65	80		49

declines since peaking around 1950. Today, they each host between thirteen and twenty-nine eds and meds. At forty-eight square miles, Boston, with thirty eds and meds, had in 2010, 618,000 residents (having lost 23 percent of its population since 1950); Baltimore's eighty-one square miles with sixteen eds and meds has a population of 620,000 (down 35 percent since 1950); and Washington's sixty-eight square miles has sixteen eds and meds and a population of 602,000 (down 25 percent since 1950). The population losses since the mid-twentieth century have not only left these cities much less densely settled but also opened land for redevelopment that some anchor institutions have purchased for present and future operations.

In terms of economic impact, these universities and their associated medical centers are powerful. They generated 60 percent or more of the aggregated operating budgets of all anchors (including museums, performing arts centers, and stadiums) in all three cities. In Boston and Baltimore, they supplied half the anchor jobs (Business Journals 2012; Crain's 2012; Birch 2012).

All three of these cities also accommodate groups of smaller universities and colleges and dedicated institutions of higher learning in the arts that, in turn, contribute to the cultural lives and arts anchor institutions of their cities and beyond.

In looking at the spatial arrangements of the eds and meds in the three cities, certain development patterns emerge. While, in each case, different configurations support the institutions' fundamental needs for space for research, instruction, and housing for staff and students, a typology—specialized district, embedded neighborhood, downtown, large-scale conversion, and quasi-suburban—emerges (see Table 11.4), with each category having distinct characteristics and needs that can provoke local or city-wide land use conflicts, often revolving around land scarcity. Boston stands out, as its layout encompasses a variety of possible ed and med land use types as well as related complexities associated with operations and growth, issues worth discussing in the local and megaregional context. Boston has four of five distinct types of anchor development: (1) specialized district (for example, the Longwood Academic and Medical Area with its concentration of educational, scientific and arts functions [twenty-three institutions including the Harvard Medical, Dental and Public Health Schools, seven hospitals and institutes, six colleges, and the Isabella Stewart Gardner Museum]; (2) embedded neighborhood (for example, Tufts Medical Center, squarely in the densely occupied Chinatown District); (3) downtown (for example, Emerson College, Suffolk University, and the Berklee College of Music); and (4)

Table 11.3. Eds and Meds in Boston, Baltimore, and Washington, D.C.

City	2010 population (% change since 1950 peak)	Area (land only) sq. mi.	No. of eds and meds institutions	Institutions college or university alone (%)	Institutions arts and culture (%)	Institutions university with medical center (%)
Boston	618,000 (−23%)	48	30	52	16	32
Baltimore	620000 (−35%)	81	16	50	6	13
Washington	601000 (−25%)	68	16	69	5	25

Table 11.4. Eds Anchor Institution Arrangement in Cities

Type	Example
Specialized district	Longwood Academic and Medical Area
Embedded neighborhood	Tufts Medical Center
Downtown	Emerson College
Large-scale conversion	Allston/Brighton
Quasi-suburban	Johns Hopkins Homewood campus

large-scale conversion (for example, Harvard and Boston College are key actors in the transformation of the Allston/Brighton area). The fifth type, quasi-suburban, is exemplified by Baltimore's Johns Hopkins Homewood campus and Morgan State's campus, which are embedded in older, established suburban-like city neighborhoods.

Beyond dealing with issues of land scarcity, the eds and meds and their home cities often experience other land use-related problems that range from residential and commercial displacement, change of character in the face of institutional expansion, undergraduate rowdiness in residential neighborhoods, transportation of goods and services (for example, food provisioning, ambulances), and parking.

Eds and Meds in Providence, Hartford, and Bethlehem

Like the larger cities in the megaregion, smaller cities benefit from the presence of eds and meds. Within Providence's nineteen square miles are seventeen eds and meds. As a city of 178,000 that has experienced a 28 percent decline in population since 1950 and that seeks to rebrand itself, Providence has a several-decade history of major infrastructure investments (for example, relocation of its railroad, day-lighting the Providence River, expanding its airport). Its latest project, the relocation of I-95, freed up twenty acres in the center of the city's 360-acre former jewelry manufacturing district, now christened the Knowledge District. Conceived in 2007 as a creative economy strategy, the city has attracted Brown University's new medical school facilities and associated laboratories, an extension unit of Johnson and Wales, and two creative industries (Hasbro and Video 38) to the area.

With twelve eds and meds, Hartford has a profile similar to that of Providence. Having lost 29 percent of its population since 1950, in addition

Table 11.5. Eds and Meds in Providence, Hartford, and Bethlehem

City	2010 population (%) change since 1950 peak	Area sq. mi.	No. of higher education institutions	No. of hospitals	Economic development concept
Providence	178, 042 (−28%)	19	11	6	City implementing eds and meds develop- ment strategy in new Knowledge District
Hartford	124,775 (−29%)	17	8	4	City anchors one end of Knowledge Corridor
Bethlehem	75,266 (+14%)	20	2	2	

to hosting the local institution, it also anchors the bistate Connecticut/ Massachusetts Knowledge Corridor that extends twenty-nine miles north to Springfield. Among the Knowledge Corridor projects is a high-speed rail link to enhance synergies among the corridor's industries, including thirty-two institutions of higher education and 120,000 students.

The Bethlehem/Allentown eds and meds are equally influential in northeastern Pennsylvania. Unlike the other small cities discussed here, Bethlehem has experienced a 14 percent increase in population since 1950, despite the crushing loss of Bethlehem Steel in 2001. It is perhaps less dependent on its two eds and meds than the other cities in this category because it has other economic assets, such as a regional casino and a large industrial/warehouse park. Nonetheless, its St. Luke's University Hospital, associated with Temple University Medical School, is the second largest employer in the Lehigh Valley, having more than 5,000 employees in its flagship facility in Bethlehem and in another unit in nearby Allentown's West End neighborhood. The combined budget of the two facilities is $683 million. Bethlehem's Lehigh University ($400+ million budget, 1,700 employees, and more than 7,000 students) and Moravian College ($76 million budget, 1,595 employees, and 2,000 students) make additional contributions to Bethlehem's economy.

Maximizing the Positive Impact of Anchor Institutions Locally and Megaregionally

While eds and meds are an important industry cluster in the Northeast Megaregion, their economic functionality is not well understood and, therefore, little scholarly or practice-based thought has gone into maximizing their impacts. Two major themes emerge: first, improving local planning and land use decision making; and second, undertaking regional planning and projects to help resolve problems that cannot be solved locally and improve the efficiency of the institutions in their primary functions of instruction or service provision and research. At the local level, smoothing the environment for institutional growth is of utmost importance. A key measure here is to improve communications among elected officials and city agencies, citizens, and anchor institution leadership to facilitate institutional growth while recognizing the needs and rights of the communities in which they operate—that is, improving the democratic decision-making process. Although there are many ways to achieve this, Boston provides one example with its requirement for Institutional Master Plans as a prerequisite for land use permissions. While time-consuming and expensive in the short run, this device, a city-wide requirement applying to all institutions, allows for transparency and negotiation in a relatively neutral environment. And, in many cases, it provides direction for agency work. For example, for Harvard's project in Allston, the Boston Redevelopment Authority undertook the broad planning work necessary to contextualize upcoming institutional efforts (BRA 2005).

In considering the many megaregional approaches possible, one stands out: promoting and participating in sustainable development practices along the northeast transportation corridor. Supporting high-speed rail, better local public transit, and transit-oriented land development offers many possibilities for improving the efficiency and functionality of the eds and meds. Improving staff and student/visitor housing and accommodations, facilitating research, and promoting instructional and patient service exchanges—much is already happening—could be advantageous to all. The most important point of this discussion is the necessity of conceptualizing the eds and meds as critical to the economic base of a megaregion and its component parts and taking appropriate actions to improve their functioning.

CHAPTER 12

Fields, Factories, and Workshops: Green Economic Development on the Smaller-Metro Scale

Catherine Tumber

"I hope no reader will try to transfer my observations into guides as to what goes on in towns, or little cities, or in suburbs," Jane Jacobs wrote in a rarely cited passage of *The Death and Life of Great American Cities*. "Towns, suburbs, and even little cities are totally different organisms from great cities. We are in enough trouble already from trying to understand big cities in terms of the behavior, and the imagined behavior of towns. To try to understand towns in terms of big cities will only compound confusion" (Jacobs 1961: 16).

All too often, urban planners and economic developers working in smaller industrial cities have ignored Jacobs's warning. Since the 1980s, they have superimposed on these once-thriving manufacturing centers economic development and design templates that have worked fairly well in large, strong-market cities such as New York, with mixed results in places like Syracuse, Rockford, and Youngstown. Indeed, it is fair to say, in the words of one urban historian, "the metropolis has become the quintessential urban form" (Connolly 2008: 4). Seldom has anyone paused to ask whether older cities of smaller scale might require significantly different economic development and planning strategies.

Today's odd neglect of urban scale has origins in mid-twentieth-century federal and state policies and demographic-cultural shifts. Postwar urban disinvestment in favor of suburban development had a deleterious effect on all older cities, to be sure, but it was particularly hard on smaller urban form.

Massive urban highway systems, designed by the likes of Robert Moses for New York, sliced these central cities in half—or even into quarters, as in the case of Hartford. Complementarily, urban and interurban rail transit was systematically removed from these places, leaving them exclusively dependent on the automobile. As a result, sprawl in smaller metros was more intense relative to their size and, thus, had a disproportionately devastating effect on center-city commerce. Meanwhile, the decline and later full-on exodus of manufacturing south, west, and overseas did not thwart sprawl in smaller industrial metros but made it less dense and relatively more far-flung than in large or growing metros, in a pattern identified as "sprawl without growth" by the Brookings Institution (Pendall 2003). In 2000, the Buffalo-Niagara metro, for example, had the same population as it did in 1950, but its footprint was three times larger. This means that the same number of people supports three times the infrastructure and services. As development inches outward, with all the expense of building and maintaining roads, schools, sewage, water, gas, and electrical lines, a stationary tax base is not only left on the hook for older legacy costs but also must help pay for new development and services (Banas 2010). One need not be suburbia-averse to see that our peculiarly disposable way of constructing and subsidizing exurban development is unsustainable and profoundly inequitable—especially in smaller industrial cities.

Things have always worked differently in these places, from their earliest flourishing between the 1880s and 1920s to the course of their economic descent after World War II. It stands to reason, then, that sustainability should be pursued on a different model in these cities too, one tailored to their scales, their historical legacies, and their natural assets. Given the disruptions to the global economy that climate change and peak oil are likely to inflict, smaller industrial cities are peculiarly well suited to the economic and ecological adjustments that will be necessary in the years ahead.

I will argue that their manufacturing legacies and rich natural resources in farmland and water—combined with their smaller yet substantial urban markets—render these metros crucial to the *productive* green economy. Furthermore, these former one- or two-industry factory cities are in a position to diversify economically for both for-export industry and increased local self-reliance. And in the tradition of critic Lewis Mumford, I will draw on late nineteenth-century Russian anarchist Petr Kropotkin's notion of "fields, factories, and workshops" to make my points (Kropotkin 1901). One need not be an anarchist or a contemporary anti-"government" libertarian to find Kropotkin's triptych a useful way of conceiving economic resilience on the smaller-metro scale. Smaller industrial cities—in contrast with small towns and big cities—have the resources in fields (agriculture), factories (manufacturing), and workshops (technical innovation) to develop all three in tandem. Controlling sprawl, I will further argue, is critical to that three-part project.

Fields

As it happens, most smaller industrial cities—particularly in upstate New York, southern New England, the upper Piedmont, and throughout the Midwest—sit amid some of the most fertile soil on earth. Between 2002 and 2007 alone, more than 4 million acres of agricultural land—roughly equivalent to the size of Massachusetts—were converted to developed uses (American Farmland Information Center 2008). In the age of global warming, we squander this land through sprawl and petroleum-drenched industrial agriculture at our ecological peril and at risk of endangering our food security. For smaller industrial cities, though, the economic stakes in preserving nearby farmland for local food production run even deeper, for three reasons. First, preserving and developing their local food sheds in a sustainable manner can help these metros retain community wealth currently drained off by corporate agribusiness. Second, unlike small towns, they constitute significant local urban markets that can be tapped by local farmers with profit. And third, smaller metros can ground local agricultural economies serving large cities seeking to source their own food closer to home rather than halfway across the world. Local food production, in other words, can become an important economic driver in these former one- or two-industry cities.

Let us look at each of these claims in order, taking the argument for retaining community wealth first. Numerous recent studies bear out the findings of a 2003 report on how commodity agriculture drains the regional economy in southeastern Minnesota. Between 1997 and 2003, local farmers in the region's seven counties sold an annual average of $912 million into the global commodity market, but they spent $996 million in petroleum-based inputs, genetically engineered seeds, feed, and such, most of it sourced outside the region, at a net loss of $84 million each year. The deficit was covered by federal subsidies and off-farm work. And because local farmers produce commodities instead of food, local consumers spent $500 million annually on food produced and processed outside the region. The current subsidy-dependent system also drives up the cost of land and feed, which blocks efforts by small food-producing farmers to offer alternatives. Yet, if the area's consumers were to buy just 15 percent of their food from local sources, the report's authors show, it would generate as much income for the region as two-thirds of farm subsidies—which at the time cost U.S. taxpayers $98 million a year in southeastern Minnesota alone (Meter and Rosales 2001). Another study demonstrates that if Michigan residents met the minimal USDA fruit and vegetable consumption guidelines by eating more seasonally available Michigan-grown fresh produce, it would result in 2,000 more jobs and $200 million in new income for the state (Conner et al. 2009). Imagine what the economics might look like if local food systems were more fully developed.

Here, we come to the second reason relocalizing agriculture near smaller cities makes economic sense: it is both feasible for small farmers and creates jobs in related distribution, retail, and processing work, as well as through the multiplier effect. Small adaptive farms of ten to fifty acres on the suburban fringe and beyond can garner a decent livable income selling to both local and more distant urban markets, while providing access to off-farm work in the city. Recent studies bear out the testimony of Henry Brockman. In 2009, Henry's twenty-four-acre organic farm, located twenty miles equidistant between Peoria and Bloomington, brought in more than $200,000 in gross sales. Since he is land-debt-free, uses only a small tractor and no expensive fertilizer or pesticide "inputs," and rotates his crops instead of relying on farm insurance, his expenditures are minimal. Henry sells most of his wares once a week, six months a year, at a Chicago-area farmer's market, 150 miles away, where he has been doing business for sixteen years. He also has a small community-supported agriculture (CSA) market in Bloomington, which he expects to expand as he grows older (Tumber 2012: 42–48).

Henry Brockman has been hard at it for a long time, with an established metro-Chicago customer base to which he is fiercely loyal. What is missing for most farmers interested in producing food rather than commodities, Brockman included, is local market infrastructure: facilities for distribution, warehousing, refrigeration, retail, value-added processing, and transportation. To understand the reason this need is particularly acute in the "nation's breadbasket," consider the broad agricultural history of the Midwest. The region was settled by farmers in debt for land purchase who produced cash crops and livestock for distant commodity markets in order to pay back their loans. Meanwhile, farmers had little commercial incentive to produce for local markets since neighboring farm families produced food for themselves. Even this form of self-reliance dropped away over the latter part of the twentieth century, as large commercial lenders demanding high returns or supporting secondary markets supplanted small local banks, grocery-store chains took over what small retail had been in place, and federal commodity subsidies for both individual farmers and long-distant marketing supports compelled farmers to take all of their land out of food production. At the same time, gross inequities were introduced to the agricultural system, rewarding a few commodity farmers handsomely while driving up land values and throwing the majority into economic peril and instability.

A 2012 study of the Indiana farm and food economy commissioned by the state's department of health shows that $14.5 billion flows out of the state each year in food sourced elsewhere, while personal income for food-industry workers has fallen. Author Ken Meter remarks wryly that, while Indiana prides itself on "feeding the world" with its commodity products, the state does not feed itself. Addressing this state of affairs, he argues, requires not simply "restoring" local market infrastructure but creating it in the first place. This "historic opportunity" is being met by emergent entrepreneurial business clusters, some forty years in the making, that have recently received a boost from the rising demand for fresh local food. Direct marketing through CSAs, retail development of farmers markets, and institutional marketing of the sort pioneered by Farm to School programs all play a role here, but it is insufficient to meet the uptick in demand. To reach this growing market, farm operators also need greater distribution, logistics, storage, retail, and transportation capacity, and facilities for refrigeration, processing, and meat rendering. Meter argues that what this emergent food system requires of government is not direct subsidies for individual food producers or products—that would only perpetuate the system of picking winners and losers—but policy and subsidy support for the market structure local food economies so sorely lack (Meter 2010). Urban farmers also need better local market structures. They play an especially important role in "shrinking" cities by cultivating food on these cities' abundant vacant lots, which helps stabilize depopulated neighborhoods while generating income for inner-city residents, imparting skills in agriculture, construction, and business management and safeguarding food security in cities often deemed food deserts in their entirety. With its *Regional Food Hub Guide*, released in April 2012, the USDA Agricultural Marketing Service now offers policy, financing, and technical guidance to meet this need and is tracking regional food system hubs nationwide (Barham et al. 2012).

Given their lower land-market pressures and potential access to sizable local metro markets, farmers in smaller city hinterlands are poised to prosper from these emergent food systems. A study of the six-state upper Midwest by University of Iowa economist Dave Swensen projects that supporting the region's twenty-eight metropolitan area markets (250,000 population or more) with twenty-eight fresh fruits and vegetables would require 195,669 acres, resulting in $637.44 million in farm-level sales, 6,694 jobs, and $284.61 million in more equitably distributed labor income. Compare that with the jobs and income resulting in corn and soybean production on the same number of acres: 1,892 jobs and $42.517 million in labor income (Swensen 2010).[1]

As valuable as these studies are, in focusing on consumer markets they do not account for the disproportionate *production* advantages for small-metro agricultural economies exporting to big-city markets. Another report, commissioned by Manhattan Borough president Scott Stringer on sourcing food for New York City 200 miles out, offers a case in point: it overlooks the tremendous economic benefits that would accrue to smaller upstate cities should such a plan be carried out. To be sure, the report discusses the plan's importance to the statewide economy and calls for more aggressive farmland protection in the Empire State, but it does not analyze its benefits for the cities settled amid its richest soil—Syracuse, Utica, Ithaca, Binghamton, Albany, and others (Stringer 2010: 12–14). Something like a Venn diagram comes to mind here, with one large circle representing New York City's massive food market, overlapping with a series of smaller circles representing these more modest yet significant urban food markets.

Open agricultural land also can be used to produce wind, solar, and biomass energy, with added profit for individual farmers and local economies alike. Although arrangements vary widely, energy companies supplying the grid pay some $6,000 per wind turbine for land-leasing arrangements. Off-grid distributed wind and solar energy installations, meanwhile, can reduce a farmer's costs significantly and leave him or her less beholden to spiking energy prices. Either way, the end result is more profit for the farmer and more dollars circulating in the local economy.[2]

Factories

At the outset of the Great Recession, which played out amid the 2008 presidential primary campaigns, almost everyone—from the candidates to state and local economic development officials—believed that American manufacturing was in its final death throes. Following on the heels of electronics, consumer durables, and garment making, all largely off-shored by the 1990s, automotive, computer, and emergent clean energy manufacturing had been moved overseas at an alarming rate over the course of the 2000s. China, most controversially, has captured much of this capacity, with its monetary and trade policies, its low wages, and its growing internal consumer market (Klier and Rubenstien 2008, 2010; United Nations Environment Programme and Bloomberg New Energy Finance 2011; Hart 2012). Advocates of neoliberal globalization policy argued that the arrangement was a "win-win." It drove down prices while benefitting shareholders, it introduced innovation-based market efficiencies, and it elevated the standard of living in developing nations. Neoliberal economic restructuring would also lead to greater American prosperity, this line of thinking went, as the United States replaced its low-skilled factory jobs with knowledge work in high-tech R&D and services. Given assists from a succession of speculative bubbles induced by a poorly regulated, exploding financial sector, it is easy to see why this strategic worldview met little significant resistance until recently.

It was, in any case, unsustainable, and not only because it introduced harrowing levels of wealth inequality to our fragile democracy. As far back as 1987, economists Stephen S. Cohen and John Zysman spelled out just why *Manufacturing Matters*—the title of their book. Against the idea of the "coming post-industrial society," they argued that "We are experiencing a transition not from an industrial economy to a service economy, but from one kind of industrial economy to another." Taking a cautious, essentially conservative approach at odds with the tone of irrational exuberance that would mark the 1990s, they maintained that "If the United States loses control and mastery of manufacturing production . . . the high-paying service jobs that are directly linked to manufacturing will, in a few short rounds of product and process innovation, seem to wither away, only to sprout up off-shore, where the manufacturing went" (Cohen and Zysman 1987: xiii, 20–21). That is, of course, what happened. By the 2000s, American industries began off-shoring their high-end services and knowledge work as well, developing intellectual property easily appropriated by their overseas competitors. For that reason and others, U.S. manufacturers are beginning to re-shore. Business leaders are also taking into account growing wage convergence, the incompatibility of just-in-time sourcing and long supply chains, the expense of management time and travel, and quality-control problems due to language and long-distance communication barriers. Peak oil and global warming play a part, too: rising oil prices and disruptive weather of the sort that caused the 2011 Fukushima nuclear power plant disaster add to the instability of global production (Sirkin, Zinser, and Hohner 2011; Phillips 2012; Pisano and Shih 2009).

It seems, then, that, after thirty years of neoliberal excess, we finally may be moving "from one kind of industrial economy to another." The form manufacturing takes as it re-shores and benefits from the bailout and restructuring of the automotive industry is as urgent now as it was in 1987. Once again, the task is disproportionately paramount for smaller industrial cities. They not only ground the just-in-time supply chain for automotives— manufacturing infrastructure, skills, and culture that can be repurposed to include clean energy production—but, since they comprise the regional geography of wealth inequality and disinvestment, smaller cities desperately need the work. Economists and policy analysts are beginning to track new manufacturing's depressed wages and their effects on national consumer markets; skill mismatches in advanced manufacturing; and efforts to overhaul secondary and higher education to meet new vocational needs (Longworth 2011; Davidson 2012; Sirkin, Zinser, and Hohner 2011). I would like to draw attention to another matter, especially important to smaller industrial metros seeking to reinvent themselves for a more environmentally and economically sustainable future: the threat of manufacturing sprawl. Americans are not accustomed to this problem—in contrast with that caused by the expanding industrial economy in China—and few have studied it (Gunther 2003; Gaswami 2010). In *Pastoral Capitalism: A History of Suburban Corporate Landscapes*, Louise A. Mozingo argues for reining in the low-density, auto-dependent office-park form that has spearheaded sprawl since the early 1940s and reintegrating it with the urban transportation and residential fabric (Mozingo 2011). Doing the same with manufacturing would be more difficult, given that the noise and grime of industry was a major spur to the rise of Euclid, separate-use zoning in the 1920s. But much of today's light and advanced manufacturing is not as hazardous as the heavy industry of yore and could be far more easily integrated with existing urban and suburban development, accessible to alternative modes of transportation.

Such far-sighted location planning seems rare, however. I say "seems" because no one is tracking manufacturing sprawl, from government agencies and scholarly think tanks to policy advocates such as Smart Growth America and the National Brownfields Coalition. Yet anecdotal evidence suggests that many manufacturers are setting up shop on greenfields, with all the associated new infrastructure and environmental costs and at further distance from urban labor pools. In 2009, metro Muncie, Indiana, for example, emptied its entire economic development budget to develop twenty acres of suburban greenfields for Brevini Wind's U.S. headquarters (lured from suburban Chicago) and wind-turbine gearbox manufacturing facility. Local officials also purchased land for the construction of a new one-and-a-quarter-mile freight-rail spur, funded with $2.3 million in federal stimulus support. This, adjacent to a city crowded with former manufacturing infrastructure, including rail, was once occupied by a thriving gear and auto-transmission industry (Tumber 2012: 93–95).[3] More recently, Janesville, Wisconsin, competed with two other Wisconsin communities to land a medical isotope manufacturer and its hundred or so jobs. As part of the deal, the city will purchase and develop an eighty-four-acre parcel of prime farmland to site the facility, among other incentives, for a total cost of about $9 million—leaving an adjacent shovel-ready site lying fallow (Nelesen 2012).

Over the past ten years, the practice of smokestack chasing has continued unabated and perhaps escalated given the desperate need for jobs in the industrial heartland. State subsidy programs that fuel this competition have led not only to job loss and lower pay but also to sprawl far from urban centers. Even worse, companies have feathered their own nests with these subsidies while moving their plants around *within the same metropolitan region*. It is nearly impossible to get a comprehensive picture of this phenomenon. As documented by two 2012 reports, states keep incomplete, inconsistent records on the five most common property-tax incentives for business, which cost $5 to 10 billion annually in lost revenue, and most have only meager programs in place to evaluate their effectiveness (Kenyon, Langley, and Paquin 2012: 2–3, 30–44; Pew Center on the States 2012). None track manufacturing subsidies specifically.

One study, however, sheds lights on pervasive patterns. In "Paid to Sprawl," Greg LeRoy and Leigh McIlvaine analyze the incomplete data on Cleveland and Cincinnati between 1996 and 2005. They show that the vast majority of moves subsidized by just two state economic development programs designed to revitalize underserved urban communities (and not including TIFs, which are not state tracked at all), sent facilities and jobs outward to less settled, more affluent communities on the exurban fringe. In Cleveland, four-fifths of these relocations were outbound and, on average, sited five miles from the urban core; in Cincinnati, almost three-quarters of these projects sprawled outward at an average three-mile distance from the central city. Altogether, 164 firms and some 14,500 jobs were moved—presumably to greenfields—by taking advantage of lucrative incentive programs intended to alleviate blight and reduce poverty. Since much of this support comes in the form of property-tax abatement, it diminishes the tax base for public schools, and the data do not track for other rich subsidies such as job training grants and investment tax credits. It is not even clear whether "incentive shopping" within the same labor market produces a net gain in jobs (LeRoy and McIlvaine 2011).

What is clear is that, to varying degrees, economic development programs intended to combat sprawl now subsidize it. In the words of the LeRoy and McIlvaine, "they reduce economic opportunity in neighborhoods with higher rates of poverty, many people of color, and/or households receiving public assistance," thus deepening inequity and further burdening taxpayers already paying for these subsidies. "Moreover, as the subsidies help more jobs locate further from urban cores, they are less likely to be transit accessible," the authors argue. "This contributes to traffic congestion, global warming and air pollution, while isolating carless workers." And they are costly. Of the 152 projects in Cleveland and Cincinnati receiving property-tax abatements between 1996 and 2005, adequate data are available for 116. They alone totaled $29.7 million (2011: 2–3, ii).

So, what value does arresting subsidized workplace sprawl have for smaller industrial cities in particular—in addition to that of preserving nearby farmland for agriculture? Here I will outline three considerations: the role of next-generation manufacturing in the productive green economy, the availability of brownfields suited to this new work, and the role that scale plays in the metro-wide cooperation required to curb sprawl—manufacturing and otherwise. Due to the dearth of data on all three scores and because urban scale is rarely taken into account in any case, I will have to be somewhat suggestive and broad rather than conclusive.

By the mid-1910s, the auto industry anchored the historic center of American manufacturing in the Northeast and Midwest. When Detroit automakers began to deconcentrate during and after World War II, they did so in a pattern that spread the work to smaller industrial cities, eventually reaching into the right-to-work states of the South. Today, "Detroit" comprises the vast supply-chain network known as Auto Alley, stretching from Ohio, Indiana, and Michigan and running south to Georgia and Alabama, feeding parts into some forty assembly plants. Just-in-time sourcing has kept much of this business afloat, serving Japanese automakers generally concentrated in the South, along with U.S. firms in the North. The revival of the auto industry under the Obama administration has breathed new, if tentative, life into these third- and second-tier component firms (Helper 2011). If we get serious about cultivating a clean-energy economy, through a national renewable energy standard (RES), transferal of subsidies from Big Oil, and/ or some type of carbon tax, smaller industrial cities have the manufacturing skills and infrastructure to produce the thousands of components comprising windmill turbines, solar arrays, next-generation hydro, and biomass processing equipment; weatherizing material and green building HVAC systems; energy-efficient appliances; lighting systems; water-efficient and recycled-content products; and, of course, low-carbon automotives and other forms of transportation. A recent Brookings study shows that the low-carbon economy is almost three times as manufacturing-dependent as the overall economy and achieves twice the export intensity of the average American job—this, in 2009—and has great potential to grow, with strength to lower the trade deficit. Although it may seem counterintuitive, low-carbon manufacturing makes a disproportionately large contribution to ecosystem preservation and could disproportionately benefit the smaller industrial cities that ground its future supply chain as well (Muro, Rothwell, and Saha 2011; Helper, Krueger, and Wial 2012a: 14–15).

It would be a shame of incalculable proportions if this work were allowed to sprawl on to greenfields, offsetting gains made in the reduction of greenhouse gas emissions, encroaching on economically valuable farmland, and putting jobs at greater distance from the urban working poor. And it is hardly necessary since the Northeast and Midwest are home to the lion's share of the country's brownfields. (These regions also have a relatively high volume of suburban grayfields, with similar reuse capacity.) A provisional 2008 study shows that 4.5 acres of open land are conserved for each acre of redeveloped brownfields. Brownfield development also saves between 20 and 40 percent of both vehicle miles traveled and transportation-related greenhouse gas emissions (GHG). The economics are also favorable. Each dollar of public investment in brownfields leverages $8 in total investment. Brownfields (and greyfields) generally require much less in costly new infrastructure since they are already outfitted with sewer and electrical lines, water service, and service roads. One study puts the savings at $1 versus $10, though such figures are highly project dependent. And where HUD and the

U.S. Small Business Administration estimate that one job requires $35,000 in public investment, that figure for brownfield site preparation is $5,700. Brownfield development also leads to a higher tax base for cities strapped by legacy costs and a disproportionate population of working poor. A 2010 survey of redeveloped brownfields by the U.S. Conference of Mayors found that, since 1993, fifty cities had generated $309 million in additional local tax revenue from these projects; fifty-eight cities estimated that they could collect as much as $1.3 billion annually in local taxes on redeveloped brownfield sites (Paull 2008; U.S. Conference of Mayors 2010).

For a variety of reasons, over the past ten years, brownfields increasingly have been redeveloped for housing—both market-rate and affordable (Bartsch 2006). This laudable infill-development trend facilitates density while preserving a city's architectural heritage and urban fabric. Yet "weak-market" smaller industrial cities in need of good jobs accessible through a variety of transportation choices should pursue such a course with caution. Once a property has been taken out of zoning for industrial uses, the designation is difficult to restore. Given their still-active place in the automotive value chain and signs of U.S. manufacturing growth, smaller industrial cities can fairly anticipate future demand for industrial activity. Like all "postindustrial" cities, large and small, their older, urban multilevel brownfields can be repurposed for housing, commercial uses, and retail. The next section will explore these facilities' potential reuses as urban workshops for artisanal manufacturing and the fine arts—reuse activities that have been around since the 1980s—but also for new-manufacturing-based innovation and production work. Farther from the urban core, however, small industrial cities also have an abundance of vacant industrial property that is relatively newer—that is, postwar—and requires little investment in infrastructure upgrades for current use by larger manufacturing firms.

The economic and environmental benefits of repurposing these brownfields for new manufacturing could redound disproportionately to smaller industrial cities. Urban planners and economic developers are again seeing value in keeping brownfields in industrial use (Badger 2011). But unless the maze of localities comprising metropolitan regions can find ways of working together, cities will face an upward battle competing for businesses preferring to start afresh—without layers of legacy codes and restrictions and with access to plentiful subsidies—on greenfields. Yet smaller industrial cities could have an advantage in putting together the kinds of cooperative metropolitan agreements necessary to prevent sprawl, since their surrounding communities have themselves been disproportionately hurt by the seemingly inexorable march toward fringe development. Moreover, in contrast with big metros accountable to multiple layers of bureaucracy (particularly in transportation planning) and numerous constituencies, smaller cities are "more nimble," as Center for Community Progress president Dan Kildee has observed. That is, they can get interested parties to the table more easily and thus get things done faster (Tumber 2012: 69). Dayton metro area officials, for example, developed a cooperative, largely voluntary regional system in 2006 to promote economic growth within the city and established suburbs and to stanch the fiscally, environmentally, socially self-defeating competitive pressures induced by exurban sprawl. Urban regions in Cuyahoga and Summit Counties (Cleveland, Akron, and Canton) have more recently developed similar plans on the Dayton model (*Creative Government in the 21st Century* 2006). State policies—such as subsidy incentives that deter poaching and tie support to transit accessibility, devise systems for tracking all subsidy programs, and encourage regional tax-revenue sharing—could facilitate such cooperative arrangements and give them teeth (LeRoy and McIlvaine 2011: iii–iv).

Workshops

A strange conceptual turn took place as we made our way through the digital revolution: it became conventional wisdom that, as the United States morphed into a knowledge economy, flailing smaller industrial cities should make the switch—and fast—lest they find themselves casualties of the big sort being carried out by globalization. Yet it never made much sense for these places to base their economic development plans on Silicon Valley's basic-science, "breakthrough" model of innovation, which bifurcates knowledge and production work and supports neoliberal justification for distant outsourcing. What can work are strategies that repurpose a community's "working knowledge"—the shop floor skills, engineering and technical acumen, and business management experience honed over generations—for new work (Collins 1998). For the new low-carbon products for which market demand is rising, "transformational" strategies and new forms of applied-science process innovation, which build on a community's historical skill base and infrastructure, show particular promise. Toledo, for example, has become a center of solar-energy innovation, based on its industrial roots in glassmaking. Taking a transformational approach, the mid-size city long worked to transition from Glass City to Solar Valley, now specializing in thin-film photovoltaics. Researchers at the University of Toledo had focused on solar technology since the mid-1980s. By 2007, the school had launched the Wright Center for Photovoltaics, Innovation, and Commercialization, which has provided research and business incubation services that, to date, have spun off some twelve solar firms, one of which (FirstSolar) is a world leader (Fitzgerald 2010: 12–18, 56–59). By 2011, Ohio's (meaning Toledo's) solar manufacturing success was second only to that of Oregon, and the Spanish firm Isofoton had announced plans to open a plant near Toledo (on the site of a former auto supplier) employing 330 workers (Cable 2011; Harrison 2011; Sklar 2011).

For a variety of reasons, including dubious Chinese trade practices and growing pains within the industry, it remains to be seen whether Toledo will be able to hold on to its solar manufacturing jobs, much less to increase their number. The same is true of the tens of thousands of manufacturing jobs—created primarily in the Midwest and the South—by a revitalized U.S. auto industry and the re-shoring of production work over the past two years (Chavez 2011; Helper, Krueger, and Wial 2012b). To retain and multiply these jobs, firms large and small must capture the manufacturing-dependent knowledge work called for by Cohen and Zysman in 1987. This incremental product and processing innovation takes place on or near the shop floor. Process innovation requires intricate collaboration among corporate leaders, engineers, applied-science R&D specialists, and workers. It involves scaling R&D at an early stage of production and, thus, requires continuously fine-tuning the entire manufacturing process down the value chain. Process refinement reverberates throughout the thousands of small and medium-size firms that constitute the supply chain, and increasingly it has been captured by our foreign manufacturing-based competitors. Although these businesses employ some 30 percent of American industrial workers and are positioned to expand with the anticipated growth of U.S. manufacturing, they receive little funding for applied research or workforce development. With improved access to financing and lifelong education for both workers and management, decent wages, and policies that facilitate community investment rather than runaway subsidies, smaller industrial cities stand to prosper from successful, process-refined for-export industries (Helper, Krueger, and Wial 2012a; Breznitz and Cowhey 2012; Fuchs 2012).

Another form of working knowledge to which smaller industrial cities are peculiarly suited by cultural inheritance is a bit more obscure but no less crucial to the entrepreneurial ethos of the new industrial economy as it reckons with global warming. It involves restoring respect for manual work, of making and repairing things in response to an age of consumption and disposability, and of reintegrating intellectual abstraction—high-tech and otherwise—with craft knowledge. Older brownfield sites (mills, warehouses, and manufacturing facilities often located on rivers and railways near residential neighborhoods), which smaller industrial cities have in abundance, are well-suited to housing this work and the cross-pollination of ideas and skills such proximity facilitates. As small-and-shrinking industrial cities struggle to resize their urban footprints, they have a historic opportunity to repurpose their brownfield and vacant industrial sites not only for manufacturing but also for workshops devoted to expanding their citizens' applied "working knowledge"—high-tech knowledge work included, but not unduly privileged as in years past.

Over the past three years, in response to the Great Recession and the longer-term shift toward contract work, an urban workshop movement has mushroomed throughout the world, notably in smaller industrial cities such as Rochester, Dayton, Fort Wayne, and Portland, Maine. Generically referred to as hackerspaces or makerspaces, each is idiosyncratic, in keeping with its independent-yet-community-based spirit, but generally it provides individual space and shared equipment for light manufacturing and small business start-ups and artisanal facilities for metalworkers, fabric and jewelry designers, woodworkers, and fine artists, whose technical skills and conceptual acumen are indispensible to the generative mix (Tweeney 2009; Hackerspaces.org/wiki/, accessed March 4, 2012).

Somerville, Massachusetts, is home to one of the largest of these nonprofit facilities, called Artisan's Asylum. Situated in a former envelope factory, it has grown from a 1,000 square-foot operation, in May 2010. By March 2012 it took up 31,000 square feet of the building's 300,000-square-foot footprint. With seven full shop and craft areas and 200 regular paying members, it has a wait list and is poised to grow larger: in March 2012, founder and president Gui Cavalcanti was negotiating a lease with a nearby, expanding office co-working outfit. Between the twenty-five or so classes it offers and its inexpensive membership fees and rents, Artisan's Asylum is self-supporting, with no additional public subsidies or private support.

When I paid a visit to Artisan's Asylum, I half expected to find a hipster rendition of earlier countercultural arts collectives, blending fine artists with crafts people making pottery, jewelry, wooden salad bowls, and fix-up bikes, with a few computer geeks thrown in for good measure. Instead, the place was filled with computer-numerical control (CNC) machining and metalworking equipment, electronic oscillators, sophisticated woodworking machinery, and a $20,000 3-D printer. Half of the tenants are professional contract manufacturers, according to Cavalcanti, making custom medical devices, upgrading the electronics of commercial-scale appliances, and fine-tuning robotics tools, among other projects. Cavalcanti himself is a mechanical and robotics engineer formerly employed by a major defense contractor who found the work too stifling. He is quick to point out, however, that the Somerville community workshop does not cater to its professional contract manufacturers. Its fundamental purpose is to share equipment, skills, and ideas, and to make them available to whoever is interested in expanding his or her working knowledge.

Urban community workshops could also work hand in glove with community colleges and vo-tech high schools to train the next generation of skilled manual laborers. In Massachusetts alone, tens of thousands of machinist jobs will age out as the baby-boom generation retires, with not nearly enough younger workers equipped with the skills simply to replace them (Massachusetts Technology Collaborative 2011: 21). Over the past thirty years, as the United States moved into a short-sighted version of the knowledge economy, planned for the end of manufacturing, and embraced consumer culture as never before, the educational infrastructure that once supported shop-floor skills has died. Vocational programs in shop and "home economics"—sewing, food preparation, and domestic budgeting— that, until the 1970s, were a part of even nonvocational public schools, have been replaced by beautician and hospitality-service programs in the vo-tech schools and by an exclusive focus on math, science, and the liberal arts in the regular public schools. With the rising costs of tuition at institutions of higher learning and the need to develop practical skills for the next industrial economy, state and federal governments are just beginning to boost funding for community colleges and vo-tech programs: the Obama administration has pledged $8 billion dollars to community college redevelopment. (Federal support, which had supplemented local funding since the postwar GI-bill era, had been cut drastically by the Reagan administration.) As these programs expand, they too could take up space in urban workshops, rather than in costly new physical plants, where students can learn practical skills in close proximity to experienced workers, artists, and innovators in their fields. This sort of setting, nestled into a compact urban fabric, can facilitate the sort of business clustering and cross-specialty knowledge spillovers that economic development theorists from Adam Smith to Jane Jacobs and Michael Porter have long observed is critical to economic strength.

As Matthew Crawford argues in *Shop Class as Soulcraft*, the very notion of "knowledge work" is a ghastly macroeconomic descendent of the old industrial assembly line, which radically separated management from manual labor, thinking from making, control from execution (Crawford 2009). Today, the popular lament that we, as a country, no longer "make things," while not entirely true, takes most poignant form on the personal level, from the skills mismatch between the desperately unemployed and available jobs, to a generation of computer-savvy college students so inundated by niche marketing and the disposable ethic of advanced consumer culture that they do not know how to cook, sew, or grow, much less make simple home or car repairs. Working knowledge, reintegrating head and hand work, not only instills self-respect and agency but also is necessary to grasp the big intellectual picture. For too long, business, design, and engineering students, as well as liberal arts majors, have been thinking in a contracting vacuum of abstraction. As liberal arts colleges and universities struggle through something of an identity crisis, those located in smaller industrial cities could make valuable use of urban workshops, along with efforts to develop local food systems and manufacturing, to revitalize their civic-intellectual purposes (Carlson 2012).

Conclusion: The New Environmentalism and Economic Development

The term "new environmentalism" has been coined to reflect the ideals of sustainable urban placemaking, a constructive vision that balances the restrictive measures introduced by the twentieth-century environmentalist movement. Where the latter concentrates on wilderness protection and pollution controls, the new environmentalism attends to the "people habitat" of built form and shared public spaces and thus fosters local civic participation in community planning (Benfield 2012). In focusing on the structured environment and social equity, however, it tends to overlook the third element in what sustainability advocates call the triple bottom line: economic development.

Green placemaking in long-struggling smaller industrial cities must involve more than redesigning public places, restoring ecological habitats, and (where appropriate) resizing urban footprints, as critical as such projects are to the long-term economic health of these places (Mallach 2012c). It also requires culling true economic diversity from the historical and natural resources at hand and occupying the regional landscape in a more resilient, more equitable fashion than that advanced by either the old industrial economy or the "new" neoliberal one. As smaller industrial cities reinvent themselves for a more prosperous future, their fields, factories, and workshops offer unrivaled opportunity for putting new ideas to work in a low-carbon world.

CHAPTER 13

Promoting Workforce Readiness
for Urban Growth

Laura W. Perna

Between 2003 and 2009, the gap between the educational attainment of the population and the educational demands of available jobs (that is, "structural unemployment") increased in all but four of the nation's hundred largest metropolitan areas (Rothwell and Berube 2011). Given that a larger education gap between the demand and supply of educated workers is associated with a higher unemployment rate in the metropolitan area (2011), these data demonstrate the need to improve educational attainment in all metropolitan areas.

Equally troubling, educational attainment tends to be lower for demographic groups that tend to be relatively overrepresented in our nation's metropolitan areas' central cities. *The State of Metropolitan America* report reveals a consistent pattern of racial/ethnic group differences: educational attainment is higher for Whites and Asians than for Blacks and Hispanics in all hundred of the nation's largest metropolitan areas (Berube 2010a). These racial/ethnic group differences in educational attainment likely contribute to observed racial/ethnic group differences in unemployment and other labor market outcomes, as unemployment rates are notably higher for Blacks and Hispanics than for Whites (14.1 and 10.7 percent versus 7.3 percent in February 2012; Bureau of Labor Statistics 2012).

As Edward Glaeser argues in his chapter in this volume, education is key to a city's economic and social success. This chapter goes one step further. It argues that educational attainment is a reasonable proxy for workforce readiness and documents the low levels of workforce readiness in urban areas. Recognizing some of the challenges associated with improving educational attainment, the chapter draws from a review of available data and research to offer seven recommendations for promoting workforce readiness of workers in our nation's urban areas.

What We Know: Educational Attainment Improves Labor Market Outcomes

With higher levels of educational attainment come improved labor market outcomes in both central cities and suburbs of metropolitan areas. Table 13.1 shows that labor market outcomes are lower on average in central cities and that, on average, in the central city as for the metropolitan area as a whole, labor market outcomes improve as the level of educational attainment rises. As just one example, in 2009 labor force participation rates in Baltimore city ranged from 34.7 percent for those who had not completed high school, to 57.8 percent for those who had graduated from high school, to 70.4 percent for those with some college or an associate's degree, to 73.6 percent for those who had completed at least a bachelor's degree (Bureau of Labor Statistics 2009). Unemployment rates also improve as educational attainment rose, declining in Baltimore (as one example) from 26.2 percent for those with less than high school, to 14.0 percent for high school graduates, to 6.8 percent for those with some college or an associate's degree, to 4.9 percent for those with at least a bachelor's degree (Bureau of Labor Statistics 2009). Table 13.1 also shows that these patterns are replicated in other metropolitan areas and center cities across the United States.

The benefits of higher levels of educational attainment are especially dramatic in an economic downturn. The negative implications of the Great Recession have been particularly severe for both individuals and metropolitan areas with the lowest levels of educational attainment (Berube 2010b). Even with the continued high overall unemployment rate in July 2011 (9.1 percent), unemployment rates were substantially lower for individuals who held a bachelor's degree (4.3 percent) than for those who held only a high school diploma (9.3 percent) and those who did not complete high school (15.0 percent) (Rothwell and Berube 2011). Between 2007 and 2009, metropolitan areas with the highest levels of educational attainment experienced smaller declines in employment rates than other metropolitan areas, even among workers without a high school diploma (Berube 2010b).

Table 13.1. Labor Market Outcomes in Selected Metropolitan Areas for Noninstitutional Population Age 25 Years and Older, 2009 Annual Average

Metro area	Educational attainment	Civilian labor force (%)		Unemployment rate (%)	
		Metro area	Central city	Metro area	Central city
Baltimore	Less than high school	40.9	34.7	13.6	26.2
	High school graduate	63.0	57.8	9.5	14.0
	Some college/associate	74.2	70.4	5.1	6.8
	Bachelor degree	79.9	73.6	2.9	4.9
Chicago	Less than high school	51.6	47.0	15.2	16.4
	High school graduate	62.5	57.9	10.4	11.6
	Some college/associate	73.5	71.3	9.7	10.6
	Bachelor degree	79.7	81.7	5.7	7.0
Cleveland	Less than high school	36.9	38.8	17.3	24.0
	High school graduate	64.1	52.7	12.7	15.4
	Some college/associate	69.9	65.4	6.9	12.4
	Bachelor degree	81.9	77.1	6.2	13.5
Dallas	Less than high school	62.3	65.7	9.5	11.9
	High school graduate	68.5	65.2	7.4	11.4
	Some college/associate	74.5	70.7	6.8	9.9
	Bachelor's degree	80.6	76.0	3.9	1.6
Denver	Less than high school	58.6	54.9	13.2	14.2
	High school graduate	68.7	66.5	6.5	12.0
	Some college/associate	75.8	78.6	8.3	9.4
	Bachelor's degree	80.1	86.4	3.5	4.2
Detroit	Less than high school	34.5	33.8	21.5	38.8
	High school graduate	56.2	50.6	20.2	26.7
	Some college/associate	67.8	55.4	14.0	18.1
	Bachelor's degree	75.4	64.5	7.9	6.2
Houston	Less than high school	57.8	60.3	11.1	11.0
	High school graduate	66.9	65.8	8.1	10.5
	Some college/associate	71.7	71.3	7.5	9.3
	Bachelor's degree	77.7	74.9	3.7	3.7
Las Vegas	Less than high school	60.9	55.2	19.4	17.3
	High school graduate	68.7	70.4	11.5	13.4
	Some college/associate	72.5	73.5	9.6	10.4
	Bachelor's degree	76.6	72.1	6.6	4.2
Los Angeles	Less than high school	58.1	64.2	13.5	13.9
	High school graduate	64.3	64.6	11.3	12.5
	Some college/associate	70.9	67.7	9.8	13.8
	Bachelor's degree	78.4	80.6	6.6	8.5

Table 13.1. (continued)

Metro area	Educational attainment	Civilian labor force (%)		Unemployment rate (%)	
		Metro area	Central city	Metro area	Central city
Minneapolis	Less than high school	44.6	48.6	20.3	25.4
	High school graduate	62.9	69.6	9.8	12.3
	Some college/associate	78.6	77.0	7.7	12.9
	Bachelor degree	81.8	84.5	4.1	5.8
New York	Less than high school	46.2	42.7	11.2	10.4
	High school graduate	60.2	57.9	8.0	8.2
	Some college/associate	72.2	70.2	9.0	9.9
	Bachelor degree	78.3	79.0	5.6	6.2
Philadelphia	Less than high school	35.1	32.8	13.3	18.1
	High school graduate	59.2	55.7	10.0	12.3
	Some college/associate	71.3	68.4	10.0	10.3
	Bachelor degree	79.0	72.4	4.8	4.7
Phoenix	Less than high school	55.5	54.6	12.2	10.8
	High school graduate	63.5	69.8	9.7	8.6
	Some college/associate	68.7	68.2	8.6	9.3
	Bachelor degree	77.1	82.1	4.8	5.3
San Diego	Less than high school	54.0	55.3	9.6	10.4
	High school graduate	55.6	61.6	9.0	6.0
	Some college/associate	68.3	73.8	8.7	7.0
	Bachelor degree	77.5	83.8	4.7	4.7
St. Louis	Less than high school	41.0	36.4	21.2	18.1
	High school graduate	65.2	59.0	11.8	19.9
	Some college/associate	76.9	72.0	8.0	7.4
	Bachelor degree	79.9	78.6	5.0	8.7
Washington	Less than high school	58.3	49.9	10.9	13.6
	High school graduate	67.8	58.4	8.2	16.5
	Some college/associate	74.3	64.4	5.7	11.2
	Bachelor degree	83.0	83.5	3.5	3.9

Bureau of Labor Statistics 2009, Table 28, www.bls.gov/opub/gp/pdf/gp09_28.pdf.

Metropolitan areas with higher levels of educational attainment are also better able to recover from deindustrialization. The metropolitan areas that experienced the largest increases in unemployment rates during the Great Recession were those that had both large gaps between the educational attainment of the population and the educational requirements of available jobs (that is, high "structural unemployment") and high concentrations of such industries as wood product manufacturing, textile mills, construction, and transportation equipment manufacturing. More specifically, between 2005 and 2011 the average unemployment rate was about 2 percentage points lower in the metropolitan areas with the lowest education gap and the most resilient industry composition than in the metropolitan areas with the highest education gap and most vulnerable industry composition (Rothwell and Berube 2011).

The Challenge: Low Levels of Workforce Readiness

One reason for the positive relationship between educational attainment and desirable labor-market outcomes is that educational attainment is a measure of the readiness of individuals to perform available jobs. According to one survey of 400 human resource professionals across the United States, employers wish that individuals with all levels of educational attainment had a broader set of basic and applied skills (Casner-Lotto and Benner 2006). But employers' dissatisfaction is substantially greater for workers who possess only a high school diploma than for those who hold at least a bachelor's degree. Nearly half (40 percent) of employers perceive high school graduates to be "deficient" in overall preparation for entry-level employment, with particular weaknesses in such basic skills as writing in English, mathematics, and reading comprehension and such applied skills as written communications, critical thinking/problem solving, and professionalism/work ethic. In contrast, only a small fraction of employers perceive that two-year college graduates (11 percent) and four-year college graduates (9 percent) are insufficiently prepared for the entry-level jobs they hold.

Various other indicators point to the increasing importance of educational attainment to workforce success. For instance, additional results from the survey by Casner-Lotto and Benner (2006) reveal that, over the next five years, a substantial share of employers expect to hire fewer workers who possess only a high school diploma (27.7 percent of respondents). In contrast, more than half (59 percent) expect to hire more four-year college graduates and about half (50 percent) expect to hire more two-year college graduates (Casner-Lotto and Benner 2006).

Given the benefits of higher levels of educational attainment to the economic and social well-being of metropolitan areas and individuals, efforts to raise college-degree attainment especially among Blacks and Hispanics, individuals from low-income families, and individuals living in our nation's central cities must not only continue but also become more effective. Also, available data suggest the benefits of an approach that increases the emphasis on high-quality educational programs that result in workforce readiness but not necessarily a college degree. Projections of the educational attainment required for future jobs suggest the value to both individuals and local labor markets of credentials beyond high school but less than an associate's or bachelor's degree.

Drawing on data from the Bureau of Labor Statistics and their assumptions about the continued "upskilling" of current jobs (Zumeta 2011), Anthony Carnevale, Nicole Smith, and Jeffrey Stohl (2010) report that 63 percent of jobs in 2018 will require some level and type of postsecondary education. In contrast, only 28 percent of jobs in 1973 required workers with education beyond high school. Moreover, while Carnevale and colleagues estimate that, in 2007, 59 percent of all jobs required some postsecondary education, nearly a fifth (17 percent) of these jobs required some college but not a degree. Of all jobs in 2007, 10 percent required an associate's degree, 21 percent required a bachelor's degree, and 11 percent required more than a bachelor's degree (Carnevale, Smith, and Stohl 2010). Consistent with these estimates, data collected from focus groups and interviews of leaders of large and mid-sized businesses in Texas and Ohio in 2011 suggest that, although a four-year degree may have many benefits, this degree is not required for economic and social prosperity (Farkas 2011).

Employers are also critical of the basic and interpersonal skills of all workers, including those with only a high school education. Among other recent reports (see Perna 2012 for a review), the National Governors Association's 2011 report, *Degrees for What Jobs?*, notes the mismatch between the qualifications of workers and the skills required for available jobs. The report concludes that "businesses and states are not getting the talent they want—and students and job seekers are not getting the jobs they want" (8).

Particularly important is the availability of workers prepared for "skilled jobs," that is jobs that require more than a high school diploma (Carnevale, Smith, and Stohl 2010). Based on their review of labor market trends, Anthony Carnevale and his colleagues predict that the economy will continue a transformation begun in the early 1980s from an industrial to "a new services economy that demands more education and different skills of its workers"

(Carnevale, Smith, and Stohl 2010: 6). The occupations with the greatest projected job openings from 2008 through 2018—management, business operations specialists, financial specialists, computer and mathematical science occupations, architects and technicians, life and physical scientists, social scientists and technicians, among others—all tend to require at least some postsecondary education (Carnevale, Smith, and Stohl 2010).

Changes in technology underlie these changes in the nature of available jobs (Carnevale, Smith, and Stohl 2010). Regardless of the industry, technological changes, particularly changes in information technology, are creating greater demand for "workers with more education" as these individuals "have the expertise to handle more complex tasks and activities" (2010: 15). At the same time, technological changes reduce the demand for workers with low levels of education, by eliminating the need for these jobs across industries (2010). Summarizing the changes in the economy and the implications of these changes for individual workers and metropolitan areas, Carnevale et al. conclude that

> Jobs created in recent recoveries looked nothing like those that were lost, and the people hired for those new positions looked nothing like the people laid off from the old ones. In the past two recessions, the typical job loser was a high school-educated male in a blue collar job, such as manufacturing or construction, working in the middle of the country. In the past two recoveries, the typical job gainer was a female with a postsecondary education who lived on either coast and worked in a service occupation—particularly healthcare, education, or business services. That picture is not changing. (16)

Seven Recommendations for Promoting Workforce Readiness in Urban Areas

Much of the existing research examining the effects of initiatives designed to improve the readiness of workers for current and future jobs has a number of limitations (Perna 2012). Perhaps most importantly, existing research provides few insights into which programs and approaches cause improved outcomes or how existing programs may be producing desired results (Perna 2012). Moreover, existing research not only uses varying definitions of workforce readiness but also considers only a narrow range of short-term outcomes (typically earnings), ignoring the noneconomic and longer-term outcomes that individuals and society also value.

Nonetheless, one recent review (Perna 2012) identifies many dimensions of the perceived mismatch between the readiness of workers and the skills and qualifications that current and future jobs require. While acknowledging the weaknesses in the existing knowledge base, the volume also offers a number of useful perspectives for understanding how to improve workforce readiness, particularly among workers in our nation's metropolitan areas. The final chapter identifies seven recommendations for preparing students for work that cut across the volume's chapters (Perna 2012). The seven recommendations are the following:

1. Provide a range of high-quality educational opportunities that recognize that not all individuals will earn college degrees.

2. Develop mechanisms that enable students to choose to participate in different education and career pathways without "tracking" them into specific options.

3. Ensure that all individuals have the information and knowledge required to choose the most appropriate education and career pathways.

4. Recognize that both generic and specific skills are required for jobs and careers in metropolitan America.

5. Develop mechanisms that support meaningful collaboration between education providers and employers.

6. Provide the supports and structures required to ensure that students successfully complete the educational programs that they enter.

7. Use public policy to encourage and support improved linkages between education and employment. (263)

The first two recommendations recognize that a traditional four-year bachelor's degree program is not the only, or even the ideal, postsecondary educational goal for all students and acknowledges the advantages of the diverse array of postsecondary educational options available in the United States. These two recommendations are also consistent with the Pathways to Prosperity Project's (2011) emphasis on the benefits of multiple high-quality pathways from high school into adulthood. A multiple pathways approach assumes that some type of postsecondary education and training is increasingly required for economic and social well-being, even if a traditional four-year college degree is not the optimal path for everyone (Pathways to Prosperity Project 2011).

Along the same lines, the volume also notes the promise of various different educational sectors and providers in promoting workforce readiness (Perna 2012). In the United States, a diverse set of educational providers is available to promote the readiness of workers for current and future jobs. These providers include career and technical education, for-profit postsecondary educational institutions, community colleges, and four-year colleges and universities.

Nonetheless, in their current forms, these multiple pathways are not without challenges (Perna 2012). For example, designating career and technical education (CTE) as a viable option requires first overcoming the legacy of the past failure of these programs. Noting the success of CTE in other nations, Nancy Hoffman (2012) describes the potential of career and technical education for effectively preparing youth for productive employment. But as Hoffman and others (Pathways to Prosperity Project 2011) note, attention to career and technical education as a potential effective and productive pathway for promoting workforce readiness requires improving the quality of CTE programs and changing negative perceptions of value of CTE. Along the same lines, William Tierney (2012) discusses the many questions that currently exist about for-profit postsecondary education institutions, including the strengths and weaknesses of relying on for-profit postsecondary education institutions in preparing students (both traditional age and adult) for work.

The third recommendation underscores the importance of improving information and knowledge about available educational and career choices (Perna 2012). Along the same lines, the Pathways to Prosperity report also recognizes the need to provide mechanisms including personalized career and college counseling that enable individuals to identify the option that best meets their goals and requirements. Developing mechanisms that provide individualized counseling that ensures that all students have the opportunity to participate in the full range of options is critical. Such efforts must avoid and correct a history in which low-income students and students of color were disproportionately tracked into career and technical education programs that had consistently poor outcomes, as well as the current tendency of Black, Hispanic, and low-income students to enroll in high-cost for-profit institutions of unknown quality (Perna 2012).

The fourth recommendation pertains to the nature of the education and skills that should be provided. Although "workforce readiness" has not been consistently defined or operationalized, available data and research suggest that workers need both generic and specific skills (Perna 2012). Moreover, existing research demonstrates the positive outcomes that are associated with participation in programs that intentionally connect and integrate vocational training into academic courses. Known as pathways programs, career pathways, and work-based learning initiatives, these initiatives include career academies; Washington State's Integrated Basic Education and Skills Training (I-BEST) program; Youth Corps, Job Corps, and ChalleNGe programs; and the U.S. Department of Labor Youth Opportunities Program.

The fifth recommendation pertains to the relationship between educational providers and employers (Perna 2012). By developing meaningful collaborative relationships with employers, educational providers may help improve students' readiness for work (Perna 2012). Similarly, the Pathways to Prosperity Project (2011) notes the need for greater employer involvement in preparing students for work, suggesting the benefits of employer-sponsored internships and employer assistance with program development. The Pathways to Prosperity Project also observes that a collaborative relationship with employers may improve students' exposure to work environments and provide students with beneficial mentoring and supervision.

The sixth recommendation stresses the importance of enabling students to finish the educational programs that they start (Perna 2012). Regardless of the type of educational program a student chooses, students must also have access to the resources and supports that are required to persist to program completion. As illustrated by the degree completion data in Table 13.2, too few students are completing the postsecondary educational programs in which they enroll. The failure to complete these programs has substantial costs for individuals and society. Individuals lose the real costs of funds invested (via savings, earnings, and/or loans) in tuition, fees, books, supplies, and such, as well as the costs of earnings not received from working rather than attending class. Society loses the costs of financial aid provided to students as well as the funds a state government appropriates to the educational institution to offset the costs of providing the education. "Society"—and metropolitan areas in particular—loses the opportunity to improve the individual's productivity and future labor market contributions, and the resulting enhancements to the economic health and well-being of the community.

Table 13.2. Graduation Rates of First-time Postsecondary Students Who Started as Full-Time Degree-seeking Students, by Sex, Race/Ethnicity, and Level and Control of Institution Where Student Started

Level & Control of Institution	Total		White		Black	
	Male	Female	Male	Female	Male	Female
% completing bachelor's degrees in 4 years (2002 start)						
All 4-year institutions	31.3	40.5	33.8	43.9	14.7	24.3
For-profit institutions	17.0	11.6	20.9	14.0	11.8	8.7
Public institutions	24.5	34.3	26.6	37.2	11.0	20.9
Not-for-profit institutions	46.3	54.7	49.1	57.8	22.9	34.0
% completing bachelor's degrees in 6 years (2002 start)						
All 4-year institutions	54.1	59.7	57.3	62.5	34.0	44.2
For-profit institutions	23.6	20.5	27.8	23.1	16.6	16.1
Public institutions	51.7	57.5	54.4	59.9	32.9	43.7
Not-for-profit institutions	61.9	66.7	64.8	69.1	38.6	49.4
Open admissions	25.4	28.6	31.2	34.4	14.8	21.1
90 percent or more accepted	42.5	48.8	44.9	51.2	26.0	33.6
75.0 to 89.9 percent accepted	51.3	57.2	53.8	59.6	34.9	44.2
50.0 to 74.9 percent accepted	56.4	62.7	59.5	65.5	36.9	48.4
25.0 to 49.9 percent accepted	71.0	74.7	77.2	80.2	39.8	51.7
Less than 25.0 percent accepted	82.3	83.5	84.5	84.4	53.4	60.8
% completing certificates or associate's degrees within 150% normal time (2005 start)						
All 2-year institutions	25.3	29.3	27.0	29.9	18.6	25.2
For-profit institutions	57.7	57.7	64.8	61.6	43.1	49.4
Public institutions	19.9	21.2	22.1	23.8	12.0	12.1
Not-for-profit institutions	44.5	51.3	49.1	54.9	38.7	44.9

National Center for Education Statistics (2011). Digest of Education Statistics 2010, Table 341.

Finally, available data and research also point to the role of public policy in encouraging and improving workforce readiness (Perna 2012). Among the promising public policies are those that include attention to sectoral initiatives that promote the development of human capital in a metropolitan area (Wolf-Powers and Andreason 2012), as well as government support for other workforce training initiatives (Holzer 2012). A component of broader or regional development strategies, sectoral initiatives typically involve collaborations between employers, educational institutions (such as community colleges), and industry representatives (such as economic devel-

Hispanic		Asian/ Pacific Isander		American Indian/ Alaska Native		Non-resident alien	
Male	Female	Male	Female	Male	Female	Male	Female
21.8	29.9	37.4	47.4	17.2	23.0	36.6	41.0
20.1	18.1	33.3	23.9	17.6	6.0	4.0	3.1
15.8	23.4	30.4	40.8	12.7	18.5	30.3	37.0
38.8	47.8	57.6	63.6	32.1	39.9	50.6	59.2
44.1	52.5	64.0	69.8	35.1	40.7	53.9	56.7
26.7	28.3	38.4	31.3	23.5	12.0	11.7	13.0
41.4	50.0	61.3	67.7	32.2	38.3	52.5	59.0
55.4	62.2	73.8	76.3	46.6	52.1	65.4	71.5
21.9	29.0	31.8	28.9	12.1	14.6	17.3	16.4
28.5	38.5	51.1	54.8	33.0	37.2	48.8	58.5
42.1	50.4	52.5	58.1	29.7	37.1	53.0	62.2
46.4	55.9	61.7	68.2	42.8	48.1	56.8	61.9
57.7	65.2	79.4	84.5	61.2	71.5	72.9	77.4
80.4	87.3	91.2	94.8	72.4	80.2	89.6	91.9
21.8	28.6	28.4	34.6	23.4	25.9	29.4	34.8
57.5	63.3	65.7	65.8	56.3	55.7	56.3	58.6
14.6	16.4	23.5	28.2	18.7	17.8	27.4	32.2
42.9	49.6	43.7	40.1	10.4	18.0	47.7	55.2

opment agencies or industry associations) and focus on preparing students for employment in targeted industries and occupations. State and local governments can encourage the development of sectoral initiatives that improve workforce readiness within a metropolitan area by strategically investing resources that incentivize such initiatives (Wolf-Powers and Andreason 2012). Public policymakers should focus available resources, including technical assistance, on initiatives designed to improve the connections between education and employment among individuals within a metropolitan area who are least prepared to meet workforce demands, that is those with the lowest educational attainment (Holzer 2012; Wolf-Powers and Andreason 2012). Through the federal Elementary and Secondary Education Act (ESEA), the Workforce Investment Act (WIA), the Perkins Act, and other legislation, the federal government should allocate grants that encourage the development of education-employment connections in our nation's metropolitan areas (Holzer 2012).

Some data indicate the benefits of initiatives designed to promote the readiness of workers in particular industries. Such approaches may be particularly appropriate for addressing the upskilling of jobs that is occurring in response to technological changes, as described earlier in this chapter and identified by Carnevale, Smith, and Stohl (2010). For instance, sponsored by the U.S. Department of Labor Employment and Training Administration, the High Growth Job Training Initiative awarded 161 grants between 2001 and 2007 to create industry-focused job training and capacity-building projects (Eyster et al. 2010). About one-fourth of grantees were in the health care sector (24 percent and one-fifth were in advanced manufacturing (21 percent). All initiatives included attention to job training, which was typically provided via apprenticeships or internships. Most initiatives included activities designed to increase the quantity and quality of training and education programs for preparing workers in the targeted industry (for example, creating new curricula and pedagogical approaches, establishing career training models, recruiting more students for the programs, increasing the number of instructors, and so forth). Although various forces limited the extent to which evaluators could isolate the effects of the program on various outcomes, descriptive analyses suggest that participants in these programs realized small improvements in employment and earnings (Eyster et al. 2010).

Concluding Note

The current and future economic and social vitality of our nation in general and of many of our nation's metropolitan areas in particular depends on the readiness of its residents to work available jobs. Yet, as measured by educational attainment, the readiness of many workers, especially those in metropolitan areas that are experiencing deindustrialization, is problematically low. While increasing bachelor-degree attainment is an important and worthwhile goal, available data also suggest the benefits to individuals and metropolitan areas of increasing the shares of students who are completing other high-quality education and training programs. Institutional and public policymakers should carefully consider not only the ways to use available resources to promote educational attainment but also the potential contributions of multiple educational sectors and providers for improving the connections between workers' skills and the requirements of current and future jobs. Although more research is required to understand more completely "what works" and how and why particular initiatives produce beneficial results, this chapter offers suggestions to guide future efforts in this area.

Afterword

Jeremy Nowak

The nation's economy has slowly evolved from an agricultural to an industrial to a postindustrial base, transforming our cities along the way. Some cities have grown, reinventing their economies and physical landscapes. Other cities have deteriorated. How, when, and where does revitalization occur? What factors contribute to cities' capacities to prosper despite a changing economic environment? What strategies have successful cities used to reinvent their economies in response to economic disruption? This volume presents some answers, showing how cities have revitalized by recreating their economic, social, or physical systems to fit a new economic environment. There is one lesson that appears in every chapter in this book: revitalization will not happen by itself. It requires action—action based on a clear understanding of the drivers of growth and an appropriate vision and plan.

In the first section of this book, we focus on understanding the drivers that encourage and enhance growth:

- Glaeser explores the historic drivers of city growth, demonstrating the enduring vitality of the city center; how the successful city provides essential services and, beyond this, the role that human capital—in particular levels of education and "collective entrepreneurship"—plays in explaining growth in city "outperformers."
- Duranton points to the evidence the research literature provides on factors that cause metropolitan areas to grow. Research shows

the critical role played by transportation, industry clusters and, again, human capital.

- Fee and Hartley identify the important relationship between density at the center and metro area growth, with new empirical results, noting the competitive advantage of cities that attend to their central business districts.

- Cochrane, Koropeckyj, Smith, and Ellis provide data on the historical losses of manufacturing jobs in the nation's 100 largest metro areas and highlight trends in city versus suburban growth. Historically, employment and population gains have occurred in the suburbs with cities' growth share declining over time; surprisingly, most recent suburban employment and population growth is outpaced by employment and population gains in central cities, for the first time in the data, in 2010–2011.

Authors of chapters in the second section ground their discussions in the experiences of cities with various degrees of success in revitalizing themselves, including a comparative examination of capacity to adapt to economic change.

- Kodrzycki and Muñoz examine mid-size cities that have successfully weathered shocks over the past half-century and identify common strategies and characteristics, what worked and what did not, and the factors associated with cities changing course and recovering from decline.

- Zeuli compares historically similar cities that have undergone similar economic shocks with dissimilar consequences, pointing to how the capacity of local actors to effect change matters and the importance of diversifying local economies in cities where one industry predominated.

- Mallach creates a typology of vitality and resilience for small cities which that have lost their industrial base. He shows how cities that have succeeded in "coming back" leverage strengths and project a vision to attract citizens based on their assets, from natural resources to historical significance to blossoming artistry.

The chapters in the book's third section discuss policies to grapple with the legacy of the deteriorated physical fabric of many cities in the wake of deindustrialization.

- Brophy argues for the importance of targeted neighborhood policies, including for the "forgotten middle" to buttress the ability of cities to deliver quality of life outcomes. He emphasizes the importance of efficient provision of essential services, such as good schools and low crime rates, which improve economic outcomes for the city's citizens, as well as expanding the tax base to improve fiscal resilience.
- Mallach tackles the question of urban spatial reconfiguration, pointing to the virtues of an incremental approach to physical transformation that addresses real-world political and practical obstacles.
- Alexander describes options for new legal and regulatory frameworks on the state and local levels, to confront the legacy of physical decline in order to repurpose land and rebuild communities.

Chapters in the book's final section showcase new strategies cities are using to revitalize, including building their capacity to adapt to change:

- Birch shows the role of anchors in revitalizing small- and mid-sized cities. She shows how "eds and meds"—educational and health care institutions—have positive spillovers that translate into clusters of productive businesses.
- Tumber looks at new economic activities cities can explore, making the argument that mid-size cities are in an especially strong position to excel in the green economy. She shows how vestiges of the old industrial model can become the foundation of new green technology production with the proper investments in job training, energy efficient architecture, and other upgrades for the new economy.
- Perna discusses the challenges cities face in connecting education with workforce needs, recommending a number of strategies cities can adopt to ensure a strong workforce. She recognizes the importance of college but the practical impossibility of "college for all" and focuses on targeted programs with a strong track record of training that provides skills to link students to employment opportunities in the new economy.

Taken together, the idea that emerges most strongly is the importance of human capital as a factor in urban productivity and in the adaptive transformation that must occur in the face of change through collective entrepreneurship.

At the heart of this ability to adapt to change is resiliency, a concept that has been most prominently employed in the fields of psychology and ecology—and, more recently, economic growth. From the field of psychology, two concepts—emerging from work on individuals who do well despite very difficult conditions—are particularly relevant: the concepts of "capacity" and of "enabling social connections." Capacity, as applied to cities, refers to the authentic strengths found within a city. Building capacity requires identifying those institutions, leaders, firms, and markets that survive and thrive in difficult circumstances and determining whether those strengths can form the building blocks for renewal. What is actually working in the city, and how can its growth and adaptation be enabled? Many of the contributors to this book argue that the basis of strength in cities is always human capital (or capacity) and the web of social networks within which it develops.

In order to revitalize, a city must transition from the old, industrial model, including the physical vestiges of that model. All cities have vacant land, but this is especially true of cities that have been losing population and manufacturing firms. Deindustrialization impacted the physical landscape, leaving many U.S. cities and urban neighborhoods with vacant or underutilized land. Similarly, vestiges of discredited mid-twentieth-century federal policies (that intended to help struggling cities and neighborhoods but that often compounded their problems) remain as well. Thus, these chapters present new tools and approaches to deal with the legacy of blight that affects many neighborhoods in declining cities. They underscore the complexity of repurposing the physical environment of these cities to offer an attractive environment to city residents while ensuring the fiscal sustainability of cities. These authors present practical solutions, cognizant of political obstacles, to problems common to many of America's struggling cities.

The social wiring of a city or a neighborhood (or a family or an institution) includes a wealth of formal and informal, planned and random connections. Cities are defined by these interactions, and these relationships form a natural starting point for reinvention. Renewal happens best when certain enabling capacities (in the form of human capital) are present; building new city and economic forms requires creativity. We cannot predetermine the exact path to this new form, but we can invest in the processes or climate of innovation. Downsizing a city's housing stock, rethinking what a school district looks like, realigning service delivery, or changing the character of governance and management through consolidation with other political entities are some examples. In these cases, political imagination and the courage to move forward in new ways—in other words, leadership—are necessary.

Repeatedly, contributors to this volume return to the necessity of building human capital through education, noting the enormous challenge of so many poorly performing urban school systems. The ability to imagine new institutions—the best charter schools, the best magnet schools, the best contract schools—indicates potential for redevelopment. As Glaeser reminds us, our cities have been continually adapting to an evolving economy since the nineteenth century. Once again, they face the challenge of building an efficient support system for the rapidly growing industries of the new economy: education, health care, skilled manufacturing, technology, and green energy, among others.

The backbone of our resiliency as a nation has been our cities. Today, they face a new challenge: the transition from an industrial society to a postindustrial one. The makings of postindustrialism have been in the works for a long time, but the final outcome is not yet clear. Nonetheless, the lesson from this book is one of optimism: the capacity to adapt and revitalize lies in the cities themselves, through the strength of local innovation and leadership. While a city needs connections to the outside for sources of new ideas, energy, and resources, the capacity for renewal lies within its boundaries.

NOTES

Chapter 2. The Growth of Metropolitan Areas

1. The few summary statistics given in this chapter all refer to metropolitan areas. This is also the geography used by most of the studies surveyed below. For policy purposes, cities might be viewed as more relevant given their greater autonomy. However, municipalities seldom form self-contained units of analysis and are extremely heterogeneous. Some metropolitan areas are clearly dominated by one city, whereas others are highly fragmented.

2. For very different reasons (e.g., better access to markets), one may also expect roads external to cities, and more generally market access, to affect urban growth. Redding and Sturm (2008) use the division of Germany after World War II as a natural experiment to show that cities close to the Iron Curtain declined after it was imposed in Western Germany.

3. Obtaining experimental evidence would of course be better. Unfortunately, true experimental evidence on this kind of topic would be hard to obtain. It is difficult to imagine that politicians would accept a random allocation of highways. "Natural experiments" (real-life events that would recreate experimental evidence) are also extremely scarce (the reference mentioned in the previous note notwithstanding). As a result, using the type of approach described here and leveraging sources of exogenous variation in the data to mimic indirectly experimental conditions is often the best that is available to the analysts.

4. See Angrist and Pischke (2008) for a more detailed exposition of this type of approach.

5. Jacobs (1969) also forcefully defended very similar ideas insisting on the importance of cross-fertilization between sectors.

6. This "Chinitz" finding about the importance of many small establishments is confirmed by Rosenthal and Strange (2010), who suggest that small establishments matter because they provide a greater diversity of specialized suppliers to local firms. This would be consistent with the explanation developed above that highlights the dynamic implications of static externalities.

Chapter 3. The Relationship Between City Center Density
and Urban Growth or Decline

1. For recent reviews of this literature, see Duranton and Puga (2004); Rosenthal and Strange (2004); and Puga (2010).

2. Rosenthal and Strange (2003); van Soest, Gerking, and van Oort (2006); Fu (2007); and Arzaghi and Henderson (2008) are examples of this work. Elvery and Sveikauskas (2010) find the strongest agglomeration effects at longer distances (ten, twenty, or twenty-five miles) but also show that short distance effects (within two-and-a-half miles) tend to be stronger when the workforce is more educated and belonging to similar occupational categories, suggesting the importance of the exchange of ideas for short-distance agglomerative effects.

3. Available at http://www.census.gov/geo/tiger/cbdct.pdf.

4. Available at http://www.s4.brown.edu/us2010/Researcher/Bridging.htm.

5. See Rosenthal and Strange (2004).

6. See Glaeser and Saiz (2004).

7. LeRoy and Sonstelie (1983) show how a pattern of high-income people moving back to the CBD from the suburbs could occur when modes of transportation such as the car are adopted first by high-income and then by low-income people. Lin (2002) provides empirical support for this hypothesis. Brueckner, Thisse, and Zenou (1999) posit that variation in amenity levels may explain variation across cities in the degree to which high-income households tend to be concentrated in the suburbs versus near the CBD.

8. For the curious reader, two-stage least squares results from the specification noted above with an F of 10.37 yield a coefficient on change in population density near the CBD of 0.527 and a standard error of 0.182.

Chapter 4. Central Cities and Metropolitan Areas: Manufacturing
and Nonmanufacturing Employment as Drivers of Growth

1. The U.S. economy has long been concentrated in metropolitan areas, and that concentration is increasing. In 1970, metro areas accounted for 80 percent of the U.S. population. This share grew to 84 percent in 2001, with the rate of growth accelerating over the past decade. Similarly, the metro area share of total nonfarm payroll employment in the U.S. has risen from 83 to 86 percent.

2. Metropolitan Statistical Areas (MSA) comprise counties or county-equivalent areas and have at least one urbanized area of 50,000 or more population, plus adjacent territory, also defined by counties, that have a high degree of social and economic integration with the core as measured by commuting ties (OMB 2009). Some metropolitan areas have more than one principal city. For the purpose of this study, we

assume the largest is the central city or the most urbanized area. If the metro area's other principal cities are located in its other counties, they are grouped together in the noncentral or suburban portion of the metro area.

3. In this chapter, the service share is defined as private services and is constituted of nonfarm private employment in Financial Activities, Professional and Business Services and Trade, Transportation and Utilities.

4. This deindustrialization trend is not unique to the U.S. and its metropolitan areas. Manufacturing as a share of the overall economy is falling in many Western European countries, 10 percent of GDP in France and the UK, nearly the same as in the U.S.; indeed, the share of manufacturing in the overall economy tends to fall as an economy grows wealthier. Nonetheless, manufacturing still represents 19 percent of GDP in Germany, in part thanks to an educational system that provides vocational training to develop a skilled manufacturing workforce (*Economist* 2012; McKinsey Global Institute 2012).

5. While manufacturing has declined dramatically over the past forty years, the reality may not be quite as drastic as the raw numbers imply, as employers during this time period were increasingly using temporary or contract workers in place of permanent workers. The practice of using temporary or contract workers surged between 1980 and 2000. Because the Bureau of Labor Statistics (BLS) groups all temporary workers together regardless of which industry they work in, it is difficult to determine directly how many work in manufacturing. However, the BLS has been able to establish a high degree of correlation between areas with high concentrations of temporary workers and high concentrations of manufacturing (Luo, Mann, and Holden 2010). Despite the hidden (to BLS data) use of temporary workers, manufacturing employment has clearly declined.

6. See Brauer 2008. Even as manufacturing employment has fallen dramatically, output per worker has increased by 4.3 times since 1978. This is much greater than the 1.6 times growth in the economy overall. A large share of the gain is in only two industries: computer and electronic products and petroleum and coal products (Atkinson, Stewart, Andes, and Ezell 2012: 35). Output per worker in computer and electronic products has increased by an astounding 1,265 times according to the Bureau of Economic Analysis (BEA), while output per worker in the petroleum and coal products industry has grown by 26 fold. Excluding these industries, productivity in the remaining manufacturing sectors has increased by a more modest 2.9 times. This phenomenon was discussed by William J. Baumol and William G. Bowen (Baumol and Bowen 1966).

7. See note 4 above. Chairman Ben Bernanke points to skill mismatch as a cause of the current weak recovery. Despite the high unemployment rate, firms are experiencing difficulty in hiring qualified workers, slowing job growth in the recovery. The so-called Beveridge Curve, which measures the inverse relationship between job openings and unemployment rate, appears to have shifted (Bernanke 2012). See also the discussion of a structural mismatch that requires changes in educational and

training programs to provide workers with the skills needed in an evolving economy as discussed by Laura Perna in her chapter.

8. Thus, the mix of products manufactured in the U.S. has changed. Specialization in higher-value-added production goes a long way toward explaining the extraordinary productivity in the computer and electronic products industries.

9. Overall, we calculate a rank correlation coefficient of 0.47 for the 100 metro areas between manufacturing employment concentration and manufacturing decline. The ten largest percentage declines in central city manufacturing from 1970 to 2011 were in the metro areas of New York, Baltimore, Philadelphia, Washington, New Orleans, St. Louis, Richmond, Boston, and San Francisco. The ten largest percent declines in suburban counties of metro areas were in Allentown, Youngstown, Buffalo, Scranton, Poughkeepsie, New York, Providence, Pittsburgh, Philadelphia, and Albany.

10. For example, the Finance Insurance and Real Estate (FIRE) sector that typically concentrates high-income earners is found to have more of its jobs in central cities (63 percent) than any other sector. In addition, it accounts for a higher percentage of the jobs in central cities than those in the suburbs: 8.2 percent of city jobs are in FIRE, compared to only 5.3 percent of suburban jobs (Ihlanfeldt 1995).

11. Wage data by place of work, rather than place of residence, are available from the BLS Quarterly Census of Employment and Wages, although historical data are limited. On the basis of place of work, the central cities fared better as income generators. Aggregate wage income earned from jobs located in central cities was 1.6 times the suburban figure in 2011. Furthermore, this relationship has held steady since 2002. In 2011, wage income earned in central cities per resident population amounted to $25,300. Income from jobs in suburbs amounted to only $18,000 per suburban resident.

12. As of 2010, the median household income was $59,878 in suburbs, compared to $44,815 in cities and overall. The U.S. poverty rate increased by 23 percent between 2000 and 2010. The poverty rate in cities (20.9 percent) remains far higher than in suburbs (11.4 percent) as of 2010. Nonetheless, poverty in suburbs is increasing; the number of suburban poor increased by 53 percent between 2000 and 2010 and, since 2005, more than half of the poor living in metropolitan areas reside in suburbs (Berube and Kneebone 2011).

13. In an earlier study, a very strong relationship was found between growth of median household income in central cities and suburbs (Barnes and Ledebur 1998: 39–48). This work suggests that the "economic fates and fortunes of cities and suburbs are inextricably intertwined" (42) Barnes and Ledebur found that, from 1979 to 1989, among the twenty-five metro areas with the fastest growing suburbs, "no suburbs experienced income growth without corresponding growth in their central cities. This also means that no central city in this high-growth sample experienced income growth in the absence of suburban growth" (42). They found a similar correlation between central cities and their suburbs where metro area median household income declined.

14. The narrower differences in population and resident wage income growth between central cities and suburbs offer potential for new employment to expand more evenly in the future as well. The potential in central cities is higher for nonmanufacturing industries that provide services for city residents. Particularly in the Northeast, there is good potential for central cities to at least grow concurrently with their suburban neighbors, even if they do not lead their respective metro areas. Employment and population in the Northeast may have a higher probability of narrowing the growth gap between central city and suburb in the coming decade.

15. According to the National Bureau of Economic Research (NBER) definition of the recession that is based on an analysis of changes in gross domestic product, as well as measures of employment, industrial production, income, and sales for determining when the economy changes direction.

16. Over the recession, suburban decline slightly outpaced the central city decline, but both exceeded downturns of 12 percent. The other regions were not far behind, with declines ranging from 10 to 11 percent in central cities and suburbs. Recovery finally came in 2011 when manufacturing employment turned positive, led by the suburban counties of metro areas in all four regions. Central city growth also was positive, except in the Northeast.

17. Apple Inc. CEO Tim Cook announced in an interview with Bloomberg on December 6, 2012, http://www.bloomberg.com/news/2012-12-06/apple-to-invest-in -manufacturing-macs-in-u-s-ceo-cook-says.html, that "Next year we're going to bring some production to the U.S." While no details are available on what will be produced or where, this comment is evidence that the U.S. is seen as a competitive location for manufacturing.

18. These results need to be interpreted with caution, since central counties in some metro areas are quite a bit larger than their central cities. This is particularly true in the West and South.

19. A similar result is derived by using the Brookings definition of core "primary cities" of the nation's 51 metropolitan areas with populations exceeding one million. In this definition principal cities include the largest city in each metropolitan area, plus additional cities that meet specific population size and employment requirements. By this definition, the central cities' population growth rate of 1.1 percent for the first time, in the four decades we cover in this chapter, had an edge over the 0.9 percent growth rate in the suburbs.

Chapter 5. Lessons from Resurgent Mid-Sized Manufacturing Cities

This chapter draws heavily on the authors' essay, "Lessons from Resurgent Cities," published in the 2009 Annual Report of the Federal Reserve Bank of Boston. The authors are grateful to Teresa Huie and Catherine Spozio of the Federal Reserve Bank of Boston for extensive research assistance and to external experts for sharing their knowledge of individual cities. The research was performed in collaboration with the other members of Toward a More Prosperous Springfield: A Federal Reserve Bank of Boston Initiative. The focus of the project has been to help reinvigorate Springfield, Massachusetts, and support revitalization strategies that would enable more city residents to prosper.

1. Three neighborhoods in Springfield were part of a concentrated poverty report that included case studies of sixteen high-poverty communities across the country. The study was a joint project of the Community Affairs Offices of the Federal Reserve System and he Metropolitan Policy Program at the Brookings Institution (2008). For details, see http://www.frbsf.org/cpreport/.

2. U.S. Bureau of the Census, American Community Survey five-year average (2006–2010). For details about Springfield neighborhoods, see Kodrzycki, Muñoz et al. (2009b).

3. In addition to Springfield, Massachusetts, the peer group consists of the following cities: Akron, Ohio, Allentown, Pennsylvania, Bridgeport, Connecticut, Dayton, Ohio, Erie, Pennsylvania, Evansville, Indiana, Flint, Michigan, Fort Wayne, Indiana, Gary, Indiana, Grand Rapids, Michigan, Greensboro, North Carolina, Hartford, Connecticut, Jersey City, New Jersey, New Haven, Connecticut, Paterson, New Jersey, Peoria, Illinois, Providence, Rhode Island, Rochester, New York, Rockford, Illinois, South Bend, Indiana, Syracuse, New York, Waterbury, Connecticut, Winston-Salem, North Carolina, Worcester, Massachusetts, and Youngstown, Ohio.

4. Furdell and Wolman's sample of 302 cities encompassed 22 of the 26 cities considered in our study. Their 65 "weak market" cities were those that fared poorly in terms of economic growth during the 1990s (measured by employment, payroll, and number of business establishments) and economic well-being of city residents in 2000 (measured by per capita income, median household income, poverty rate, unemployment rate, and labor force participation rate). These cities included only two of the nine overlapping resurgent cities (New Haven and Providence), but ten of the overlapping thirteen nonresurgent cities. Another seven overlapping cities (four resurgent and three nonresurgent) were characterized by Furdell and Wolman as having moderate residential economic well-being but weak city economic conditions. The final two overlapping cities (both resurgent) had moderate residential economic well-being and moderate city economic conditions.

5. Many of the resurgent cities annexed land to prevent their populations from shrinking. Annexation was easier in areas where cities were bordered by unincorporated land.

6. According to the U.S. Bureau of Labor Statistics, Providence's unemployment rate increased from 6.3 percent in 2005 to 13.7 in 2012.

7. For details see tables 4 and 5 in Kodrzycki, Muñoz et al. (2009a).

8. A study done at the Federal Reserve Bank of Boston documented inequities in the distribution of municipal aid that have further disadvantaged Springfield and certain other old industrial cities in Massachusetts (Zhao et al. 2010). Based heavily

on that study, legislation was introduced in the state legislature to adopt a new approach to allocating unrestricted municipal aid. This bill was not passed during the 2011–2012 session.

Chapter 6. Revitalizing Small Cities: A Comparative Case Study of Two Southern Mill Towns

The author gratefully acknowledges the following individuals who helped shape the content of this chapter: Tammie Hoy, Nika Lazaryan, Shannon McKay, and Urvi Neelakantan.

1. For a thorough discussion of the factors behind the decline, see Minchin (2009).

Chapter 7. Parallel Histories, Diverging Trajectories: Resilience in Small Industrial Cities

1. The criteria used to select these cities were that they were all in the Third Federal Reserve District, were founded in the nineteenth century or earlier, had at one time a strong manufacturing base, and had at one point a population of at least 50,000. The full study, titled *In Philadelphia's Shadow: Small Cities in the Third Federal Reserve District*, was published in 2012 by the Federal Reserve Bank of Philadelphia.

2. Ten were colonial settlements, many founded in the wake of the founding of Philadelphia late in the seventeenth century, and others Swedish settlements taken over and renamed by the British in the second half of that century. A few have a more recent origin. Scranton and Wilkes-Barre were initially settled by migrants from New England and remained small towns until well into the nineteenth century, while Altoona did not exist until its creation by the Pennsylvania Railroad in 1849.

3. The company built a large facility in a suburb of Buffalo, subsequently incorporated as Lackawanna, New York. The company was acquired by Bethlehem Steel in the 1920s and closed its doors permanently in 1984.

4. Scranton was the economic center of the nation's principal anthracite coal mining region, which also included Wilkes-Barre and other smaller centers. Anthracite or "hard" coal was particularly valuable for its high BTU content and clean-burning character. Its use declined significantly after World War II, and it is not a major energy source today.

5. In addition to Cumbler (1989), the extent to which forces of decline had been working in cities since the 1920s and 1930s is discussed extensively by Jon C. Teaford (1993) and documented in detail in Douglas W. Rae's insightful case study of New Haven, Connecticut (2003).

6. For a more detailed discussion of the process of change and the current social, economic, and housing market conditions in these cities, see Mallach (2012b).

7. The outlet mall, however, is not in Reading but in the adjacent Borough of West Reading.

8. ExplorePAhistory.com, "Reading [Labor] Historical Marker," http://explore pahistory.com/hmarker.php?markerId=1-A-245, accessed July 17, 2011.

9. The redevelopment of the lands since 1996 along the Christina River in Wilmington is a strong example of a postfederal revitalization strategy. The results include art, cultural, and entertainment facilities; public open space; office and retail space; and some 1,200 units of market-rate housing. This effort was led by a special-purpose corporation created by the Delaware legislature in 1995, and provided with state funds to initiate the redevelopment effort.

10. The case for a positive economic impact resulting from these facilities is weak (Zimbalist and Noll 1997), although the potential value of the intangible effect should not be ignored (Chapin 2002). One area that has not been as well explored in the literature is the opportunity cost associated with diversion of substantial public resources to these projects, rather than being used either for improved public services or alternative economic development strategies.

11. The national organization CEOs for Cities has put it unequivocally: "We know that educational attainment is the biggest predictor of success for cities and metro areas today. The research is unassailable." They refer to this as the "talent dividend." http://www.ceosforcities.org/work/talentdividendtour accessed August 24, 2011.

12. I consider this ratio more telling than the percentage of households in poverty as such. Households earning below the poverty level are disproportionately likely to be receiving public assistance, including food stamps, housing vouchers, and Medicaid, and less likely to be paying much in either income or property taxes; moreover, for the most part, they draw resources from the rest of the community. Conversely, households earning more than double the poverty level (or roughly $45,000 or more for a family of four) are highly likely to contain employed household members and to be paying income and property taxes, less likely to be relying on subsidized services and transfer payments, and largely contributing resources to the community. Households between these two groups are likely to be a mix of both categories and, thus, a wash for analytical purposes. Thus, the ratio between the two—referred to here as the "household economic dependency ratio"—reflects the extent to which a community's population is economically dependent or independent. A higher ratio indicates a stronger household economic base. Altoona, with a ratio of 3.04, has three households with incomes more than double the poverty level for every household under that level; Camden, with a ratio of 0.89, has more households below the poverty level than with incomes more than double that level. Nationally, the ratio is 5.08 (just over five households with incomes more than double the poverty level for every household below that level).

13. School quality itself is another factor that is clearly relevant to a city's social and economic condition. School quality directly affects intergenerational economic

mobility and opportunity and significantly affects housing markets, influencing consumer choice not only on the part of households with children but arguably among others who may see it as a surrogate for stability and potential appreciation of house values (Ramsay, Sanchez, and Wanzer 2006; Varady and Raffel 1995). Drawing meaningful comparisons between school districts, however, is highly problematic, reflecting both serious data problems as well as a more fundamental issue of what is to be measured. Applying the sorts of measurements that might potentially make a comparative analysis of these thirteen cities and their school districts meaningful is a task well beyond the scope of this chapter.

14. The interplay between homeownership as a tenure choice and residential stability, whether as owner and renter, with respect to many of the social benefits associated with homeownership is a complicated one. There is some research evidence that the favorable child outcomes associated with homeownership may have as much or more to do with stability (Barker and Miller 2009). The association between homeownership and stability, however, is so powerful, at least in an American context, that this distinction is far less significant than it may appear.

15. This is a powerful, although approximate, measure of the relative weight of homebuyers and investors in the residential market. According to data from Campbell/Inside Mortgage Finance *HousingPulse* Survey for February 2011, 75 percent of investor home purchases are all-cash transactions. FHA, Fannie/Freddie, and VA mortgages in toto amount to only 7 percent of investor purchases, while 18 percent of transactions use some other type of financing, most of it unlikely to be subject to reporting under the Home Mortgage Disclosure Act. It is important to stress that the ratio of sales to mortgages is an *approximation* of the relationship between absentee buyers and owner-occupiers, not an exact measure of the relationship. Roughly 20 to 25 percent of owner-occupant homebuyers purchase their homes through all-cash transactions, a percentage that may be higher in areas with strong cash-based service economies.

16. Given the permeability of municipal boundaries to economic activity, one can question the significance of measuring the level of economic activity within an arbitrarily defined area within the region as distinct from that of the region as a whole. While this is a legitimate question, those boundaries are politically, socially, and fiscally significant. As long as that remains the case, the economic activity inside these cities is relevant to their present and future well-being and must be viewed separately from that of the region.

17. These measures, unfortunately, are not as robust as those used in the other categories of urban vitality, owing to the limitations of economic data available at the small city level.

18. Hill, Wolman, Kowalczyk and St. Clair. (2012) found a strong positive relationship between the size of the health care sector and the severity of a city's population decline.

19. Fiscal pressures are a looming threat to the future of nearly all older American cities (Mallach and Scorsone 2011). To the extent that these cities are forced to take steps that reduce the quality of service delivery, infrastructure, or physical environment, that is likely to impair future revitalization prospects. Given the extent to which the municipal revenue base is determined by state law and the extent to which these cities rely on state assistance, the issue will ultimately have to be addressed at the state rather than the local level.

20. Of the two cities among the thirteen that have shown the strongest population growth in recent decades, Allentown is in the middle of the pack with respect to measures of vitality, while Reading is among the weakest.

21. Between 2006 and 2010, the state of New Jersey provided Camden an average of $115 million per year to support municipal operations, roughly two-thirds of all city government costs, and $250–300 million per year to support the Camden school district, over 90 percent of total school costs. Total local tax collections for city services amounted to roughly $20 million per year, less than 15 percent of the city budget (CamConnect 2010). In conjunction with the state takeover of Camden city government in 2002, the legislature approved $175 million in bonds to finance redevelopment in the city. Additional state investment—in housing, infrastructure, and other facilities—over the decade is far greater.

22. Anecdotal reports late in 2011 by Camden residents suggest these fears are being borne out.

23. It should be noted that this finding, which appears to be based on the one-year 2010 American Community Survey, is based on a relatively small sample and is subject to a wide margin of error, something acknowledged, but only in passing, in the *New York Times* article.

24. Six of the thirteen cities fit all three of Rusk's criteria for having passed the point of no return, including Wilmington, which has seen significant revitalization.

25. Camden, Chester, Harrisburg, Trenton, and Wilmington accounted for 81 percent of the African American population of the thirteen cities in 2000.

Chapter 8. A Market-Oriented Approach to Neighborhoods

1. The Knight Foundation Soul of the Community project, conducted in partnership with Gallup, finds that resident attachment to a neighborhood or city is based on three leading drivers: openness of the community, aesthetics, and social offerings. See http://www.soulofthecommunity.org.

2. The *Legal Dictionary* defines blockbusting as "The practice of illegally frightening homeowners by telling them that people who are members of a particular race, religion, or national origin are moving into their neighborhood and that they should expect a decline in the value of their property. The purpose of this scheme is to get the homeowners to sell out at a deflated price."

3. See, e.g., articles in *Cityscape: A Journal of Policy Development and Research* 14, 2 (2012).

4. A quick history is available at http://www.nw.org/network/aboutUs/history/default.asp.

5. This underutilized approach may be less important in cities with robust neighborhood markets virtually everywhere, but, even in strong cities, there may be need for neighborhood-by-neighborhood strategies based on improving market conditions (Brophy and Burnett 2003).

6. For a good example of an MVA map, see http://baltimorecity.gov/Portals/0/agencies/planning/public%20downloads/Typology2011%20Final.pdf.

7. The Dynamic Neighborhoods final report is at http://www.rw-ventures.com/ftp/DNT%20Final%20Report.pdf.

8. This phenomenon also needs to be viewed in a regional context. During the 2000s, for example, the number of households in the Baltimore metropolitan area increased by 62,000, but approximately 71,000 housing units were produced. The effect of this supply/demand imbalance is that housing units some place in the regional market become surplus—which eventually become vacant. The vast bulk of these units are in Baltimore City and its older suburbs.

9. Baltimore is not the only U.S. city to take a "middle-neighborhoods approach." Similar efforts are underway in Milwaukee, Philadelphia, Cleveland, and elsewhere. Richmond, Virginia, carried out a successful Neighborhoods in Bloom Program in the early 2000s (see Accordino, Galster, and Tatian 2005).

10. Disclosure: the author has been a member of the board since 2004.

11. The city uses scarce city tax funds to support the program, because the federal funds it would otherwise have access to are income restricted, making them unattractive for the purpose of attracting and holding households regardless of income.

12. The U.S. Department of Education Promise Neighborhoods program has the ambition that all children and youth growing up in Promise Neighborhoods have access to great schools and strong systems of family and community support that will prepare them to attain an excellent education and successfully transition to college and a career. The purpose of Promise Neighborhoods is significantly to improve the educational and developmental outcomes of children and youth in our most distressed communities.

Chapter 9. Transformation Is Messy Work: The Complex Challenge of Spatial Reconfiguration in America's Legacy Cities

1. The term "legacy cities" for older cities, particularly in the Northeast and Midwest, that have experienced sustained population and job loss and are the principal focus of this paper, was coined during an American Assembly in Detroit in April

2011. The report (American Assembly 2011) from that Assembly, "Reinventing America's Legacy Cities," is an excellent introduction to policy thinking about these cities.

2. Another important volume is *The City After Abandonment* (Dewar and Thomas 2012).

3. As Brent Ryan (2012) points out, the concept inherent in the term, that of finding the "right size" for a city, is largely meaningless, as "no city in history has ever attained a fixed size." Cities by their nature will continue to grow, or in some cases decline, for reasons largely outside planners' and politicians' control. Nonetheless, the term is widely used, including in the title of the Rightsizing Task Force of the Advisory Council on Historic Preservation, as well as a recent publication prepared for that body (Bertron and Rypkema 2012).

4. According to one source, there is no documented evidence Burnham actually ever said these particular words, although they appear consistent with his thinking; http://en.wikipedia.org/wiki/Daniel_Burnham, accessed January 29, 2012.

5. It is important to distinguish between cities in which population loss has taken place to such an extent, as is true of Youngstown, Detroit, and many other cities such as Gary, Flint, or Buffalo; and cities on which, although their population loss has been significant, it has not had such pervasive effects. Such cities would include, in all likelihood, Philadelphia and many smaller cities such as Syracuse or Albany.

6. I led the Detroit Sustainable Design Assessment Team and was principal author of this report. A far more ambitious effort, Detroit Future City, the long-term strategic framework plan of the Detroit Works Project, was unveiled in January 2013.

7. From a conceptual standpoint, one could argue that a competitive industrial district is really a form of viable neighborhood, in which the unit of measurement is jobs and businesses, rather than homes and families.

8. The diagram is, of course, an abstract diagram that does not represent any specific city.

9. Remarks at Lincoln Institute of Land Policy roundtable, February 7, 2012.

10. This is indeed happening and, in some cities like Detroit, accelerating, a subject I addressed in a presentation at the 2012 Urban Affairs Association conference titled "Market Collapse and the Future of the Middle-Ground Neighborhood in Shrinking Cities."

11. Those involved in planning in legacy cities face a constant challenge in coming up with names for these areas that offer positive connotations and are, therefore, not politically or socially objectionable.

12. At least during any time frame meaningful for planning purposes. While it is unlikely that Detroit will retain any appreciable part of its historic population within the next few decades, the long haul is unpredictable. Rome reached its first population peak, according to most historians, at roughly 1 million around 300 AD. It subsequently declined, falling to a population that may have been as low as 15,000 to 20,000 by the twelfth century. Over the years, however, it gained back that population, and reached the million mark again in 1931, only 1,600 or so years later.

13. In many respects, the most ambitious planning effort of all is underway in Detroit, where under the rubric of the Detroit Works Project, a multidisciplinary planning team is trying to develop a comprehensive citywide vision of change grounded in physical reconfiguration. For a variety of reasons, however, the process is taking place outside the city government framework—although coordinated with it— and the extent to which it will result in implementation remains in question.

14. What to call the process of change in heavily disinvested areas is another subject where terminology remains in flux. What Dayton calls "reimaging" is essentially the same as Cleveland's "reimagining" or some other city's "reconfiguration." In each case, the goal is to convey that the process of change is not one of abandonment or withdrawal of resources but one of transformation to something different, and not necessarily less desirable. Clearly, it is a difficult task.

15. Lennon apparently used this line on a number of occasions, including his 1980 song "Beautiful Boy (Darling Boy)," http://en.wikipedia.org/wiki/Beautiful_Boy_ (Darling_Boy).

16. In the case of Camden, no better off than before the state took over the city in 2002.

17. Analysis by Frank Ford, Neighborhood Progress, Inc., November 18, 2011.

18. Estimate by the author. The Detroit Works Project consultants estimated that approximately 60,000 people reside in the most extensively abandoned parts of the city that would be considered "green zones" under any reconfiguration scenario. Approximately 50 percent of these residents were owner-occupants, with an average household size of 2.0. Assuming that only owner-occupants would be actively relocated and that relocation would require providing each household with a "move-in" house elsewhere in Detroit at nominal cost, it was estimated that 15,000 households would have to be relocated at an average cost of $50,000 per household.

19. Examples of all three can be found in Michigan in recent years. Flint has reduced the number of sworn police officers by more than two-thirds and the number of firefighters by over half since 2001. Saginaw has eliminated its capital budget, and Highland Park has removed all but 500 of 1,600 street lights (Davey 2011).

20. In one of the most significant manifestations of the backlash against the U.S. Supreme Court's 2005 *Kelo* decision, Michigan voters approved a constitutional amendment in 2006 that bars use of eminent domain for "transfer to a private entity for the purpose of economic development or enhancement of tax revenues" and establishes an exceptionally high threshold for eminent domain for removal of blight (Pesick and Reynolds 2007).

21. Finding from a policy audit of public land holdings in Detroit performed by HR&A Advisors for the Detroit Works Project (2010).

22. Comment by Douglas Weiland, executive director, Washington, D.C., September 24, 2012.

23. Perhaps the most ambitious effort was that of former Baltimore mayor (now governor of Maryland) Martin O'Malley's Project 5000, a plan to gain control of 5,000

vacant lots and buildings in that city. The target was set, to a large extent, by backing into what was considered feasible; the plan managers were quick to admit that this number made up only a modest—but not insignificant—part of the total vacant property inventory in the city.

24. The long-term strategic framework plan for Detroit contains an ambitious and well-grounded strategy designed to achieve this goal, developed by the Boston-based firm Stoss Landscape Urbanism. If successfully implemented, something that may not be known for many years, it may become a model for other cities.

25. This was not even a remote possibility in light of the provisions of Michigan law noted in note 20.

26. In contrast to other cities where growth has been fueled by immigration in recent decades, few legacy cities have drawn significant Latino or Asian communities.

27. A simple formulation of the problem is by philosopher Michael Ruse: "Suppose you are down a mine and five people are standing on the track. You see a trolley laden with coal coming down the track, you cannot warn the people, but you can flip a switch that will divert the trolley onto a side line. Unfortunately one person is standing on this line. What should you do (morally, that is)?" http://chronicle.com/blogs/brainstorm/the-trolley-problem/27627, accessed March 6, 2012.

28. The one most widely cited counterexample, Richmond, Virginia's Neighborhoods in Bloom program, did not have to overcome similar obstacles. Under that rubric, after a careful process that was both data-driven and participatory, the city in 1999 directed 80 percent of its discretionary community development funds to six of the city's forty-nine neighborhoods for the next four years, with impressive results. The program and its effects are described in Accordino, Galster, and Tatian (2005). The principal difference between Richmond and the cities discussed here, however, is that the former was not suffering from the severe imbalance of supply and demand characteristic of Detroit or Youngstown; as a result, targeting of discretionary resources to a relatively small number of areas was far from a death sentence for the neighborhoods not targeted, nor was it perceived as such.

29. What appears to be a significant exception is Pittsburgh, where change appears to have triggered significantly more and earlier reconsideration of institutional relationships than in most similar cities (Briggs 2008). Of all major cities that have experienced significant population loss over the past decades, Pittsburgh is arguably the most successful in terms of regeneration.

30. This is exacerbated by the notorious urban pattern of extremely low voter turnouts for local elections, particularly in the areas most likely to be affected by physical reconfiguration.

31. This phrase appears in my notes of Nowak's presentation at the opening session of the fifth biennial Reinventing Cities conference sponsored by the Federal Reserve Bank of Philadelphia on May 9.

32. An arguable exception was increased focus on demolishing vacant buildings, an activity, however, pursued largely in isolation without connection to a reuse or reconfiguration strategy.

Chapter 10. Tactical Options for Stable Properties

1. See 1893 Mich. Pub. Act 206, as amended by 1999 Mich. Pub. Act 123; Mich. Comp. Laws §§ 211.1 et seq.

2. Official Code of Georgia Annotated § 48-4-78(d).

3. Official Code of Georgia Annotated § 41-2-9(b)(1).

4. Chicago, Ill., Code ch. 13–12, §125(e) (2010).

5. Wilmington, Del., Code Ch. 4 § 27.125.00 (2003).

6. Chula Vista, Cal., Ordinance No. 3080 (2007).

7. Official Code of Georgia Annotated §44-14-14(b).

8. See, e.g., Ohio Rev. Code Annotation § 3767.41; Pennsylvania Statutes Annotated § 1101 et seq.; Baltimore, Md., Code § 121.1 et seq.

9. Baltimore, Md., Code § 121.1 (2011); 68 Pennsylvania Statutes Annotated § 1105.

10. New York Land Bank Act, N.Y Not-for-Profit Corporation Law § 1600 (2012).

11. Georgia Land Bank Act, Official Code of Georgia Annotated § 48-4-100 (2012).

12. Missouri Rev. Statutes § 141.980 (2012).

13. Pennsylvania Land Bank Act, 68 Pennsylvania Consolidated Statutes ch. 21 (2012).

Chapter 12. Fields, Factories, and Workshops: Green Economic Development on the Smaller-Metro Scale

1. Note that these figures are in 2008 dollars and assume food sourcing 150 miles out.

2. In 2011, the U.S. Department of Energy's National Renewable Energy Laboratory further developed its excellent 2002 tool, the Jobs and Economic Development Impact (JEDI) model, for determining the state and local economic benefits of renewable energy-generation development, http://www.nrel.gov/analysis/jedi/about_jedi.html. See also the National Resource Defense Council state-profile studies, which use JEDI along with other sources to model the economic impact of low-carbon industry development, http://www.nrdc.org/energy/renewables/states.asp.

3. In February 2012, Brevini announced that it was unable to find markets for its wind turbines, thanks to the uncertainties of the global economic climate and federal support for the renewable energy industry. It has found contracts instead for producing heavy equipment for the oil, gas, and mining industries (Roysdon 2012).

Frank S. Alexander is the Sam Nunn Professor of Law at Emory University School of Law and cofounder of the Center for Community Progress. He is the author or editor of eight books and over fifty articles on real estate finance and community redevelopment. His work has focused on homelessness and affordable housing. He served as a Fellow of the Carter Center of Emory University from 1993 to 1996; commissioner of the State Housing Trust Fund for the Homeless from 1994 to 1998; interim dean of Emory University School of Law from 2005 to 2006; and Visiting Fellow at the Joint Center for Housing Studies at Harvard University in 2007. He testified before Congress concerning the mortgage foreclosure crisis.

Eugenie L. Birch is the Lawrence C. Nussdorf Professor of Urban Research and Education; chair of the Graduate Group of City and Regional Planning, University of Pennsylvania School of Design; codirector of the Penn Institute for Urban Research; and coeditor of the City in the Twenty-First Century series, University of Pennsylvania Press. She has been published extensively. Her most recent books include *Women's Health and the World's Cities* (with Afaf Meleis and Susan M. Wachter), *Global Urbanization*, and *Neighborhoods and Life Chances: How Place Matters in Modern America* (with Harriet Newburger and Susan M. Wachter). She is cochair, UN-HABITAT World Urban Campaign and chair, Board of Directors, Municipal Art Society of New York.

Paul C. Brophy is a principal with Brophy & Reilly, LLC, a consulting firm specializing in economic development, housing and community development, and the management of complex urban redevelopment projects. One of his specialties is the improvement of older industrial cities and the neighborhoods within those cities. He is a Senior Advisor to Enterprise Community Partners and the Center for Community Progress. He is a Nonresident Senior

Fellow at the Brookings Institution and and a Senior Scholar at the Brown School at Washington University in St. Louis. He is coauthor of *Neighborhood Revitalization: Theory and Practice, Housing and Local Government,* and *A Guide to Careers in Community Development.*

Steven Cochrane is a Managing Director of Moody's Analytics. He oversees the U.S. regional forecasting service and directs the research and development activities of the research staff, including its Global Cities service. He also edits *Regional Financial Review,* a monthly publication that analyzes U.S. macro-, regional, industry, and international trends. An analyst with Moody's Analytics since 1993, Cochrane has been featured on Wall Street Radio, the PBS *NewsHour,* and CNBC. He earned a Ph.D. in regional science from the University of Pennsylvania, a master's degree from the University of Colorado-Denver, and a bachelor's degree from the University of California-Davis.

Gilles Duranton is Professor of Real Estate at the Wharton School of the University of Pennsylvania. A graduate of HEC Paris and Sorbonne University, he obtained his Ph.D. in economics jointly from the London School of Economics and the École des Hautes Études en Sciences Sociales in Paris. His research focuses on regional and urban issues. His empirical work is concerned with urban growth and the estimation of the costs and benefits of cities and clusters. He serves as coeditor for the *Journal of Urban Economics* and on the editorial boards of several other academic journals. He is a Fellow of the Centre for Economic Policy Research and was 2011 President of the North American Regional Science Association.

Sean Ellis is an Associate Economist with Moody's Analytics. He covers the Kentucky economy and contributes to the Dismal Scientist web site. He received his bachelor's degree from La Salle University.

Kyle Fee is a Senior Research Analyst in the Research Department of the Federal Reserve Bank of Cleveland. His work focuses on economic development, regional economics, and economic geography. He has a bachelor's degree in economics and business administration from John Carroll University and a master's degree in urban studies: economic development from Loyola University.

Daniel Hartley is a Research Economist in the Research Department of the Federal Reserve Bank of Cleveland. He is primarily interested in urban/regional economics and labor economics. His current work focuses on crime, public housing, neighborhood housing market dynamics, and urban growth and decline. He has a Ph.D. in economics from the University of California-Berkeley, an M.B.A. in economics and finance from the University of Chicago, and an M.Eng. and a B.S. in electrical engineering from the Massachusetts Institute of Technology.

Edward Glaeser is Fred and Eleanor Glimp Professor of Economics in the Faculty of Arts and Sciences at Harvard University, where he has taught since 1992. He is Director of the Taubman Center for State and Local Government and Director of the Rappaport Institute of Greater Boston. He regularly teaches microeconomic theory and occasionally teaches urban and public economics. He has published dozens of papers on cities, economic growth, and law and economics. In particular, his work has focused on the determinants of city growth and the role of cities of centers of idea transmission. He received his Ph.D. from the University of Chicago in 1992.

Yolanda K. Kodrzycki is Vice President and Director of the New England Public Policy Center at the Federal Reserve Bank of Boston. The Policy Center conducts research on key economic and policy issues in New England and engages with regional partners in advancing identified policy options. Prior to assuming this position, Kodrzycki was a Senior Economist and Policy Advisor in the Boston Fed's Research Department. She is a senior contributor to "Toward a More Prosperous Springfield," a multiyear commitment by the Boston Fed to support the economic revitalization of Springfield, Massachusetts. During 1991–1992, she took a leave of absence from the Federal Reserve to consult for the U.S. Treasury advisory program in Central and Eastern Europe. Prior to joining the Boston Fed in 1986, she taught economics at Amherst College.

Sophia Koropeckyj is a Managing Director for Moody's Analytics. She oversees the firm's publications and consulting projects, edits many of the publications, trains new staff members, and gives presentations to clients and trade groups. She covers labor markets, auto-related industries, and the Midwestern economy. Based in West Chester, Pennsylvania, she has been with Moody's Analytics since 1994. Previously, she worked as an economist for the Great Lakes Trade Adjustment Assistance Center and WEFA. She has completed all but the dissertation portion of her doctoral studies in economics at the University of Michigan. She earned a master's degree in finance at Drexel University and a bachelor's degree in economics and history at the University of Pennsylvania.

Alan Mallach is a Senior Fellow at the Center for Community Progress, a Nonresident Senior Fellow at the Metropolitan Policy Program of the Brookings Institution in Washington, D.C., and a Visiting Scholar at the Federal Reserve Bank of Philadelphia. A widely known speaker and writer on housing policy and urban change, Mallach has been engaged in planning, community development, and urban policy as a public- and private-sector practitioner, advocate, and scholar for over forty years. He teaches in the graduate city planning program at Pratt Institute in New York City and served as a Brookings Scholar at the University of Nevada-Las Vegas for the 2010–2011 academic year. He has written several books, including *A Decent Home: Planning, Building and Preserving Affordable Housing*. He is a member of the College of Fellows of the American Institute of Certified Planners.

Ana Patricia Muño is a Senior Policy Analyst at the Federal Reserve Bank of Boston, where she conducts research on community development. She is a member of the bank's initiative "Toward a More Prosperous Springfield, MA," which supports ongoing efforts to revitalize the city of Springfield. As part of this initiative, she analyzed the role of Latino entrepreneurship in economic development and worked on identifying growth opportunities for older manufacturing cities. In addition, Muñoz has analyzed the implementation of the Home Affordable Modification Program and worked with counseling organizations and servicers to improve the loan modification process. She previously worked as a research associate in the Boston Fed's Research Department. Muñoz holds a master's degree in economics from the University of Montreal and a master's degree in public affairs from Brown University.

Jeremy Nowak is current chair of the board of directors of the Federal Reserve Bank of Philadelphia. He is a Nonresident Senior Fellow at the Brookings Institution and a Research Scholar at Penn's Institute for Urban Research. He is the former president of the William Penn Foundation and founding

CEO of The Reinvestment Fund (TRF). During his time at TRF, the organization made more than $1 billion of investments into some of America's poorest cities. Nowak was the founding chair of the Mastery Charter schools, a network of twelve inner-city schools that has successfully turned around failing schools. He has published on a variety of issues including housing policy, creativity, and development finance. He holds a B.A. in philosophy from Pennsylvania State University and a Ph.D. in cultural anthropology from the New School for Social Research.

Laura W. Perna is Professor of Higher Education Management in the Graduate School of Education (GSE) and Faculty Fellow at the Institute for Urban Research at the University of Pennsylvania. She is vice president of the Postsecondary Education Division of the American Education Research Association and former project director of the Institute for Education Sciences-funded Pre-Doctoral Training Program in Interdisciplinary Methods for Field-Based Research in Education at Penn GSE. She is associate editor of the *Journal of Higher Education*. Perna received the 2003 Promising Scholar/Early Career Achievement Award from the Association for the Study of Higher Education, the 2010 Christian R. and Mary F. Lindback Foundation Award for Distinguished Teaching from the University of Pennsylvania, and the 2011 Robert P. Huff Golden Quill Award from the National Association of Student Financial Aid Administrators.

Aaron Smith is a Senior Economist for Moody's Analytics and Associate Editor of the North American edition of the Dismal Scientist web site, producing real-time online commentary and weekly analysis on the U.S. macroeconomy. Based in West Chester, Pennsylvania, he helps oversee the U.S. Dismal team, which generates forecasts for high-frequency economic indicators. He conducts regular briefings on the economy and is frequently quoted in national and global news outlets. Smith received his B.A. in economics and business administration from Coe College, where he graduated summa cum laude and researched asset bubbles and capital markets.

Catherine Tumber is a historian and journalist whose most recent book is *Small, Gritty, and Green: The Promise of America's Smaller Industrial Cities in a Low-Carbon World*. She is a Visiting Scholar at Northeastern University's School of Public Policy and Urban Affairs, and a Fellow of the Massachusetts Institute for a New Commonwealth's Gateway Cities Innovation

Institute. She researched and wrote *Small, Gritty, and Green* while a research affiliate with MIT's Department of Urban Studies and Planning Community Innovators Lab. Her articles, essays, and reviews have appeared in the *Boston Review, Washington Post, Boston Phoenix, Bookforum, The Nation, In These Times,* and *Democracy: A Journal of Ideas,* among other publications.

Susan M. Wachter is Richard B. Worley Professor of Financial Management, a Professor of Real estate and Finance at The Wharton School, and a Professor of City and Regional planning at PennDesign, as well as codirector of the Penn Institute for Urban Research. She served as assistant secretary for policy development and research at the U.S. Department of Housing and Urban Development.

Kimberly Zeuli is Senior Vice President and Director of Research at ICIC. Her research is focused on community and economic development. She previously held positions as a vice president at the Federal Reserve Bank of Richmond and faculty positions at the University of Kentucky and the University of Wisconsin. She received her Ph.D. in applied economics from the University of Minnesota.

BIBLIOGRAPHY

Accordino, John, George Galster, and Peter Tatian. 2005. *The Impacts of Targeted Public and Nonprofit Investment on Neighborhood Development*. Richmond, Va.: Federal Reserve Bank of Richmond.

Accordino, John, and Gart T. Johnson. 2000. "Addressing the Vacant and Abandoned Property Problem." *Journal of Urban Affairs* 22: 301–15.

Ahlbrandt, Roger S., Jr., and Paul C. Brophy. 1975. *Neighborhood Revitalization: Theory and Practice*. Boston: Lexington Books.

Albouy, David. 2008. "Are Big Cities Really Bad Places to Live? Improving Quality-of-Life Estimates Across Cities." University of Michigan, Department of Economics.

Alexander, Frank S. 2000a. *Renewing Public Assets for Community Development*. New York: Local Initiative Support Corporation.

———. 2000b. "Tax Liens, Tax Sales and Due Process." *Indiana Law Journal* 75: 747–807.

———. 2011. *Land Banks and Land Banking*. Washington, D.C.: Center for Community Progress.

Alexander, Frank S., Dan Immergluck, Katie Balthrop, Philip Schaeffing, and Jesse Clark. 2012. "Legislative Responses to the Foreclosure Crisis in Nonjudicial Foreclosure States." *Review of Banking & Financial Law* 31: 341–410.

Alexander, Frank S., and Leslie A. Powell. 2011. "Neighborhood Stabilization Strategies for Vacant and Abandoned Properties." *Zoning and Planning Law Report* 34, 8: 1–10.

Alonso, William. 1964. *Location and Land Use: Toward a General Theory of Land Rent*. Cambridge, Mass.: Harvard University Press.

America 2050. n.d. *America 2050: A Prospectus*. New York: Regional Plan Association. http://www.america2050.org/pdf/America2050prospectus.pdf.

American Assembly. 1997. *Community Capitalism: Rediscovering the Markets of America's Urban Neighborhoods*. New York: American Assembly.

———. 2003. *Keeping America in Business: Advancing Workers, Businesses, and Economic Growth*. New York: American Assembly.

———. 2011. *Reinventing America's Legacy Cities: Strategies for Cities Losing Population*. New York: American Assembly.

American Farmland Information Center. 2008. *Farming on the Edge: Sprawling Development Threatens America's Best Farmland*. Washington, D.C.: American Farmland Trust.

American Institute of Architects. 2008. *Leaner, Greener Detroit*. Sustainable Design Assistance Team Report. Detroit: American Institute of Architects, Communities by Design.

Anderson, Martin. 1967. *The Federal Bulldozer*. New York: McGraw-Hill.

Angrist, Joshua D., and Jörn-Steffen Pischke. 2008. *Mostly Harmless Econometrics: An Empiricist's Companion*. Princeton, N.J.: Princeton University Press.

Arzaghi, Mohammed, and J. Vernon Henderson. 2008. "Networking Off Madison Avenue." *Review of Economic Studies* 75, 4: 1011–38.

Atkinson, Robert D., Luke A. Stewart, Scott M. Andes, and Stephen J. Ezell. 2012. "Worse Than the Great Depression: What Experts Are Missing About American Manufacturing Decline." Information Technology and Innovation Foundation, March. http://www2.itif.org/2012-american-manufacturing-decline.pdf.

Audretsch, David B. 1995. *Innovation and Industry Evolution*. Cambridge, Mass.: MIT Press.

Badger, Emily. 2011. "Redeveloping Former Industrial Sites Doesn't Mean Giving Up on Industry." *Atlantic Cities* (blog), http://www.theatlanticcities.com/housing/2011/09/brownfield-revitalization-movement/153/.

Banas, Chuck. 2010. "Sprawl and the R-word: A Buffalo-Niagara Case Study." *Joe the Planner* (blog). http://joeplanner.blogspot.com/2010/02/sprawl-and-r-word-buffalo-niagara-case.html.

Barham, James, Debra Tropp, Kathleen Enterline, Jeff Farbman, John Fisk, and Stacia Kiraly. 2012. *Regional Food Hub Resource Guide*. Washington, D.C.: U.S. Department of Agriculture, Agricultural Marketing Service.

Barker, David, and Eric A. Miller. 2009. "Homeownership and Child Welfare." *Real Estate Economics* 39, 2 (Summer): 279–303.

Barnes, William R., and Larry C. Ledebur. 1998. *The New Regional Economies*. Thousand Oaks, Calif.: Sage.

Bartik, Timothy. 1991. *Who Benefits from State and Local Economic Development Policies?* Kalamazoo, Mich.: Upjohn Institute.

Bartsch, Charles. 2006. *Linking Brownfield Redevelopment and Housing*. Washington, D.C.: Northeast-Midwest Institute.

Baum-Snow, Nathaniel. 2007. "Did Highways Cause Suburbanization?" *Quarterly Journal of Economics* 122, 2: 775–805.

Baumol, William J., and William G. Bowen. 1966. *Performing Arts: The Economic Dilemma*. Cambridge, Mass.: MIT Press.

Benfield, Kaid. 2012. "Is Placemaking a 'New Environmentalism'?" *NRDC Switchboard* (blog). http://switchboard.nrdc.org/blogs/kbenfield/is_placemaking_a_new_environme.html.

Bernanke, Ben. 2012. "Recent Developments in the Labor Market." National Association of Business Economics Annual Conference, March 26.

Berry, Christopher R., and Edward L. Glaeser. 2005. "The Divergence of Human Capital Levels Across Cities." NBER Working Paper 11617. Cambridge, Mass.: National Bureau of Economic Research.

Bertron, Cara, and Donovan Rypkema. 2012. *Historic Preservation and Rightsizing.* Washington, D.C.: Advisory Council on Historic Preservation.

Berube, Alan. 2010a. "Educational Attainment." In *The State of Metropolitan America.* Washington, D.C.: Brookings Institution Metropolitan Policy Program. http://www.brookings.edu/~/media/Files/Programs/Metro/state_of_metro_america/metro_america_chapters/metro_america_education.pdf.

——. 2010b. "Degrees of Separation: Education, Employment, and the Great Recession in Metropolitan America." In *The State of Metropolitan America.* Washington, D.C.: Brookings Institution.

Berube, Alan, and Elizabeth Kneebone. 2011. "Parsing U.S. Poverty at the Metropolitan Level." Brookings Institution. http://www.brookings.edu/blogs/the-avenue/posts/2011/09/22-metro-poverty-berube-kneebone.

Birch, Eugenie L. 2007. "Hopeful Signs: U.S. Revitalization in the 21st Century." In *Land Policies and their Outcomes,* ed. Graham K. Ingram and Yu-hung Hong. Cambridge, Mass.: Lincoln Institute of Land Policy.

——. 2012. College, University and Associated Medical Center Database, Penn Institute for Urban Research, Philadelphia.

Bluestone, Barry, and Bennett Harrison. 1982. *The Deindustrialization of America: Plant Closings, Community Abandonment, and the Dismantling of Basic Industry.* New York: Basic Books.

Blumenthal, Pamela, Harold L. Wolman, and Edward Hill. 2009. "Understanding the Economic Performance of Metropolitan Areas in the United States." *Urban Studies* 46, 3: 605–27.

Boehlke, David. 2001. *Great Neighborhoods, Great City: Revitalizing Baltimore Through the Healthy Neighborhoods Approach.* Baltimore: Goldseker Foundation.

——. 2004. *Great Neighborhoods, Great City: The Healthy Neighborhoods Approach in Baltimore, 2004 Update.* Baltimore: Goldseker Foundation.

——. 2012. "Preserving Healthy Neighborhoods: Market-Based Strategies for Housing and Neighborhood Revitalization." In *Rebuilding America's Legacy Cities: New Directions for the Industrial Heartland,* ed. Alan Mallach, 143–62. New York: American Assembly.

Bonham, J. Blaine, Jr., Gertrude J. Spilka, and Darl Rastorfer. 2002. *Old Cities/Green Cities: Communities Transform Unmanaged Land.* Chicago: American Planning Association.

Boston Redevelopment Authority. 2005. *North Allston Strategic Framework for Planning.* http://www.bostonredevelopmentauthority.org/planning/PlanningInitsIndividual.asp?action=ViewInit&InitID=34.

Boustan, Leah Platt, and Allison Shertzer. 2010. "Demography and Population Loss from Central Cities, 1950–2000." NBER Working Paper 16435. Cambridge, Mass.: National Bureau of Economic Research.

Brachman, Lavea, and Alan Mallach. 2010. *Ohio's Cities at a Turning Point: Finding the Way Forward.* Washington, D.C.: Brookings Institution.

Bradbury, Katharine L., Anthony Downs, and Kenneth A. Small. 1980. "Some Dynamics of Central City-Suburban Interactions." *American Economic Review* 70, 2: 410–14.

Brauer, David. 2008. "Factors Underlying the Decline in Manufacturing Employment Since 2000." Congressional Budget Office, December 23.

Breznitz, Dan, and Peter Cowhey. 2012. *America's Two Systems of Innovation: Recommendations for Policy Changes to Support Innovation, Production, and Job Creation.* LaJolla, Calif.: CONNECT Innovation Institute.

Briggs, Xavier de Souza. 2008. *Democracy as Problem Solving: Civic Capacity in Communities Across the Globe.* Cambridge, Mass.: MIT Press.

Brophy, Paul C., and Kim Burnett. 2003. *Building a New Framework for Community Development in Weak Market Cities.* Denver: Community Development Partnership Network, April.

Brophy, Paul C., and Jennifer S. Vey. 2002. *Seizing City Assets: Ten Steps to Vacant Land Reform.* Washington, D.C.: Brookings Institution.

Brueckner, Jan K., Jacques-Francois Thisse, and Yves Zenou. 1999. "Why Is Central Paris Rich and Downtown Detroit Poor? An Amenity-Based Theory." *European Economic Review* 43: 91–107.

Bureau of Labor Statistics. 2009. "Table 28: Selected metropolitan areas, metropolitan divisions, and cities: civilian labor force participation rates, employment-population ratios, and unemployment rates for the noninstitutional population 25 years and over, by educational attainment, 2009 annual averages." Washington, D.C.: U.S. Department of Labor. http://www.bls.gov/opub/gp/pdf/gp09_28.pdf.

———. 2012. "Employment Situation Summary." Washington, D.C.: U.S. Department of Labor, February. http://www.bls.gov/news.release/empsit.nr0.htm.

Business Journals. 2012. *The Business Review Book of Lists 2012.* http://www.bizjournals.com/albany/research/bol-marketing/.

Busso, Matias, and Patrick Kline. 2008. "Do Local Economic Development Programs Work? Evidence from the Federal Empowerment Zone Program." Working Paper 36, Economics Department, Yale University. http://papers.ssrn.com/sol3/papers.cfm?abstract_id=1090838.

Butler, Samuel. 2012. "Detroit: Testing a Collaborative, Community-Driven Strategic Plan for Reconfiguring Vacant Land." In *Cities in Transition*, ed. Joseph Schilling and Alan Mallach, 133–39. Chicago: APA Planning Advisory Service.

Cable, Josh. 2011. "Solar Manufacturers Find a Home in Glass City." *Industry Week* 260, 12: 45–47.

CamConnect. 2010. *The Budget Report: The City of Camden's Fiscal Environment 2001–2010*. Camden, N.J.: CamConnect.

Carlino, Gerald A., and Albert Saiz. 2008. "Beautiful City: Leisure Amenities and Urban Growth." Working Paper 0822. Philadelphia: Federal Reserve Bank of Philadelphia.

Carlson, Scott. 2012. "The Future of American Colleges May Lie, Literally, in Students' Hands." *Chronicle of Higher Education*, February 5.

Carnevale, Anthony, Nicole Smith, and Jeffrey Stohl. 2010. *Help Wanted: Projections of Jobs and Education Requirements Through 2018*. Washington, D.C.: Georgetown Center on Education and the Workforce. http://www9.georgetown.edu/grad/gppi/hpi/cew/pdfs/FullReport.pdf.

Casner-Lotto, Jill, and Mary Wright Benner. 2006. *Are They Really Ready to Work? Employers' Perspectives on the Basic Knowledge and Applied Skills of New Entrants to the 21st- Century U.S. Workforce*. Conference Board, Inc., The Partnership for 21st Century Skills, Corporate Voices for Working Families, and the Society for Human Resource Management. http://www, 21.org/storage/documents/FINAL_REPORT_PDF09-29-06.pdf, accessed March 25, 2012.

Center City District and Central Philadelphia Development Corporation. 2012. *State of Center City Philadelphia 2012*. Philadelphia: Center City District and Central Philadelphia Development Corporation.

CEO Council for Growth, Greater Philadelphia Chamber of Commerce, and Select Philadelphia. 2010. *The Impact of Higher Education in the Greater Philadelphia Area*. Philadelphia: CEO Council for Growth, Greater Philadelphia Chamber of Commerce, and Select Philadelphia.

Chapin, Tim. 2002. "Identifying the Real Costs and Benefits of Sports Facilities." Lincoln Institute of Land Policy Working Paper. Cambridge, Mass.: Lincoln Institute of Land Policy.

Chavez, John. 2011. "Local Solar Firms Confident Despite Industry Challenges." *Toledo Blade*, December 4.

Chinitz, Benjamin. 1961. "Contrasts in Agglomeration: New York and Pittsburgh." *American Economic Review Papers and Proceedings* 51, 2: 279–89.

Cisneros, Henry S., and Lora Engdahl, eds. 2009. *From Despair to Hope: HOPE VI and the New Promise of Public Housing in America's Cities*. Washington, D.C.: Brookings Institution Press.

City of Concord, N.C. n.d."Historic Facts." http://www.concordnc.gov/Visitor/Historic-Facts, accessed March 19, 2012.

City of Eden, N.C. 2007. "Land Development Plan." http://www.ptcog.org/planning_services/regional_planning/documents/regionalplanning_EdenLDP.pdf, accessed May 23, 2012.

———. n.d: "Our History, 1970–1979." http://edennc.us/Consolidation/twelveyears.htm, accessed March 19, 2012.

Clark, Ralph Ewing. 1959. *A Treatise on the Law and Practice of Receivers.* Cincinnati: Anderson.

Coclanis, Peter, and Louis Kyriakoudes. 2007. "Selling Which South? Economic Change in Rural and Small-Town North Carolina in an Era of Globalization, 1940–2007." *Southern Cultures* 13, 4 (Winter): 86–102.

Cohen, Stephen S., and John Zysman. 1987. *Manufacturing Matters: The Myth of the Post-Industrial Economy.* New York: Basic Books.

Collins, Benjamin, Thomas McDonald, and Jay A. Mousa. 2007. "The Rise and Decline of Auto Parts Manufacturing in the Midwest." *BLS Monthly Labor Review* 130, 10 (October): 14–20.

Collins, David. 1998. "Knowledge Work or Working Knowledge? Ambiguity and Confusion in the Analysis of the 'Knowledge Age'." *Journal of Systemic Knowledge Management* 19, 1: 38–50.

Colson, N. Edward, Seok-Joon Hwang, and Susumu Imai. 2002. "The Value of Owner-Occupation in Neighborhoods." *Journal of Housing Research* 1, 2: 153–74.

———. 2003. "The Benefits of Owner-Occupation in Neighborhoods." *Journal of Housing Research* 14, 1: 21–48.

Community Affairs Offices, Federal Reserve System and Metropolitan Policy Program at the Brookings Institution. 2008. *The Enduring Challenge of Concentrated Poverty in America: Case Studies from Communities Across the U.S.A.* Washington, D.C.: Brookings Institution.

Community Research Partners and Rebuild Ohio. 2008. *$60 Million and Counting: The Cost of Vacant and Abandoned Property to Eight Ohio Cities.* Columbus: Community Research Partners.

Conner, David S., William A. Knudson, Michael W. Hamm, Christopher Peterson. 2009. "The Food System as an Economic Driver: Strategies and Results in Michigan." *Journal of Hunger & Environmental Nutrition* 3, 4: 371–83.

Connolly, James J. 2008. "Decentering Urban History: Peripheral Cities in the Modern World." *Journal of Urban History* 35, 1: 3–14.

Cove, Elizabeth, Margery Austin Turner, Xavier de Souza Briggs, and Cynthia Duarte. 2008. *Can Escaping from Poor Neighborhoods Increase Employment and Earnings?* Washington, D.C.: Urban Institute, Metropolitan Housing and Communities Center.

Crain's New York Business. 2012. *Book of Lists 2012.* Vol. 27, nos. 51–52.

Crawford, Matthew. 2009. *Shop Class as Soulcraft: An Inquiry into the Value of Work.* New York: Penguin.

Creative Government in the 21st Century. 2006. Dayton, Ohio: Wright State University Center of Urban and Public Affairs.

Cumbler, John T. 1989. *A Social History of Urban Decline.* New Brunswick, N.J.: Rutgers University Press.

Cutter, Susan, Christopher Burton, and Christopher Emrich. 2010. "Disaster Resilience Indicators for Benchmark Baseline Conditions." *Journal of Homeland Security and Emergency Management* 7(2): 141–46.

Davey, Monica. 2011. "Darker Nights as Some Cities Turn Off the Lights." *New York Times*, December 29.

Davidson, Adam. 2012. "Making It in America." *Atlantic Monthly* 309, 1.

Davis, Timothy A. 2012. "A Comparative Analysis of State and Local Government Vacant Property Registration Statutes." *Urban Lawyer* 44: 399–428.

De Tocqueville, Alexis. 1835. *Democracy in America: Volume 1.* London: Saunders and Otley.

Dewar, Margaret, and June Manning Thomas, eds. 2012. *The City After Abandonment.* Philadelphia: University of Pennsylvania Press.

Duranton, Gilles. 2007. "Urban Evolutions: The Fast, the Slow, and the Still." *American Economic Review* 97(1): 197–221.

Duranton, Gilles, Philippe Martin, Thierry Mayer, and Florian Mayneris. 2010. *The Economics of Clusters: Lessons from the French Experience.* Oxford: Oxford University Press.

Duranton, Gilles, and Diego Puga. 2001. "Nursery Cities: Urban Diversity, Process Innovation, and the Life Cycle of Products." *American Economic Review* 91, 5: 1454–77.

———. 2004. "Micro-Foundations of Urban Agglomeration Economies." In *Handbook of Regional and Urban Economics*, ed. J. Vernon Henderson and Jacques Francois Thisse, 2063–2117. Amsterdam: North-Holland.

———. 2013. "The Growth of Cities." In *Handbook of Economic Growth*, vol. 2, ed. Philippe Aghion and Steven N. Durlauf. Amsterdam: North-Holland, forthcoming.

Duranton, Gilles, and Matthew A. Turner. 2012. "Urban Growth and Transportation." *Review of Economic Studies*, 79, 4: 1407–40.

Economist. 2012. "A Lack of Enterprise." November 13.

Elvery, Joel A., and Leo Sveikauskas. 2010. "How Far Do Agglomeration Effects Reach?" Typescript, November.

Erickcek, George, and Hannah McKinney. 2006. "'Small City Blues': Looking for Growth Factors in Small and Medium-Sized Cities." *Economic Development Quarterly* 20, 3: 232–58.

Eyster, Lauren, Demetra Smith Nightingale, Burt Barnow, Carolyn O'Brien, John Trutko, and Daniel Kuehn. 2010. *Implementation and Training Outcomes of the High Growth Job Training Initiative: Final Report.* Washington, D.C.: Urban Institute.

Fainstein, Susan S., and Norman I. Fainstein. 1986. "Regime Strategies, Communal Resistance, and Economic Forces." In *Restructuring the City*, ed. Susan S. Fainstein, Norman I. Fainstein, Richard Child Hill, Dennis Judd, and Michael Peter Smith, 245–82. New York: Longman.

Farkas, Steve. 2011. *Hiring and Higher Education: Business Executives Talk about the Costs and Benefits of College*. Committee for Economic Development and the Public Agenda. http://www.publicagenda.org/files/pdf/Hiring_HigherEd.pdf., accessed March 25, 2012.

Federal Reserve Board. 2012. *The U.S. Housing Market: Current Conditions and Policy Considerations*. Washington, D.C.: Federal Reserve Board.

Ferryman, Kadija S., Xavier de Souza Briggs, Susan J. Popkin, and Maria Rendon. 2008. *Do Better Neighborhoods for MTO Families Mean Better Schools?* Washington, D.C.: Urban Institute, Metropolitan Housing and Communities Center.

Fitzgerald, Joan. 2010. *Emerald Cities: Urban Sustainability and Economic Development*. New York: Oxford University Press.

Fitzpatrick, Thomas J., and Stephan Whitaker. 2012. *Overvaluing Residential Properties and the Growing Glut of REO*. Economic Commentary 2012–3. Cleveland: Federal Reserve Bank of Cleveland.

Foot, Philippa. 1967. "The Problem of Abortion and the Doctrine of the Double Effect." *Oxford Review* 5: 5–15.

Forrant, Robert. 2009. *Metal Fatigue: American Bosch and the Demise of Metalworking in the Connecticut River Valley*. New York: Baywood.

Foster, Katherine. 2012. "In Search of Resilience." In *Urban and Regional Policy and Its Effects*, vol. 4, *In Search of Regional Resilience*, ed. Margaret Weir, Nancy Pindus, Howard Wial, and Harold Wolman, 24–59. Washington, D.C.: Brookings Institution Press.

Frey, William H. 2012. "Demographic Reversal: Cities Thrive, Suburbs Sputter." Washington, D.C.: Brookings Institution.

Fu, Shihe. 2007. "Smart-Café-Cities: Testing Human Capital Externalities in the Boston Metropolitan Area." *Journal of Urban Economics* 61, 1 (January): 86–111.

Fuchs, Erica R. H. 2012. *The Impact of Manufacturing Offshore on Technology Competitiveness: Implications for U.S. Policy*. LaJolla, Calif.: CONNECT Innovation Institute.

Fullilove, Mindy Thompson. 2004. *Root Shock: How Tearing Up City Neighborhoods Hurts America and What We Can Do About It*. New York: One World/Ballantine.

Furdell, Kimberly, and Harold Wolman. 2006. "Toward Understanding Urban Pathology: Creating a Typology of 'Weak Market' Cities." George Washington Institute of Public Policy Working Paper 021, April. Washington, D.C.: Trachtenberg School of Public Policy and Public Administration.

Furman Center for Real Estate and Urban Policy. 2009. *Transforming Foreclosed Properties into Community Assets*. New York: Furman Center for Real Estate and Urban Policy.

Galster, George. 1987. *Homeowners and Neighborhood Reinvestment*. Durham, N.C.: Duke University Press.

Gans, Herbert J. 1962. *The Urban Villagers Group and Class in the Life of Italian-Americans*. Glencoe, Ill.: Free Press.

Gaswami, Rahul. 2010. "A Pearl River Tale: Power and Pride in China." *Energy Bulletin* (website).

Glaeser, Edward L. 2011. *The Triumph of the City.* New York: Penguin.

Glaeser, Edward L., and Joshua D. Gottlieb. 2008. "The Economics of Place-Making Policies." *Brookings Papers on Economic Activity* 1: 155–239.

Glaeser, Edward L., Joshua D. Gottlieb, and Kristina Tobio. 2012. "Housing Booms and City Centers." NBER Working Paper 17914. Cambridge, Mass.: National Bureau of Economic Research.

Glaeser, Edward L., and Joseph Gyourko. 2005. "Urban Decline and Durable Housing." *Journal of Political Economy* 113, 2: 345–75.

Glaeser, Edward, Joseph Gyourko, and Raven Saks. 2006. "Urban Growth and Housing Supply." *Journal of Economic Geography* 6, 1: 71–89.

Glaeser, Edward L., and Matthew E. Kahn. 2001a. "Decentralized Employment and the Transformation of the American City." Brookings-Wharton Papers on Urban Affairs, 1–47.

———. 2001b. "Decentralized Employment and the Transformation of the American City." NBER Working Paper 8117. Cambridge, Mass.: National Bureau of Economic Research.

Glaeser, Edward L., Matthew E. Kahn, and Jordan Rappaport. 2008. "Why Do the Poor Live in Cities? The Role of Public Transportation." *Journal of Urban Economics* 63, 1: 1–24.

Glaeser, Edward L., Heidi Kallal, José A. Scheinkman, and Andrei Schleifer. 1992. "Growth in Cities." *Journal of Political Economy* 100, 6: 1126–52.

Glaeser, Edward L., and William R. Kerr. 2009. "Local Industrial Conditions and Entrepreneurship: How Much of the Spatial Distribution Can We Explain?" *Journal of Economics Management and Strategy* 18, 3: 623–63.

Glaeser, Edward L., Sari Pekkala Kerr, and William R. Kerr. 2012. "Entrepreneurship and Urban Growth: An Empirical Assessment with Historical Mines." NBER Working Paper 18333. Cambridge, Mass.: National Bureau of Economic Research.

Glaeser, Edward L., William R. Kerr, and Giacomo A. M. Ponzetto. 2010. "Clusters of Entrepreneurship." *Journal of Urban Economics* 67, 1: 150–68.

Glaeser, Edward L., and Janet E. Kohlhase. 2004. "Cities, Regions and the Decline of Transport Costs." *Papers in Regional Science* 83, 1: 197–228.

Glaeser, Edward L., Jed Kolko, and Albert Saiz. 2001. "Consumer City." *Journal of Economic Geography* 1, 1: 27–50.

Glaeser, Edward L., and Giacomo A. M. Ponzetto. 2010. "Did the Death of Distance Hurt Detroit and Help New York?" NBER Working Paper 13710. Cambridge, Mass.: National Bureau of Economic Research.

Glaeser, Edward L., Giacomo A. M. Ponzetto, and Kristina Tobio. 2011. "Cities, Skills and Regional Change." NBER Working Paper 16934. Cambridge, Mass.: National Bureau of Economic Research.

Glaeser, Edward L., and Bruce Sacerdote. 1999. "Why Is There More Crime in Cities?" *Journal of Political Economy* 107, 6: S225-58.

Glaeser, Edward L., and Albert Saiz. 2004. "The Rise of the Skilled City." *Brookings-Wharton Papers on Urban Affairs* 5: 47–94.

Glaeser, Edward L., José A. Scheinkman, and Andrei Shleifer. 1995. "Economic Growth in a Cross-Section of Cities." *Journal of Monetary Economics* 36, 1: 117–43.

Glaeser, Edward, and Jesse Shapiro. 2001. *City Growth and the 2000 Census: Which Places Grew and Why?* Center on Urban and Metropolitan Policy, May. Washington, D.C.: Brookings Institution.

Glaeser, Edward L., and Christina Tobio. 2007. "The Rise of the Sunbelt." Taubman Center Policy Briefs, Harvard University, PB-2007-5, May.

———. 2008. "The Rise of the Sunbelt." *Southern Economic Journal* 74, 3: 610–43.

Goldstein, Ira. 2011. "Market Value Analysis: A Data-Based Approach to Understanding Urban Housing Markets." In *Putting Data to Work: Data-Driven Approaches to Strengthening Neighborhoods*, ed. Anne O'Shaughnessy and Liam Nelson, 49–60. Washington, D.C.: Board of Governors of the Federal Reserve System.

Goldstein, Joseph. 2011. "Police Force Nearly Halved, Camden Feels Impact." *New York Times,* March 6.

Gottlieb, Joshua D., and Edward L. Glaeser. 2008. "The Economics of Place-Making Policies." *Brookings Papers on Economic Activity* 1: 155–239.

Gould Ellen, Ingrid, and Katherine O'Reagan. 2009. "Crime and U.S. Cities: Recent Patterns and Implications." In *The Shape of the New American City*, ed. Eugénie L. Birch and Susan M. Wachter. *Annals of the American Academy of Political and Social Science* 626, 6.

Government Accountability Office. 2011. *Vacant Properties: Growing Number Increases Communities' Costs and Challenges.* GAO-12-34. Washington, D.C.

Greenstone, Michael, Richard Hornbeck, and Enrico Moretti. 2010. "Identifying Agglomeration Spillovers: Evidence from Winners and Losers of Large Plants Openings." *Journal of Political Economy* 118, 3: 536–98.

Greenstone, Michael, and Enrico Moretti. 2004. "Bidding for Industrial Plants: Does Winning a 'Million Dollar Plant' Increase Welfare?" Working Paper 04-39. Cambridge, Mass.: MIT Department of Economics. http://ssrn.com/abstract=623122, accessed March 3, 2013.

Guerrieri, Veronica, Daniel Hartley, and Erik Hurst.. 2012. "Within-City Variation in Urban Decline: The Case of Detroit." *American Economic Review - Papers and Proceedings*, 102, 3: 120–126.

———. 2013. "Endogenous Gentrification and Housing Price Dynamics." *Journal of Public Economics* 100: 45–60.

Gunther, Robert. 2003. *Manufacturing Anywhere, Session 3: Think Globally, Manufacture Locally: Redrawing the Map of Manufacturing.* Washington, D.C.: RAND.

Gyourko, Joseph, Albert Saiz, and Anita A. Summers. 2008. "A New Measure of the Local Regulatory Environment for Housing Markets: The Wharton Residential Land Use Regulatory Index." *Urban Studies* 45, 3: 693–729.

Haar, Sharon. 2011. *The City as Campus: Urbanism and Higher Education in Chicago.* Minneapolis: University of Minnesota Press.

Hackerspaces.org wiki. http://hackerspaces.org/wiki/List_of_Hacker_Spaces, accessed March 4, 2012.

Hackney, Suzette. 2009. "Is Right-Sizing the Right Fix?" *Detroit Free Press*, July 19.

"Hanesbrands Closing N.C. Plant Earlier Than Expected." 2008. *Manufacturing.Net*, December 3. http://www.manufacturing.net/news/2008/12/hanesbrands-closing -nc-plant-earlier-than-expected, accessed March 19, 2012.

Harrison, Sheena. 2011. "Ohio Rated Second in U.S. in Solar-Panel Output." *Toledo Blade*, July 19.

Hart, Melanie. 2012. *Shining a Light on U.S.-China Clean Energy Cooperation.* Washington, D.C.: Center for American Progress.

Hayden, Dolores. 2003. *Building Suburbia: Green Fields and Urban Growth 1820– 2000.* New York: Pantheon.

Helper, Susan. 2011. *The U.S. Auto Supply Chain at a Crossroads: Implications of an Industry in Transformation.* Cleveland: Driving Change Research Consortium.

Helper, Susan, Timothy Krueger, and Howard Wial. 2012a. *Why Does Manufacturing Matter? Which Manufacturing Matters? A Policy Framework.* Washington, D.C.: Brookings Institution, February.

———. 2012b. *Locating American Manufacturing: Trends in the Geography of Production.* Washington, D.C.: Brookings Institution. April.

Hill, Edward, Travis St. Clair, Howard Wial, Harold Wolman, Patricia Atkins, Pamela Blumenthal, Sarah Ficenenc, and Alec Friedhoff. 2012. "Economic Shocks and Regional Economic Resilience." In *Urban and Regional Policy and Its Effects*, vol. 4, *In Search of Regional Resilience*, ed. Margaret Weir, Nancy Pindus, Howard Wial, and Harold Wolman, 193–274. Washington, D.C.: Brookings Institution Press.

Hill, Edward W., Harold L. Wolman, Katherine Kowalczyk, and Travis St. Clair. 2012. "Forces Affecting City Population Growth or Decline: The Effects of Interregional and Inter-Municipal Competition." In *Rebuilding America's Legacy Cities: New Directions for the Industrial Heartland,* ed. Alan Mallach, 31–80. New York: American Assembly.

Hodgson, Kimberley, Marcia Caton Campbell, and Martin Bailkey. 2011. *Urban Agriculture: Growing Healthy, Sustainable Places.* Chicago: American Planning Association.

Hoffman, Nancy. 2012. "Ordinary Teenagers, Extraordinary Results: How the Best Vocational Education Systems Launch Young People into Working Life." In *Preparing Today's Students for Tomorrow's Jobs in Metropolitan America: The Policy,*

Practice, and Research Issues, ed. Laura W. Perna, 75–92. Philadelphia: University of Pennsylvania Press.

Holmes, Thomas J. 1998. "The Effects of State Policies on the Location of Industry: Evidence from State Borders." *Journal of Political Economy* 106, 4: 667–705.

Holzer, Harry. 2012. "Creating Effective Education and Workforce Policies for Metropolitan Labor Markets in America." In *Preparing Today's Students for Tomorrow's Jobs in Metropolitan America: The Policy, Practice, and Research Issues*, ed. Laura W. Perna, 245–59. Philadelphia: University of Pennsylvania Press.

Hoornbeek, John, and Terry Schwarz. 2009. *Sustainable Infrastructure in Shrinking Cities: Options for the Future.* Cleveland: Center for Public Administration and Public Policy and Cleveland Urban Design Collaborative, Kent State University.

Hout, Michael. 2011. "Social and Economic Returns to College." *Annual Review of Sociology* 37: 1–45.

HUD. 2012. "Welcome to the Community Renewal Initiative." http://www.hud.gov /offices/cpd/economicdevelopment/programs/rc/index.cfm.

Ihlanfeldt, Keith R. 1995. "The Importance of the Central City to the Regional and National Economy: A Review of the Arguments and Empirical Evidence." *Cityscape: A Journal of Policy Development and Research* 1, 2: 125–50.

Immergluck, Dan. 2012. "Distressed and Dumped: Market Dynamics of Low-Value, Foreclosed Properties During the Advent of the Federal Neighborhood Stabilization Program." *Journal of Planning Education and Research* 32, 1: 48–61.

Immergluck, Dan, and Geoff Smith. 2006. "The External Costs of Foreclosure: The Impact of Single-Family Mortgage Foreclosures on Property Values." *Housing Policy Debate* 17: 57–80.

Isserman, Andrew. 2000. "Economic Base Studies for Urban and Regional Planning." In *The Profession of City Planning: Changes, Images and Challenges 1950–2000*, ed. Lloy Rodwin and Bishwapriya Sanyal, 174–93. New Brunswick, N.J.: Center for Urban Policy Research, Rutgers University.

Jacob, Brian A., and Jens Ludwig. 2011. "Educational Interventions: Their Effects on the Achievement of Poor Children." In *Neighborhood and Life Chances: How Place Matters in Modern America*, ed. Harriet B. Newburger, Eugenie L. Birch, and Susan M. Wachter, 37–49. Philadelphia: University of Pennsylvania Press.

Jacobs, Jane. 1961. *The Death and Life of Great American Cities.* New York: Random House.

——. 1969. *The Economy of Cities.* New York: Random House.

——. 2011. *The Death and Life of Great American Cities.* 50th Anniversary Edition. New York: Vintage Modern Library.

Jaffe, Adam B., Manuel Trajtenberg, and Rebecca Henderson. 1993. "Geographic Localization of Knowledge Spillovers as Evidenced by Patent Citations." *Quarterly Journal of Economics* 108(3): 577–98.

Karastan Rug News. 2009. April 15. http://karastanrug.org/karastan-rugs-home.html, accessed March 19, 2012.

Katz, Matt. 2009. "Camden's Waterfront—And Its Woes." *Philadelphia Inquirer*, November 9.

Kelly, James J., Jr. 2004. "Refreshing the Heart of the City: Vacant Building Receivership as a Tool for Neighborhood Revitalization and Community Empowerment." *Journal of Affordable Housing* 13, 2: 210–38.

Kenyon, Daphne A., and Adam H. Langley. 2012. *Payments in Lieu of Taxes: Balancing Municipal and Nonprofit Interests*. Cambridge, Mass.: Lincoln Institute of Land Policy.

Kenyon, Daphne, Adam H. Langley, and Bethany P. Paquin. 2012. *Rethinking Property Tax Incentives for Business*. Cambridge, Mass.: Lincoln Institute of Land Policy.

Klier, Thomas H., and James Rubenstien. 2008. *Who Really Made Your Car?* Kalamazoo, Mich.: Upjohn Institute.

———. 2010. "The Changing Geography of North American Motor Vehicle Production." *Cambridge Journal of Regions, Economy, and Society* 3, 3: 335–47.

Klosterman, R. E. 1990. *Community and Analysis Planning Techniques*. Savage, Md.: Rowman & Littlefield.

Kneebone, Elizabeth. 2009. "Job Sprawl Revisited: The Changing Geography of Metropolitan Employment." Metro Economy Series for the Metropolitan Studies Program at Brookings, April. Washington, D.C.: Brookings Institution.

Kodrzycki, Yolanda K. 2002. "Educational Attainment as a Constraint on Economic Growth." In *Education in the 21st Century: Meeting the Challenge of a Changing World*, ed. Yolanda K. Kodrzycki, 37–84. Boston: Federal Reserve Bank of Boston.

Kodrzycki, Yolanda K., Ana Patricia Muñoz, et al. 2009a. "Reinvigorating Springfield's Economy: Lessons from Resurgent Cities." Public Policy Discussion Paper 09-6. Boston: Federal Reserve Bank of Boston.

———. 2009b. "Jobs in Springfield, Massachusetts: Understanding and Remedying the Causes of Low Resident Employment Rates." Public Policy Discussion Paper 09-11. Boston: Federal Reserve Bank of Boston.

Kropotkin, Petr. 1901. *Fields, Factories, and Workshops: or, Industry Combined with Agriculture and Brain Work with Manual Work*. New York: Putnam.

Krugman, Paul. 1991. "History and Industry Location: The Case of the Manufacturing Belt." *American Economic Review* 81(2): 80–83.

Kutner, J. 2009. "A Rust Belt City Tries to Shrink Its Way to Success." *Christian Science Monitor*, May 29.

Lehigh University. 2009. *Form 990 Return of Organization Exempt from Income Tax*. http://www.guidestar.org/FinDocuments/2009/240/795/2009-240795445-05ae7f59-9.pdf.

Leinberger, Christopher B. 2005. "Turning Around Downtown: Twelve Steps to Revitatlization." Metropolitan Policy Program. Washington, D.C.: Brookings Institution, March.

Leibowitz, Stan J., and Stephen E. Margolis. 1999. "Path Dependence." In *Encyclopedia of Law and Economics*, ed. Boudewijn Bouckaert and Gerrit DeGeest. Cheltenham: Edward Elgar and University of Ghent.

LeRoy, Greg, and Leigh McIlvaine. 2011. *Paid to Sprawl: Subsidized Job Flight from Cleveland and Cincinnati*. Washington, D.C.: Good Jobs First.

LeRoy, Stephen F., and Jon Sonstelie. 1983. "Paradise Lost and Regained: Transportation Innovation, Income, and Residential Location." *Journal of Urban Economics* 13: 67–89.

Lima, A. 2011. *Boston by the Numbers: Taxes, Local Aid and Fiscal Conditions*. Boston: Boston Redevelopment Authority.

Lin, Jeffrey. 2002. "Gentrification and Transit in Northwest Chicago." *Journal of Transportation Research Forum, Transportation Quarterly* 56, 4: 175–91.

Lind, Kermit. 2012. "Collateral Matters: Housing Code Compliance in the Mortgage Crisis." *Northern Illinois University Law Review* 32: 445–71.

Logan, John R., Zengwang Xu, and Brian Stults. 2012. "Interpolating US Decennial Census Tract Data from as Early as 1970 to 2010: A Longitudinal Tract Database." *Professional Geographer*, forthcoming.

Longworth, Richard C. 2008. *Caught in the Middle: America's Heartland in the Age of Globalism*. New York: Bloomsbury.

———. 2011. *The Midwesterner: Blogging the Global Midwest* (blog). http://globalmidwest.typepad.com/global-midwest/2011/10/re-shoring-and-its-discontents.html.

Luo, Tian, Amar Mann, and Richard Holden. 2010. "The Expanding Role of Temporary Help Services from 1990 to 2008." *Monthly Labor Review, Bureau of Labor Statistics* 133, 8 (August): 3–16.

MacDonald, Christine. 2011. "Private Landowners Complicate Reshaping of Detroit." *Detroit News*, February 3.

Mallach, Alan. 2008. *Managing Neighborhood Change: A Framework for Sustainable and Equitable Revitalization*. Montclair, N.J.: National Housing Institute.

———. 2010. *Meeting the Challenge of Distressed Property Investors in America's Neighborhoods*. New York: Local Initiatives Support Corporation.

———. 2011a. "Re-Engineering the Urban Landscape: Land Use Reconfiguration and the Morphological Transformation of Shrinking Industrial Cities." In *Engineering Earth: The Impacts of Mega-Engineering Projects*, ed. Stanley D. Brunn, 1855–82. Dordrecht: Springer Science+Business Media.

———. 2011b. "Demolition and Preservation in America's Distressed Older Industrial Cities." *Building Research and Information* 39, 4 (July–August): 380–94.

———. 2012a. "Depopulation, Market Collapse and Property Abandonment: Surplus Land and Buildings in Legacy Cities." In *Rebuilding America's Legacy Cities: New Directions for the Industrial Heartland*, ed. Alan Mallach, 85–109. New York: American Assembly.

———. 2012b. *In Philadelphia's Shadow: Small Cities in the Third Federal Reserve District*. Philadelphia: Federal Reserve Bank of Philadelphia.

———, ed. 2012c. *Rebuilding America's Legacy Cities: New Directions for the Industrial Heartland*. New York: Columbia University, American Assembly.

Mallach, Alan, and Eric Scorsone. 2011. *Long-Term Stress and Systemic Failure: Taking Seriously the Fiscal Crisis of America's Older Cities*. Washington, D.C.: Center for Community Progress.

Manahan, Kevin. 2012. "Trenton Mayor Tony Mack Has a Big Mess to Clean Up: His Own." *New Jersey Star-Ledger*, January 8.

Marshall, Alfred. 1890. *Principles of Economics*. London: Macmillan.

Martin, Benton C. 2010. "Vacant Property Registration Ordinances." *Real Estate Law Journal* 39, 1: 1–43.

Massachusetts Technology Collaborative. 2011. *Building Bridges to Growth: A Roadmap for Advanced Manufacturing in Massachusetts*. Boston: John Adams Innovation Institute.

McKinsey Global Institute. 2012. *Manufacturing the Future: The Next Era of Global Growth and Innovation*, November. http://www.mckinsey.com/insights/mgi /research/productivity_competitiveness_and_growth/the_future_of_manufac turing.

Meter, Ken. 2010. *Hoosier Farmer? Emergent Food Systems in Indiana*. Report for Indiana Department of Health. Minneapolis: Crossroads Resource Center.

Meter, Ken, and Jon Rosales. 2001. *Finding Food in Farm Country: The Economics of Food and Farming in Eastern Minnesota*. Minneapolis: University of Minnesota. Updated through 2005 at http://www.crcworks.org/fffc.pdf, accessed January 23, 2012.

Mieszkowski, Peter, and Edwin S. Mills. 1993. "The Causes of Metropolitan Suburbanization." *Journal of Economic Perspectives* 7(3): 135–47.

Mills, Edwin S. 1967. "An Aggregative Model of Resource Allocation in a Metropolitan Area." *American Economic Review (Papers and Proceedings)* 57, 2: 197–210.

Minchin, Timothy J. 2009. "'It Knocked This City to Its Knees': The Closure of Pillowtex Mills in Kannapolis, North Carolina, and the Decline of the U.S. Textile Industry." *Labor History* 50: 350, 3: 287–311.

Minnesota Population Center. 2011. *National Historical Geographic Information System: Version 2.0*. Minneapolis: University of Minnesota.

Mock, Gary N. 2013a. "Cannon Mills, Kannapolis, N.C." http://www.textilehistory .org/CannonMills.html, 1.

———. 2013b. "Fieldcrest Mills." http://www.textilehistory.org/FieldcrestMills.html, accessed March 14, 2012.

Mollenkopf, John H. 1978. "The Postwar Politics of Urban Development." In *Marxism and Metropolis*, ed. William K. Tabb and Larry Sawers, 117–52. New York: Oxford University Press.

Moloney, Brenna. 2011. "Welcome to Saginaw!" *PreservationNation Blog*. National Trust for Historic Preservation. http://blog.preservationnation.org/2011/07/21 /welcome-to-saginaw/, accessed February 12, 2012.

Moretti, Enrico. 2004. "Estimating the Social Return to Higher Education: Evidence from Longitudinal and Repeated Cross-Sectional Data." *Journal of Econometrics* 121(1–2): 175–212.

Morrison, Hunter, and Margaret Dewar. 2012. "Planning in America's Legacy Cities: Toward Better, Smaller Communities After Decline." In *Rebuilding America's Legacy Cities: New Directions for the Industrial Heartland,* ed. Alan Mallach, 115–38. New York: American Assembly.

Mozingo, Louise A. 2011. *Pastoral Capitalism: A History of Suburban Corporate Landscapes.* Cambridge, Mass.: MIT Press.

Muro, Mark, and Christopher Hoene. 2009. *Fiscal Challenges Facing Cities: Implications for Recovery.* Washington, D.C.: Brookings Institution and National League of Cities.

Muro, Mark, Jonathan Rothwell, and Devashree Saha. 2011. *Sizing the Green Economy: A National and Regional Green Jobs Assessment.* Washington, D.C.: Brookings Institution.

Muth, Richard F. 1969. *Cities and Housing: The Spatial Pattern of Urban Residential Land Use.* Chicago: University of Chicago Press.

National Center for Education Statistics. 2011. *Digest of Education Statistics 2010.*

National Consumer Law Center. 2012. *The Other Foreclosure Crisis: Property Tax Lien Sales.* Boston: National Consumer Law Center.

National Governors Association. 2011. *Degrees for What Jobs? Raising Expectations for Universities and Colleges in a Global Economy.* Washington, D.C.: NGA Center for Best Practices, March 22.

Nelesen, Marcia. 2012. "Janesville City Council Approves Incentives for Shine." *Janesville Gazette*, February 14.

Nichols, Donald M. 2003. "Midwest Manufacturing, the Chinese Yuan and the Dollar." University of Wisconsin, Madison, working paper, September.

Norris, Patricia E., and Nigel G. Griswold. 2007. *Economic Impacts of Residential Property Abandonment.* MSU Land Policy Institute Report 2007-05. East Lansing: Michigan State University Land Policy Institute.

North Carolina Research Campus. n.d. "History of Kannapolis." http://www.ncresearch campus.net/about-ncrc/history-of-kannapolis.aspx, accessed March 19, 2012.

Nowak, Jeremy. 2012. "Resilience and Renewal." Remarks at Philadelphia Federal Reserve Bank Reinventing Cities Conference, May 9.

Office of Management and Budget. 2009. Bulletin 10-02, December 1.

Page, Scott E. 2006. "Path Dependence." *Quarterly Journal of Political Science* 1: 87–115.

Pathways to Prosperity Project. 2011. *Pathways to Prosperity: Meeting the Challenge of Preparing Young Americans for the 21st Century.* Cambridge, Mass: Harvard Graduate School of Education.

Paull, Evans. 2008. "Environmental and Economic Benefits of Brownfields Redevelopment" (working draft). Washington, D.C.: Northeast-Midwest Institute.

Pendall, Rolf. 2003. *Sprawl Without Growth: The Upstate Paradox*. Washington, D.C.: Brookings Institution.

Perna, Laura W., ed. 2012. *Preparing Today's Students for Tomorrow's Jobs in Metropolitan America: The Policy, Practice, and Research Issues*. Philadelphia: University of Pennsylvania Press.

Perry, David C., and Wim Wiewel, eds. 2005. *The University as Urban Developer: Case Studies and Analysis*. Cambridge, Mass.: Lincoln Institute of Land Policy.

Pesick, Jerome P., and Ronald E. Reynolds. 2007. "Recent Changes in Eminent Domain Law." *Michigan Bar Journal* 86, 11(November): 22–26.

Pew Center on the States. 2012. *Evidence Counts: Evaluating State Tax Incentives for Jobs and Growth*. Washington, D.C.: Pew Charitable Trusts.

Philadelphia Museum of Art. 2012. "Over 150,000 Tickets Booked for Van Gogh Up Close at the Philadelphia Museum of Art." Press release, March 26.

Phillips, Matthew. 2012. "For Some Manufacturers, Time to Head Home." *Bloomberg Businessweek*, February 2.

Pisano, Gary P., and Willy C. Shih. 2009. "Restoring American Competitiveness." *Harvard Business Review* 87, 7: 114–25.

Porter, Michael E. 1997. New Strategies for Inner-City Economic Development. *Economic Development Quarterly* 11, 1: 11–27.

Pritchett, Wendell E. 2008. *Robert Clifton Weaver and the American City*. Chicago: University of Chicago Press.

Puga, Diego. 2010. "The Magnitude and Causes of Agglomeration Economies." *Journal of Regional Science* 50, 1 (February): 203–19.

Rae, Douglas W. 2003. *City: Urbanism and Its End*. New Haven, Conn.: Yale University Press.

Ramsay, Christina, Cintli Sanchez and Jesse Wanzer. 2006. *Shopping for Homes and Schools: A Qualitative Study of West Hartford, Connecticut*. Hartford, Conn.: Trinity College, December 2006. Available from Trinity College Digital Repository, Hartford, Connecticut, http://digitalrepository.trincoll.edu.

Rappaport, Jordan. 2003. "U.S. Urban Decline and Growth, 1950 to 2000." *Economic Review* 88 (Third Quarter): 15–44.

———. 2007. "Moving to Nice Weather." *Regional Science and Urban Economics* 37, 3: 375–98.

Rauch, James E. 1993. "Productivity Gains from Geographic Concentration of Human Capital: Evidence from the Cities." *Journal of Urban Economics* 34: 380–400.

Redding, Stephen J., and Daniel M. Sturm. 2008. "The Costs of Remoteness: Evidence from German Division and Reunification." *American Economic Review* 98, 5: 1766–97.

Reese, Laura A. 1997. "Do Leadership Structures Matter in Local Economic Development?" In *Dilemmas of Urban Economic Development*, ed. Richard D. Bingham and Robert Mier, 224–240. Urban Affairs Annual Reviews 47. Thousand Oaks, Calif.: Sage.

Reese, Laura A., and Minting Ye. 2011. "Policy Versus Place Luck: Achieving Local Economic Prosperity." *Economic Development Quarterly* 25, 3: 221–36.

Reichtell, Bobbi. 2012. "Re-Imagining Cleveland: Pilot Land Reuse Projects." In *Rebuilding America's Legacy Cities: New Directions for the Industrial Heartland*, ed. Alan Mallach, 185–88. New York: American Assembly.

Roback, Jennifer. 1982. "Wages, Rents and the Quality of Life." *Journal of Political Economy* 90(6): 1257–78.

Rodin, Judith. 2007. *The University and Urban Revival: Out of the Ivory Tower and into the Streets.* Philadelphia: University of Pennsylvania Press.

Rosenthal, Stuart S., and William C. Strange. 2003. "Geography, Industrial Organization, and Agglomeration." *Review of Economics and Statistics* 85, 2 (May): 377–93.

———. 2004. "Evidence on the Nature and Sources of Agglomeration." In *Handbook of Regional and Urban Economics*, ed. J. Vernon Henderson and Jacques-François Thisse, 2119–72. Amsterdam: North-Holland.

———. 2010. "Small Establishments/Big Effects: Agglomeration, Industrial Organization and Entrepreneurship." In *The Economics of Agglomeration*, ed. Edward L. Glaeser, 277–302. Cambridge, Mass.: National Bureau of Economic Research.

Rothwell, Jonathan, and Alan Berube. 2011. *Education, Demand, and Unemployment in Metropolitan America.* Washington, D.C.: Metropolitan Policy Program at Brookings.

Rowthorn, Robert, and Ramana Ramaswamy. 1997. "Deindustrialization: Its Causes and Implications." Working Paper of the IMF. Washington, D.C.: International Monetary Fund.

Roysdon, Keith. 2012. "Brevini Says Contract Means 30 to 50 Jobs." *Muncie Star Press*, February 25.

Rusk, David. 1993. *Cities Without Suburbs.* Washington, D.C.: Woodrow Wilson Center Press.

Ryan, Brent D. 2012. "Rightsizing Shrinking Cities: The Urban Design Dimension." In *The City After Abandonment*, ed. Margaret Dewar and June Manning Thomas, 268–88. Philadelphia: University of Pennsylvania Press.

Saiz, Albert. 2010. "The Geographic Determinants of Housing Supply." *Quarterly Journal of Economics* 125, 3: 1253–96.

Schilling, Joseph. 2009. "Code Enforcement and Community Stabilization: The Forgotten First Responders to Vacant and Foreclosed Homes." *Albany Government Law Review* 2: 105–62.

Schilling, Joseph, and Jonathan Logan. 2008. "Greening the Rust Belt: A Green Infrastructure Model for Right Sizing America's Shrinking Cities." *Journal of the American Planning Association* 74, 4 (Autumn): 451–66.

Schilling, Joseph, and Alan Mallach. 2012. *Cities in Transition: A Guide for Practicing Planners.* Chicago: American Planning Association.

Schuyler, David 2002. *A City Transformed: Redevelopment, Race, and Suburbanization in Lancaster, Pennsylvania, 1940–1980.* University Park: Pennsylvania State University Press.

Shapiro, Jesse M. 2006. "Smart Cities: Quality of Life, Productivity, and the Growth Effects of Human Capital." *Review of Economics and Statistics* 88, 2: 324–35.

Sherrieb, Kathleen, Fran Norris, and Sandro Galea. 2010. "Measuring Capacities for Community Resilience." *Social Indicators Research* 99, 2: 227–47.

Simmons, Ellis Garner, Jr. 1981. "Evaluation of the Federally Assisted Code Enforcement Program: A Case Study of Denver, Colorado." *Journal of Planning Education and Research* 1, 1: 49.

Simon, Curtis J. 1998. "Human Capital and Metropolitan Employment Growth." *Journal of Urban Economics* 43: 223–43.

Simon, Curtis J., and Clark Nardinelli. 2002. "Human Capital and the Rise of American Cities: 1900–1990." *Regional Science and Urban Economics* 32, 1: 59–96.

Sirkin, Harold, Michael Zinser, and Douglas Hohner. 2011. *Made in America, Again: Why Manufacturing Will Return to the U.S.* Boston: Boston Consulting Group.

Sklar, Scott. 2011. "Pure Fantasy on Green Manufacturing, Solar Jobs, and the Mainstream Media." *Renewableenergyworld.com.* http://www.renewableenergyworld.com/rea/news/article/2011/09/pure-fantasy-on-green-manufacturing-solar-jobs-and-the-mainstream-media.

Starr, Roger. 1976. "Making New York Smaller." *New York Times Magazine*, November 14.

Stimson, Robert, Roger Stough, and Brian Roberts. 2006. "Capacity Building, Institutions and Leadership for Regional Economic Development." In *Regional Economic Development: Analysis and Planning Strategy*, ed. Robert Stimson, Robert Stough, and Brian Roberts, 319–47. New York: Springer-Verlag.

Stringer, Scott. 2010. *Food NYC: A Blueprint for a Sustainable Food System.* New York: New York University and Just Food.

Swensen, Dave. 2010. *Selected Measures of the Economic Values of Increased Fruit and Vegetable Production and Consumption in the Upper Midwest.* Ames, Iowa: Leopold Center for Sustainable Agriculture.

Tavernise, Sabrina. 2011. "Reading, Pa., Knew It Was Poor. Now It Knows Just How Poor." *New York Times*, September 26.

Teaford, Jon C. 1993. *Cities of the Heartland: The Rise and Fall of the Industrial Midwest.* Bloomington: Indiana University Press.

Tiebout, C. M. 1962. *The Community Economic Base Study.* New York: Committee for Economic Development.

Tierney, William G. 2012. "The Promise and Challenge of For-Profit Higher Education." In *Preparing Todays's Students for Tomorrows Jobs in Metropolitan America: The Policy, Practice, and Research Issues*, ed. Laura W. Perna, 149–74. Philadelphia: University of Pennsylvania Press.

Tumber, Catherine. 2012. *Small, Gritty, and Green: The Promise of America's Smaller Industrial Cities in a Low-Carbon World*. Cambridge, Mass.: MIT Press.

Tweeney, Dylan. 2009. "DIY Freaks Flock to 'Hacker Spaces' Worldwide." *Wired*, March 29. http://www.wired.com/gadgetlab/2009/03/hackerspaces/.

U.S. Census Bureau, American Community Survey. 2009. "Commuting in the United States: 2009." American Community Survey Reports. http://www.census.gov/prod /2011pubs/acs-15.pdf.

U.S. Conference of Mayors. 2010. *Recycling America's Land: National Report on Brownfields Redevelopment*. Washington, D.C.: U.S. Conference of Mayors.

United Nations Environment Programme and Bloomberg New Energy Finance. 2011. *Global Trends in Renewable Energy Investment*. Frankfurt: Frankfurt School of Finance and Management.

University of Pennsylvania. 2011. *Penn Economic Impact Report FY 2010*. Philadelphia: University of Pennsylvania, Office of the Executive Vice President.

Van Soest, Daan P., Shelby Gerking, and Frank G. van Oort. 2006. "Spatial Impacts of Agglomeration Externalities." *Journal of Regional Science* 46 (December 5): 881–99.

Varady, David P. and Jeffrey A. Raffel. 1995. *Selling Cities: Attracting Homebuyers through Schools and Housing Programs*. Albany: State University of New York Press.

Vey, Jennifer S. 2007. *Restoring Prosperity: The State Role in Revitalizing America's Older Industrial Cities*. Washington, D.C.: Brookings Institution.

Wallace, R. 1990. "Urban Desertification, Public Health and Public Order: 'Planned Shrinkage,' Violent Death, Substance Abuse and AIDS in the Bronx." *Social Science and Medicine* 31: 801–13.

Wang, X., and R. Vam Hofe. 2007. *Research Methods in Urban and Regional Planning*. Berlin and Beijing: Springer Verlag and Tshighua University Press.

Webber, H. 2012. Universities as Anchors, Paper presented at National Conference of Planning, Los Angeles. April 14.

Whitaker, Stephan, and Thomas J. Fitzpatrick IV. 2011. "The Impact of Vacant, Tax-Delinquent and Foreclosed Property on Sales Prices of Neighboring Homes." Federal Reserve Bank of Cleveland Working Paper 11023. Cleveland: Federal Reserve Bank of Cleveland.

Wolf-Powers, Laura, and Stuart Andreason. 2012. "Creating Effective Education and Workforce Policies for Metropolitan Labor Markets in America." In *Preparing Today's Students for Tomorrow's Jobs in Metropolitan America: The Policy, Practice, and Research Issues*, ed. Laura W. Perna, 224–44. Philadelphia: University of Pennsylvania Press.

Wolman, Harold, Edward W. Hill, and Kimberly Furdell. 2000. "Evaluating the Success of Urban Success Stories: Is Reputation a Guide to Best Practice?" *Housing Policy Debate* 15, 4: 965–97.

Yeoman, Barry. 2012. "The Death and Life of Detroit." *American Prospect*, April 30, at http://prospect.org/article/death-and-life-detroit.

Youngstown, City of. 2005. *Youngstown 2010 Citywide Plan*. Youngstown, Ohio: City of Youngstown and Youngstown State University.

Youngstown Neighborhood Development Corporation. 2012. http://www.yndc.org/about, accessed March 16, 2013.

Zhao, Bo et al. 2010. "Does Springfield Receive Its Fair Share of Municipal Aid? Implications for Aid Formula Reform in Massachusetts?" NEPPC Working Paper Series 10–2. Boston: Federal Reserve Bank of Boston.

Zimbalist, Andrew, and Roger G. Noll. 1997. "Sports, Jobs & Taxes: Are New Stadiums Worth the Cost?" Washington, D.C.: Brookings Institution.

Zumeta, William. 2011. "Does the U.S. Need More College Graduates to Remain a World Class Economic Power?" Paper for National Discussion and Debate Series, Miller Center of Public Affairs, University of Virginia.

INDEX

Figures and tables are represented by **boldface** page numbers followed by **f** or **t** (e.g., **20f**, **58t**).

leadership (continued)
necessity of, 259; and private, nonprofit
organizations, 94, 95–96
Ledebur, Larry C., 264n13
legacy cities: fiscal problems, 177; and
neighborhood improvement approaches,
151; population declines, 168–69; racial
divides, 180; as term, 271n1. *See also*
spatial reconfiguration in legacy cities
Lehigh University, 217, 222
LeRoy, Greg, 232–33
LeRoy, Stephen F., 262n7
Lin, Jeffrey, 262n7
Living Cities, 158
Local Initiatives Support Corporation
(LISC), 102
Logan, John R., 48
Longitudinal Tract Database (LTDB),
47, 48
Los Angeles, California, **244t**

Making Connections initiative, 102
Mallach, Alan, 125–45, 168–88, 257, 258
manufacturing and nonmanufacturing
employment, 1–2, 65–80, 87, 257;
deindustrialization and decline of
manufacturing, 1–2, 65, 66–68, **86f**, 87,
263nn4–5; and Great Recession, 2, 75–76,
265n16; median household income,
73–74, **75t**, 264nn12–13; methodology,
65; metropolitan population and employment, **66f**, 262n1; nonmanufacturing employment in central counties/suburban
counties, 72–73, **73f**; nonmanufacturing
employment in cities, by region, 73, **74f**,
77–79, **78f**; population growth in cities,
by region, 71–72, **72f**, 79, **79f**, 265n19;
population growth of suburban counties,
71, **72f**; and poverty rates, 73–74, 264n12;
resurgence (post-Great Recession), 2,
76–79; and service employment (private
services), 66, **67f**, 263n3; shift from cities
to suburbs, 68–71, **69f**, **70f**; technology
manufacturing, 77, 263n6, 264n8, 265n17;
trends in population, nonmanufacturing
employment, and wage income, 71–75,
264nn10–13, 265n14; wage income,
71–75, **74f**, **75f**, **76f**, 264nn10–11, 265n14.
See also mid-sized manufacturing cities,
resurgent

Manufacturing Matters (Cohen and
Zysman), 230
Market Value Analysis (MVA), 156–58;
housing market descriptions by neighbor-
hood type, 156, **157t**; percent of housing
units located in middle neighborhoods,
156–58, **158t**
Marshall, Alfred, 9, 35
Maryland Housing Fund, 162
Massachusetts Biomedical Initiatives, 98
Massachusetts Biotechnology Institute
(MBRI), 98
Massachusetts General Hospital (Boston),
213, 215, **216t**
McDonald, Frank F., II, 94–95
McIlvaine, Leigh, 232–33
McKinney, Hannah, 92
Meter, Ken, 228
middle neighborhood approaches, 149–67,
258, 271n9; Baltimore, 160–64; characteristics of middle/distressed neighborhoods,
160, 271n8; characteristics of strong vi-
brant neighborhoods, 150–51; federal
programs that consider market conditions, 164–65; Federally Assisted Code
Enforcement (FACE) program, 153;
Healthy Neighborhoods Program (Baltimore), 161–63; and history of federal
neighborhood policy, 151–55; HOPE VI
program, 154; housing market descriptions (by neighborhood type), 156, **157t**;
Live Baltimore, 164, 271n11; Market
Value Analysis (MVA) and housing,
156–58, **157t**, **158t**; Neighborhood Self-
Help Development Program, 153–54;
NeighborWorks America, 154–55; new
urban research, 165; people-oriented, 166;
percent of housing units located in
middle neighborhoods, 156–58, **158t**;
place-oriented, 165–66; RW-Ventures'
"Dynamic Neighborhoods" analysis,
158–59; Social Compact and Drill-
Down™ methodology, 159; techniques
for understanding neighborhood
market conditions, 155–60, **157t**, **158t**,
271n5
mid-sized manufacturing cities, resurgent,
83–104, **85f**, 257; cities analyzed, 84,
85–87, **85f**, **86f**, **89t**, 266n3; distinguish-
ing features of resurgent cities, 87–90,

ACKNOWLEDGMENTS

The complex and interrelated problems of population decline and the loss of legacy manufacturing industries have left many of the nation's older industrial cities facing a range of economic and social challenges. To explore strategies that communities can use to address these challenges, the Community Development Studies and Education Department of the Federal Reserve Bank in Philadelphia chose to focus the Fifth Biennial *Reinventing Older Communities* conference on the theme *Building Resilient Cities.* The conference, held May 9–11, 2012, at the Hyatt Regency Philadelphia at Penn's Landing, inspired this volume.

Conference organizers, including many community development staff members from across the Federal Reserve System, designed a meeting that integrated timely research and practical experience. To this end, the majority of the conference sessions included presentations by both scholars and practitioners, highlighting the tools and strategies that have been effective in cities across the nation. This effort would not have been possible without the support of the Federal Reserve Bank of Philadelphia, its President and CEO, Charles Plosser, and the thoughtful leadership of senior vice president Milissa Tadeo, community affairs officer Theresa Singleton, and the hard work of Erin Mierzwa, research manager, and former community affairs officer, Dede Meyers, who retired in December 2011.

We are also grateful to the conference cosponsors who contributed their financial and intellectual resources, including the Federal Reserve Banks of Boston, Chicago, Cleveland, New York, Richmond, and St. Louis; the William Penn Foundation; the Penn Institute for Urban Research (Penn IUR); the Ford Foundation; the U.S. Department of Housing and Urban Development Office of Policy Development and Research; and the Federal Home Loan Bank of Pittsburgh.

Over 400 researchers, policymakers, community development leaders, government officials and staff, bankers, foundation representatives, and students brought their energy, ideas, and expertise to the three-day event. In addition, the gathering featured keynote speeches from President of the Federal Reserve Bank of Philadelphia Charles Plosser, Chair of the Federal Reserve Bank of Philadelphia Jeremy Nowak, Harvard University Professor and Director of the Taubman Center for State and Local Government and the Rappaport Institute for Greater Boston Edward Glaeser, and United States Secretary for Housing and Urban Development Shaun Donovan, all of whom added immensely to the conference. We hope the enthusiasm of the speakers and the participants is reflected in this book.

The leadership and editorial staff at Penn Press made this book, which is part of the Press's The City in the Twenty-First Century series, possible. We would particularly like to thank Peter Agree, Editor-in-Chief, for his careful and thoughtful review of the manuscript's drafts.

On our team, we would like to thank Arthur Acoca, Cara Griffin, and Anthony Orlando, who provided invaluable research and editorial assistance in the production of this book.

Finally, we would like to thank the book's contributors, without whom there would be no book, for their willingness to share their expertise and to work graciously under very tight deadlines.